SPOKEN SOUL

SPOKEN SOUL

The Story of Black English

John Russell Rickford
and
Russell John Rickford

Foreword by Geneva Smitherman

John Wiley & Sons, Inc.

New York • Chichester • Weinheim • Brisbane • Singapore • Toronto

Copyright © 2000 by John Russell Rickford and Russell John Rickford.
All rights reserved

Published by John Wiley & Sons, Inc.
Published simultaneously in Canada

This publication is designed to provide accurate and authoritative information in regard to the subject matter covered. It is sold with the understanding that the publisher is not engaged in rendering professional services. If professional advice or other expert assistance is required, the services of a competent professional person should be sought.

Library of Congress Cataloging-in-Publication Data:

Rickford, John Russell
    Spoken soul : the story of black English /
John Russell Rickford and Russell John Rickford.
        p.   cm.
    Includes bibliographical references and index.
    ISBN 0-471-32356-X (cloth)
    ISBN 0-471-39957-4 (paper)
    1. Black English—United States. 2. English language—Spoken
English—United States. 3. English language—Social aspects—United
States. 4. Afro-Americans—Language.   I. Rickford, Russell John.
II. Title.
PE3102.N42R54   2000
427'.089'96073—dc21   99-37796

From Russell John:

For the Almighty, for whom our souls are a witness.

*For my godfather Uncle Teddy, the swashbuckler who taught me
to take life in my teeth and leap.*

*For my father, the pacifist who showed me how to skip a rock,
build a kite, and be a do-right man.*

From John Russell:

*For Angela, my beloved, and for our children, Shiyama, Russell,
Anakela, and Luke, the pride and joy of our lives.*

*For my fallen/risen siblings: Peter Howell, Edward Noel, Patricia Stella,
and all my kinfolk, here and there. May the circle be unbroken.*

*For soul speakers everywhere. May their language be better understood
and appreciated, and may their enormous potential in school
and life be more richly realized.*

Contents

Part Five
The Double Self

Foreword

It's been a long time coming, as the old song goes, but the change done come. Back when I was working with the parents and legal team in *King* v. *Ann Arbor* (the "Black English" federal court case, 1977–79), public confusion and misunderstanding about Black English came as a shock to many linguists and scholars. Then shock waves again, almost two decades later, when the Ebonics controversy erupted among the mistletoe and Kinara of the 1996 Christmas-Kwanzaa season. The scholarly community has written volumes of commendable work on Spoken Soul (not by that name, of course), dating back at least to 1884, when Harrison published "Negro English" in the academic journal *Anglia*. However, with one or two exceptions over the past three decades, scholarly research on this language spoken by millions of African Americans has not been written up for the public at large. *Spoken Soul* steps to the challenge. The book breaks it down and makes it plain. At long last, the academic world of morphemes and phonemes reaches beyond ivied walls, connecting town and gown.

The Rickfords—in this case not husband and wife, but father and son—take their title from the name that writer Claude Brown gave to our language back in the 1960s. They present myths and realities about Spoken Soul, and in the process do much soul-speaking themselves, covering topics from the language of great comedians and actors to that of "preachers and pray-ers." In writing that is rich and powerful—and funky and bold when it bees necessary—they dissect black writing and black speech, the grammar and history of Spoken Soul, the Ebonics controversy and media coverage of it.

The story of Spoken Soul is not an easy one to tell because it is not *just* about language. To tell the story right, you have to talk about the culture and lived experience of African Americans. You have to talk about a language inextricable from the complex social structure and political history of people of African descent in these United

ix

States. To get it right, you have to do what the Rickfords have done: you have to represent. Otherwise, there is no way to understand the linguistic double consciousness of black Life, as revealed here in the 1997 Howard University graduation scene with renowned broadcast news pioneer Sista Carole Simpson as commencement speaker, a push-pull scenario reenacted countless times in different versions in African America, and about which the Rickfords write with insight and eloquence in chapter 5, "Singers, Toasters, and Rappers." Their message to us—in a book that is truly da bomb—is that we must "claim both Spoken Soul and Standard English as our own, empowering our youth to appreciate and articulate each in their respective forums," for only then "will we have mastered the art of merging our double selves into a better and truer self."

John Russell and Russell John were both at the Million Man March. And now they have come together to speak the truth to the people about what it means to talk black in America. An African American father and son writing together as a team—now that in itself is a moment of history to be cherished. One a journalist, the other a linguist; one in the academy, the other in public media. *Spoken Soul* is testimony to the power of this combination of *kin*dred spirits.

—Geneva Smitherman, Ph.D.
University Distinguished Professor
Michigan State University
Author, *Black Talk: Words and Phrases from the Hood to the Amen Corner, Talkin and Testifyin: The Language of Black America,* and *Talkin That Talk: Language, Culture and Education in African America*
October 1999

Acknowledgments

Thanks to the Stanford Humanities Center, where the proposal and much of John's writing for this book were completed, and to the Department of Linguistics and the Program in African and Afro-American Studies at Stanford, which were both supportive throughout. Gina Wein, Trudy Vizmanos, Diann McCants, and Linda Watson were especially helpful. Thanks are due, too, to former Stanford Deans of Humanities Ewart Thomas and John Shoven. Funding from the Martin Luther King Jr. Centennial Fellowship is gratefully acknowledged.

Stanford students Admas Kanyagia, Naomi Levin, Emma Petty, Sarah Roberts, Mary Rose, and Andrew Wong were first-rate research assistants, as were Joy Hsu and Damian Schnyder. Arnold Rampersad, Houston Baker, and Meta Duwa Jones provided helpful feedback with the "Writers" chapter, as did Tom Wasow with the "System" chapter. Lisa Green was generous with her native-speaker intuitions; her theoretically sophisticated work on the structure of Black English is most perceptive, and we look forward to her books. Elaine Ray and Linda Cicero of the Stanford News Service were both encouraging and helpful, and students in John's classes at Stanford, particularly African American Vernacular English, were invaluable in clarifying many points and forcing him to clarify others.

John's study and understanding of Black English have been facilitated by many current and former Stanford students, including Arnetha Ball, Renee Blake, Catherine Chappel, Keith Denning, Dawn Hannah, Raina Jackson, Andrea Kortenhoven, Nomi Martin, Bonnie McElhinny, John McWhorter, and Jacquelyn Rahman. He has also learned from his former research associates and coauthors, Faye McNair-Knox, Christine Theberge-Rafal, and Angela Rickford. His mentors, J. Herman Blake and William Labov, taught him a good deal, respectively, about black life and language. Other scholars and colleagues, many of them cited in the endnotes, also contributed to this learning. But his most significant instructors were the vernacular speakers throughout African America and the Caribbean—particularly in East Palo Alto, Philadelphia, New York City, the South Carolina Sea Islands, Barbados, Guyana, and Jamaica—who gave him the privilege of hearing, observing, analyzing, and appreciating the language.

John wishes, finally, to thank his son Russell for the many pleasures and insights that collaborating on this book involved, and especially for teaching him, by precept and example, how to write for the people. No project has ever been more rewarding.

Many thanks to the brothers of Alpha Phi Alpha Fraternity, Inc., Beta Chapter, Howard University, who guided Russell across the hinterlands of underground hip-hop culture, and who had faith that Spoken Soul was no jive, and to the editors and reporters of the *Philadelphia Inquirer*, whose support and curiosity about this book helped shape its content and style. Thanks also to Venus, who loves books.

Thanks from both of us to Noah Lukeman of Lukeman Literary Management, who first proposed this project and waited patiently for us to sign on, and to Carole Hall, our editor at John Wiley & Sons, without whose faith and convictions this book would not have seen the light of day, and without whose editorial experience and good sense it would not have been the same. Copyeditor Anna Jardine did a fantastic job. We also thank Benjamin Hamilton, associate managing editor, for seeing this book through the production process so efficiently and promptly. For their assistance in procuring photos for this volume, we thank Yaeko Ozaki of the Stanford News Service, and Mary Yearwood and Jim Huffman of the Schomburg Center for Research in Black Culture, New York Public Library. Special thanks are due to the generous cooperation of celebrated photographer Jill Krementz, whose famous photos of distinguished African American writers grace our pages. And for anyone whose contributions we have forgotten to mention, our apologies.

Thanks to Dr. G. (Geneva Smitherman) for righteously encouraging us and for writing the foreword to this book, and to all our colleagues, family members, and friends whose interest in and contributions to this book helped make it what it is. We particularly wish to recognize Angela Rickford, spouse and momma, whose counsel we drew on repeatedly.

Finally, our faith in God sustained us throughout and helped us over many of the bumps along the way.

Part One

Introduction

1

What's Going On?

For what shall it profit a man, if he shall gain the whole world and lose his own soul?

—Mark 8:36

SOUL [sōl] 1. The animating and vital principle in humans . . . 5. The central or integral part; the vital core . . . 9. A sense of ethnic pride among Black people and especially African Americans, expressed in areas such as language, social customs, religion and music.

—*The American Heritage Dictionary of the English Language* (4th edition, 2000)

"Spoken Soul" was the name that Claude Brown, author of *Manchild in the Promised Land,* coined for black talk. In a 1968 interview he waxed eloquent in its praise, declaring that the informal speech or vernacular of many African Americans "possesses a pronounced lyrical quality which is frequently incompatible to any music other than that ceaselessly and relentlessly driving rhythm that flows from poignantly spent lives." A decade later, James Baldwin, legendary author of *The Fire Next Time,* described black English as "this passion, this skill . . . this incredible music."

Now, at the beginning of the twenty-first century, the Spoken Soul these writers exalted is battered by controversy, its very existence called into question. Though belittled and denied, however, it lives on authentically. In homes, schools, and churches, on streets, stages, and the airwaves, you can hear soul spoken every day. Most African Americans—including millions who, like Brown and Baldwin, are

3

fluent speakers of Standard English—still invoke Spoken Soul as we have for hundreds of years, to laugh or cry, to preach and praise, to shuck and jive, to sing, to rap, to shout, to style, to express our individual personas and our ethnic identities ("'spress yo'self!" as James Brown put it), to confide in and commiserate with friends, to chastise, to cuss, to act, to act the fool, to get by and get over, to pass secrets, to make jokes, to mock and mimic, to tell stories, to reflect and philosophize, to create authentic characters and voices in novels, poems, and plays, to survive in the streets, to relax at home and recreate in playgrounds, to render our deepest emotions and embody our vital core.

The fact is that most African Americans *do* talk differently from whites and Americans of other ethnic groups, or at least most of us can when we want to. And the fact is that most Americans, black and white, know this to be true.

In this book, we will explore the vibrancy and vitality of Spoken Soul as an expressive instrument in American literature, religion, entertainment, and everyday life. We will detail the features and history of Spoken Soul. We will then return to the Ebonics firestorm that flared up at century's end, considering its spark (the Oakland, California, School District's resolutions and their educational significance), its fuel (media coverage), and its embers (Ebonics "humor"). In the final chapter we will reflect on the vernacular's role in American life and society, and seek the truth about the dizzying love-hate relationship with black talk that is as old and new as the nation itself. Who needs this information and insight? We all do, because Spoken Soul is an inescapable vessel of American history, literature, society, and popular culture. Regardless of its status, we need to come to terms with this beloved and beleaguered language.

In coming to terms with Spoken Soul, what it is and why it matters, the first thing to know is how high it ranks in the esteem of its maestros. Echoing the sentiments of Claude Brown and James Baldwin, Nobel Prize–winning author Toni Morrison insisted in 1981 that the distinctive ingredient of her fiction was

> the language, only the language. . . . It is the thing that black people love so much—the saying of words, holding them on the tongue, experimenting with them, playing with them. It's a love, a passion. Its function is like a preacher's: to make you stand up out of your seat, make

you lose yourself and hear yourself. The worst of all possible things that could happen would be to lose that language. There are certain things I cannot say without recourse to my language. It's terrible to think that a child with five different present tenses comes to school to be faced with books that are less than his own language. And then to be told things about his language, which is him, that are sometimes permanently damaging. He may never know the etymology of Africanisms in his language, not even know that "hip" is a real word or that "the dozens" meant something. This is a really cruel fallout of racism. I know the standard English. I want to use it to help restore the other language, the lingua franca.

June Jordan, celebrated essayist and poet, in 1985 identified "three qualities of Black English—the presence of life, voice and clarity—that testify to a distinctive Black value system." Jordan, then a professor at Stony Brook College, chided her students for their uneasiness about the colloquial language in Alice Walker's novel *The Color Purple,* and went on to teach them about the art of the vernacular.

The second thing to bear in mind is that between the 1960s and 1990s, a dramatic shift occurred. By the end of the 1990s, we could find scarcely a spokesman or spokeswoman for the race who had anything flattering to say about Spoken Soul. In response to the Oakland school board's December 18, 1996, resolution to recognize "Ebonics" as the primary language of African American students in that California district, poet Maya Angelou told the *Wichita Eagle* that she was "incensed" and found the idea "very threatening." NAACP president Kweisi Mfume denounced the measure as "a cruel joke," and although he later adopted a friendlier stance, the Reverend Jesse Jackson on national television initially called it "an unacceptable surrender, borderlining on disgrace." Jackson found himself curiously aligned with Ward Connerly, the black University of California regent whose ultimately successful efforts to end affirmative action on University of California campuses and in the state as a whole Jackson had vigorously opposed. Connerly called the Oakland proposal "tragic," and went on to argue, "These are not kids who came from Africa last year. . . . These are kids that have had every opportunity to acclimate themselves to American society, and they have gotten themselves into this trap of speaking this language—this slang, really, that people can't understand. Now we're going to legitimize it."

Other African Americans from different ends of the ideological spectrum fell into step. Black conservative academic and author Shelby Steele characterized the Oakland proposal as just another "gimmick" to enhance black self-esteem, while black liberal academic and author Henry Louis Gates Jr., chairman of Afro-American Studies at Harvard, dismissed it as "obviously stupid and ridiculous." Former Black Panther Eldridge Cleaver agreed, as did entertainer Bill Cosby.

The virtual consensus blurred political lines among white pundits as well. Conservative talk-show host Rush Limbaugh assailed the Ebonics resolution, while leading Republican William Bennett, former U.S. secretary of education, described it as "multiculturalism gone haywire." Leading liberal Mario Cuomo, former governor of New York, called it a "bad mistake," and Secretary of Education Richard Riley, a member of President Clinton's Democratic cabinet, declared that Ebonics programs would not be eligible for federal bilingual education dollars, maintaining that "elevating black English to the status of a language is not the way to raise standards of achievement in our schools and for our students." At the state level, anti-Ebonics legislation was introduced both by Republicans, such as Representative Mark Ogles of Florida, and by Democrats, such as Georgia state senator Ralph Abernathy III.

Millions of other people across the United States and around the world rushed in to express their vociferous condemnation of Ebonics and the proposal to take it into account in schools. ("Ebonics" in fact quickly became a stand-in for the language variety and for Oakland's proposal, so the recurrent question "What do you think about Ebonics?" elicited reactions to both topics.) Animated conversations sprang up in homes and workplaces and at holiday gatherings, as well as on television and radio programs, in letters to the editor, and on electronic bulletin boards that were deluged after the Oakland decision. According to *Newsweek*, "An America Online poll about Ebonics drew more responses than the one asking people whether O. J. Simpson was guilty."

The vast majority of those America Online responses were not just negative. They were caustic. Ebonics was vilified as "disgusting black street slang," "incorrect and substandard," "nothing more than ignorance," "lazy English," "bastardized English," "the language of illiteracy," and "this utmost ridiculous made-up language." And Oakland's resolution, almost always misunderstood as a proposal to teach Ebonics instead of as a plan to use Ebonics as a springboard to Standard English, elicited superlatives of disdain, disbelief, and derision:

"Idiocy of the highest form." (December 21, 1996)

"Man, 'ubonics will take me far back to de jungo!" (December 21, 1996)

"I think it be da dumbest thing I'd eber heard be." (December 23, 1996)

These comments, dripping with scorn, are far removed from the tributes that Brown, Baldwin, Morrison, and Jordan had paid to the African American vernacular in earlier decades. Why the about-face? What had happened to transform Spoken Soul from an object of praise to an object of ridicule?

For one thing, the focus was different. The Ebonics controversy of the 1990s was about the use of the vernacular in school, while the earlier commentaries were more about the expressiveness of the vernacular itself in literature and informal settings.

Moreover, the general misconception that the Oakland school board intended to teach and accept Ebonics rather than English in the classroom—perhaps assisted by the resolution's vague wording and the media's voracious coverage—made matters worse. Most of the fuming and fulminating about Ebonics stemmed from the mistaken belief that it was to replace Standard English as a medium of instruction and a target for success.

This misunderstanding was not new, nor was it unique to the United States. The 1979 ruling by Michigan Supreme Court justice Charles Joiner that the negative attitudes of Ann Arbor teachers toward the home language of their black students represented a barrier to the students' academic success was similarly misinterpreted as a plan "to teach ghetto children in 'black English'" (in the words of columnist Carl Rowan). And from the 1950s on, proposals by Caribbean linguists to take students' Creole English into account to improve the teaching of Standard English (in Jamaica, Trinidad, and Guyana) have been similarly misinterpreted and condemned as attempts to "settle" for Creole instead of English.

But the backlash against Ebonics in the 1990s was certainly fueled by new elements, and by considerations unique to the contemporary United States. There is more concern today about what we have in common as Americans, including English. Some who thrashed Ebonics in Internet forums voiced this concern:

> There seems to be a movement with the cultural diversity, bilingualism, and quota-oriented affirmative action campaigns to balkanize the country and build walls between people and dissolve the concept of being an American. This Ebonics . . . will . . . keep a segment of the black community in ghetto mode. (December 20, 1996)

As in this case, critiques of Ebonics were often couched in larger objections to bilingual education, affirmative action, and any measure that seemed to offer special "advantages" to ethnic minorities and women—despite the centuries of disadvantage these groups have endured. A month before Oakland passed its Ebonics resolution, Californians endorsed Proposition 209, outlawing affirmative action in education and employment, and in June 1998, they approved Proposition 227, prohibiting most forms of bilingual education. Many states passed English-only legislation in the 1980s and 1990s, and lawmakers continue to lobby for similar legislation at the federal level.

The 1990s also saw internal divisions within the African American population—by socioeconomic class, generation, and gender—grow more pronounced than they had been in the 1960s. This accounts for some of the stinging criticism of Ebonics that originated "within the race." While the 1960s featured "*The* March on Washington," a united protest by African Americans and others against racial and economic inequality, blacks in the 1990s participated in separate "Million Man" and "Million Woman" marches, and competing "Million Youth" marches. While the proportion of African Americans earning more than $100,000 (in 1989 dollars) tripled between 1969 and 1989 (from 0.3 percent to about 1 percent of all African American households), the proportion earning below $15,000 remained the same (about 43 percent of all African American households), and the mean income actually dropped in the interim (from $9,300 to $8,520). When we consider that Ebonics pronunciation and grammar are used most frequently by poor and working-class African Americans, and that it was primarily the comments of middle- and upper-middle class African Americans heard over the airwaves and read on the Internet in 1996 and 1997, their disdain is not surprising.

What's more, the distance between the younger hip-hop generation and older African American generations—marked by the politics of dress, music, and slang—has in various ways also grown more stark in the 1990s. Some middle-aged and elderly black folk have increasingly come to view baggy-jeans-and-boot-wearing, freestylin' youth as hoodlums who are squandering the gains of the civil rights movement. Not entirely coincidentally, most of the publicly aired comments on Ebonics came from black baby boomers (now in their forties and fifties) or older African Americans. When discussing the slang of hip-hop youth—which they (mis)identified with Ebonics—they often bristled with indignation. So did others, of other races, who vented their prejudices quite openly.

While today's debate is charged with new elements, the question of the role of the vernacular in African American life and literature has been a source of debate among African Americans for more than a century. When Paul Laurence Dunbar was establishing his reputation as a dialect poet in the late 1800s, James Weldon Johnson, who wrote the lyrics to "Lift Every Voice and Sing" (long hailed as "The Negro National Anthem"), chose to render the seven African American sermons of *God's Trombones* in standard English because he felt that the dialect of "old-time" preachers might pigeonhole the book. During the Harlem Renaissance of the 1920s, a similar debate raged among the black intelligentsia, with Langston Hughes endorsing and exemplifying the use of vernacular, and Alain Locke and others suggesting that African Americans ought to put the quaintness of the idiom behind them and offer the world a more "refined" view of their culture. These enduring attitudes reflect the attraction-repulsion dynamic, the oscillation between black and white (or mainstream) poles that W. E. B. Du Bois defined a century ago as "double-consciousness."

This century marks a watershed for the vernacular. One purpose of this book is to help rescue Spoken Soul from the negativity and ignorance in which it became mired during the Ebonics debate, and to correct the many misconceptions people have about black talk. Another is to offer a fresh way to think and talk about Spoken Soul that does justice to its persistence and potency.

Like virtually everyone else, we acknowledge that African Americans must master Standard English, corporate English, mainstream English, the language of wider communication, or whatever you want to call the variety of English needed for school, formal occasions, and success in the business world. But we also believe that Ebonics, African American Vernacular English, Black English, Spoken Soul, or whatever you want to call the informal variety spoken by many black people, plays an essential, valuable role in our lives and in the life of the larger society to which we all belong.

The reasons for the persistence and vitality of Spoken Soul are manifold: it marks black identity; it is the symbol of a culture and a life-style that have had and continue to have a profound impact on American popular life; it retains the associations of warmth and closeness for the many blacks who first learn it from their mothers and fathers and other family members; it expresses camaraderie and solidarity among friends; it establishes rapport among blacks; and it serves as a creative and expressive instrument in the present and as a vibrant link with this nation's past.

If we lost all of that in the heady pursuit of Standard English and the world of opportunities it offers, we would indeed have lost our soul. We are not convinced that African Americans want to abandon "down-home" speech in order to become one-dimensional speakers. Nor—to judge from the ubiquity of the distinctive linguistic style of African American music, literature, and popular culture—do whites and other people in this country and around the world want to see it abandoned either, quiet as that viewpoint is kept. Certainly it is not necessary to abandon Spoken Soul to master Standard English, any more than it is necessary to abandon English to learn French, or to deprecate jazz to appreciate classical music.

Moreover, suggesting, as some do, that we abandon Spoken Soul and cleave only to Standard English is like proposing that we play only the white keys of a piano. The fact is that for many of our most beautiful melodies, we need both the white keys and the black, in the same way that, in the Chinese dualistic philosophy, the *yin* is as essential to the whole as the *yang*. Bear in mind that language is an inescapable element in almost everyone's daily life, and an integral element of human identity. If for that and no other reason, we would all do well to heed the still-evolving truth of the black language experience. That truth promises to help us confront one of the most critical questions of our day: Can one succeed in the wider world of economic and social power without surrendering one's distinctive identity? We hope to transform the conventional wisdom.

Part Two

"This Passion, This Skill,
This Incredible Music"

2

Writers

Perhaps the proper measure of a writer's talent is skill in rendering everyday speech . . . as well as the ability to tap, to exploit, the beauty, poetry and wisdom it contains. "If you say what's on your mind in the language that comes to you from your parents and your street and your friends, you'll probably say something beautiful."

—Paule Marshall (1983)

Whereas black writers most certainly revise texts in the Western tradition, they often seek to do so "authentically," with a black difference, a compelling sense of difference based on the black vernacular.

—Henry Louis Gates Jr. (1988)

Denying or denouncing Spoken Soul requires either missing or forgetting the cadences and capabilities of the vernacular in everyday speech, and the way its "beauty, poetry and wisdom" have been tapped by black and white authors for more than two hundred years.

The earliest representations of black speech in American literature appear in the works of white writers, beginning with eighteenth-century travel books and colonial plays and novels. John Leacock's play *The Fall of British Tyranny; or, American Liberty Triumphant* was published in 1776, the year the Revolutionary War began. In the following excerpt, Cudjo, who has escaped from American slavery, is being interviewed by the Kidnapper on a ship as he and other escapees seek to enlist in the British navy.

KIDNAPPER: Very well, did you all run away from your masters?

CUDJO: Eas, massa Lord, eb'ry one, me too.

KIDNAPPER: That's clever; they have no right to make you slaves.
              I wish all the Negroes would do the same, I'll make
              'em free—what part did you come from?

CUDJO: Disse brack man, disse one, disse one, disse one, disse
              one, come from Hamton, disse one, disse one, disse one,
              come from Nawfok, me come from Nawfok too.

KIDNAPPER: Very well, what was your master's name?

CUDJO: Me massa name Cunney Tomsee.

Derived from the West African name for a male born on Monday, "Cudjo" was a common christening for black men during the colonial period. But Cudjo's language includes several features that are either rare or nonexistent in the speech of African Americans today, such as the use of the verb *come* for past tense (instead of *came*), and the appearance of *me* as subject and possessive pronouns (instead of *I* and *my*, respectively). These patterns are more frequently found in Caribbean Creole English today.

From the 1700s to the present, a legion of white writers put African American vernacular of one variety or another in the mouths of their black characters. Included are some of the most prominent names in American literature: Edgar Allan Poe ("The Gold Bug," 1843), Herman Melville (Fleece's speech in *Moby-Dick*, 1851), Harriet Beecher Stowe (*Uncle Tom's Cabin*, 1851–1852), Joel Chandler Harris (*Uncle Remus*, 1880), Thomas Nelson Page (*In Ole Virginia*, 1887), Mark Twain (Jim's Missouri black dialect in *Huckleberry Finn*, 1885), Thomas Dixon (*The Clansman*, 1905), Margaret Mitchell (*Gone With the Wind*, 1936), and William Faulkner (*Go Down, Moses*, 1942). Some of these renditions (such as Faulkner's) have been praised for their authenticity and imaginativeness. Others (such as Page's) have been severely criticized—and continue to be criticized today—for their stereotypical representations of African Americans. We will return to the work of Harris and Page later in this chapter, because reaction to them helps explain some of the hypersensitivity to black dialect that has shaped literature and criticism in the last hundred years. But our focus will be on the use of Spoken Soul by black writers, who have deployed the idiom for a broader spectrum of purposes and in a wider array of genres (including poetry, the highest mode of self-expression).

As we consider black writers, we might begin with the question: What makes a book black? Not just black enough for a slot on the bookstore's "African American Interest" shelf, but so organically black that it bears witness to a staggering sum of experiences. How does the black author articulate his or her empathy toward these experiences? How does he or she express the marriage of suffering and celebration that binds one African American to the next? What narrative style speaks from the collective soul, amplifying the race's unique pulses and leaving its men and women wondering why they haven't heard their own splendor until just then?

In our attempt to come up with a response, we would do well to borrow Stephen Henderson's notes. Speaking of black poetry, but in terms that could apply to all black literature, Henderson, the late Howard University theorist and a leading spokesman for the Black Arts movement of the 1960s and 1970s, observed: "Whenever Black poetry is most distinctly and effectively Black, it derives its form from two basic sources: Black speech and Black music." In reference to black speech, he went on to say:

> Poets use Black speech forms consciously because they know that Black people—the mass of us—do not talk like white people. They know that despite the lies and distortions of the minstrels . . . there is a complex and rich and powerful and subtle linguistic heritage whose resources have scarcely been touched that they draw upon. . . . For there is this tradition of beautiful talk with us—this tradition of saying things beautifully even if they are ugly things. We say them in a way which takes language down to the deepest common level of our experience while hinting still at things to come. White people and many academicians call this usage slang and dialect; Black people call it Soul Talk.

Charles W. Chesnutt and Alice Walker could have hung with Henderson. Those two, along with a host of black poets, fiction writers, and playwrights spanning more than a century and a half, put this "rich and powerful and subtle linguistic heritage" in the mouths of their characters, and sometimes in their narrative text, sculpting a voice that was—in linguistic and often emotional terms—distinctively black. Of course, on the question of where and how the vernacular should appear, the top thinkers in the nation's black academy rarely harmonized, clashing anew in nearly every decade. And every writer who used the vernacular also used Standard or mainstream English. Nevertheless, almost all leading black writers have exploited or embraced the vernacular at one time or another.

The soul is their witness. Characters with names like Tea Cake, Shine, Simple, and Bigger were soul-generated in the vernacular tradition. Not unlike many real-life dialect speakers, they tended to

hail from the working class and to be less "colleged" than the gentry
with whom they sometimes shared plot and page. They were heroes
and antiheroes, noble or wretched types who, depending on which
critics you cared to listen to, shuffled or strode and backpedaled or
advanced on race matters. And they turned up at every terminal in
the convoy of black American literature. But why have black writers
used the dialect when doing so sometimes means catching hell from
critics?

For many, it has been to try to express every timbre of emotion
while following the true-to-life script of the black playground and pulpit, talking with this evocative tongue, this language that traces a
labyrinth of emotions. Through the years, the caravan of black story-
tellers who spun yarns with the vernacular did so because they acknowledged, publicly or privately, that "homely" speech patterns carried currency in their own community, as in American fiction and
popular culture. As we shall see, their use of this currency was moti-
vated by the overlapping considerations of audience, authenticity,
and attitude.

Audience

For black writers looking to zero in on their community, Spoken Soul
offered a conceptual code that many whites simply could not pene-
trate. Falling back on an old African American survival strategy, such
writers packaged their work in distinctly Afro styles, establishing the
principal group they wished to engage—to "conversate" with. Now
black writers have mortgages, and certainly want their work to be
bought and read by as broad an audience as possible. As we know, the
most widely read artists of any ilk use culturally specific material to illustrate universal truths. But the most masterly African American writers of the dialect tradition kept soul people foremost in their minds
and slipped them exclusive messages in their works.

Sterling A. Brown (1901–1989) was among them. A pioneering
folk poet who produced verse, criticism, and anthologies, primarily
in the 1930s and 1940s, Brown homed in on his audience by borrowing the characteristics of the blues. Often he would repeat the initial
line of the stanza—a definitive blues feature. But Brown also adopted
blues themes, giving hard life a cathartic treatment through the celebration of the melancholy. His pieces crackled with the condition of
long labor, the surety of low luck, the promise of death, and the bur-

den of racism as told by iron-forged men. His use of dialect in *Southern Road* (1932) drew praise from James Weldon Johnson, who was generally critical of dialect literature. As the editors of *The Norton Anthology of African American Literature* have noted, *Southern Road* forced Johnson "to reevaluate the place of 'the common, racy, living speech of the Negro' in literature—so much so that he finally found more to praise in Brown's dialect pieces than in the more traditional poems in the same volume." In this verse from the title piece of that collection, a chain-gang prisoner emits a "hunh" with every swing of his hammer:

> . . . White man tells me—hunh—
> Damn yo' soul;
> White man tells me—hunh—
> Damn yo' soul;
> Got no need, bebby,
> To be tole. . . .

Audiences of the time—African Americans in particular—would have been familiar with the Jim Crow policy of condemning black men to a life of servitude in chain gangs on trivial or trumped-up charges, and would have understood the prisoner's bitterness. When you already know damn well that your family's poor, splintered, and black, that the chain gang will "nevah—hunh— / Let me go," and that you're a "Po' los' boy" (revelations from the poem's other verses), your condemnation need not be verbally confirmed. The poem's gritty qualities are derived in part from the fact that, with the exception of *bebby* ("baby"), the speaker's words are all short, forceful, and monosyllabic, befitting a man engaged in hard labor. And the use of dialect helps the poem in more ways than one; the absence of the final *d* in *tole*, for example, facilitates its rhyme with the preceding *soul*.

On the outside, the poem seems a bitter acceptance of white contempt. But inwardly, it amounts to an act of rebellion, a curse of white convention. Bluesmen would not be bluesmen if they did not slyly emancipate the African American spirit with their seemingly straightforward lyrics of heartbreak, backbreak, liquor, infidelity, crime, and death. And Brown would not have been a blues poet if he had shunned the raw language of the blues, with its praise and damnation for life all wrapped up in a bent note. The "hunh" that punctuates the poem is more than an involuntary accompaniment to the prisoner's physical exertion. It's a scoff, a jeer, a private word passed between

Brown and his black reader, a remark that recalls the energetic "hunh" of black preachers at the height of their sermons and simultaneously takes a jab at the presumptions of white folks. This duality of outer and inner meaning is intrinsic to the blues and to African American speech, especially in the sayings of the elders, who have always fought covert battles from society's basement. It is "a *way* of saying" familiar to the dispossessed. Indeed, familiar to those masses magnified by Langston Hughes.

In his verses, Hughes (1902–1967) cast not the blue-veined but the grubby-palmed, not the Negro socialite but the porter or the shoeshine. Everyday people suited him fine. In turn, the masses worshipped the jazz poet (who scraped shoulders with them as a young sailor and a busboy as easily as he did as a scribe) and ultimately granted his lyrics staying power. Even today, of all the names from the Harlem Renaissance of the 1920s, his is the most familiar to the pedestrian on Martin Luther King Jr. Avenue, U.S.A.

A dashing charmer and a prodigious talent, Hughes could talk that talk. For black people his volumes still run it all down, from the deferred dreams to the jubilees. Of course, many of his most recited pieces, such as "The Negro Speaks of Rivers," were fashioned in Standard English. But he often used the vernacular to bear witness that life for the black masses "ain't been no crystal stair." In 1920 he wrote "Mother to Son," one of his most beloved poems, and one that, as an African American journalist recently put it, would not feel the same in Standard English:

> Well, son, I'll tell you:
> Life for me ain't been no crystal stair.
> It's had tacks in it,
> And splinters,
> And boards torn up,
> And places with no carpet on the floor—
> Bare.
> But all the time
> I'se been a-climbin' on,
> And reachin' landin's,
> And turnin' corners,
> And sometimes going in the dark
> Where there ain't been no light. . . .

As his biographer Arnold Rampersad has noted, Hughes's dialect in this poem "allows a humble black woman—and through her all black women—to speak nobly." The overall effect stems from the sustained metaphor of the woman's upward movement on the staircase, despite its tacks and splinters, from the warm conversational tone ("Well, son, I'll tell you") with which she conveys her combination of admonition and encouragement, and from the simple words and phrases (often beginning with "and") that frame her message. Although the immediate audience of the poem is the woman's son, Hughes is speaking for all oppressed people who have overcome daunting circumstances, and to their progeny, male and female, who similarly must learn to persevere and triumph.

Unlike many dialect writers of the nineteenth century, Hughes is sparing in his representation of black pronunciation ("climbing," "reaching," and "turning" are represented as *climbin', reachin',* and *turnin';* but "and" is not *an',* "with" is not *wid,* and "boards" is not *boa'ds*). Thus the poem is easier for readers to follow. The powerful black vernacular effect comes almost entirely from grammatical features, sparingly and skillfully deployed: *ain't* for "hasn't," the double negative (*ain't been no light*), and a few cases of nonstandard verb agreement—*you finds* instead of "you find" (in a line not quoted here) and *I'se* instead of "I'm." Unless it represents contemporary usage that has since vanished, however, the use of *I'se* for "I've" may have been a convention of dialect writing rather than an accurate depiction. We find similar examples in the work of some nineteenth- and early-twentieth-century writers, but *I'se* is not heard today. Even the most pronounced soul speakers regularly use the contracted "I've."

In black speech, cadence is as crucial to meaning as the words themselves. The rhythm, inflection, and rhetorical style are organic to the message, the clues that the speaker provides as to his or her mood and the nature of his or her relationship with the audience. Such is the case with "Queens of the Universe" (1971), an anthem by poet-activist Sonia Sanchez (b. 1934), part of which is reprinted here:

> Sisters.
>   i saw it to
>   day. with
> My own eyes.
>   i mean like i
> got on this bus
>   this cracker wuz
> driving saw him look/
>   sniff a certain
> smell and
>   turn his head in disgust.

sisters.
              that queen of sheba
                          perfume wuz
doooooooing it.
                          strong/
                               blk/
                                    smell that it
be. i mean
         it ain't delicate/stuff
sisters.
         when u put it on
              u be knowing it on. . . .

For a poem that likens black womanhood to an overwhelming
essence, that declares it hip to shun white sensibilities and aesthetics,
the swaying tempo fits. One can almost envision the speaker strutting
through the bus. There is no question of the intended audience here,
and not just because Sanchez comes right out and addresses the sisters. It is the peculiar arrangement of the phrases that gives the verse
hips. But it is the extension of the vowel in "doooooooing it" that calls
to mind the singsong intonation of a black woman in diva mode. (Recall Don Lee's use of "woooooooooowe" in "Move Un-Noticed to Be
Noticed: A Nationhood Poem.") It is the use of the habitual *be* in
"strong/ / blk/ / smell that it / be" that punctuates that strong black
smell, adding a consonant stress exuding more attitude than the
phrase's mainstream version, "strong black smell that it regularly is."
With the line "u be knowing it on," Sanchez makes political use of
that *be* once again, signaling pride in the tense-aspect marker *be* and
in her people. The versatile word is used here as an appendage, almost like an Afro. But in a deeper sense, it is an affirmation of truths
familiar only to those within the double circles of womanhood and
blackness. It is an acknowledgment of the shared condition of race
(as in, "It *bees* that way sometimes"), and a deliberate signpost of
blackness (as in, "How you *be*, sis?").

Sanchez wrote many poems in the vernacular. But when it came
to black prose writers, the vernacular was restricted largely to dialogue. This was true of William Wells Brown, who is credited with the
first African American novel (*Clotel; or, The President's Daughter,* 1853),
and it has been true of virtually all biographers and fiction writers
since, including Claude Brown (b. 1937), Mr. "Spoken Soul" himself.
In this excerpt from his autobiographical *Manchild in the Promised*

Land (1965), the author/protagonist's parents delete *is* (*he gittin'*), use the double negative, and begin emphatic statements with an inverted *can't*—demonstrating that contrary to the media's misconceptions during the Ebonics controversy, black vernacular usage has never been limited to teenagers or "gangbangers":

> Mama started crying more and saying, "He'll be eleven years old soon, and he gittin' into that shit already."
> Dad said, "Can't nothin' real bad happen before he gits thirteen or fourteen."

The tradition of reserving English for narration and Spoken Soul for dialogue extends even to novels of the 1990s, including the crime fiction of Walter Mosley (b. 1952). In this excerpt from *Devil in a Blue Dress* (1990), the narrator/protagonist comments overtly on the expressiveness of his own dialect, but it is a variety marked primarily by a few pronunciation features (*smilin'*, *front'a*) and vernacular words (*got* for "has," for instance):

> Joppy turned his jagged lips into a frown. "Naw, he must'a come after my time."
> "Yeah, well, Mouse is a lot like Mr. Albright. He's smooth and a natty dresser and he's smilin' all the time. But he always got his business in the front'a his mind, and if you get in the way you might come to no good." I always tried to speak proper English in my life, the kind of English they taught in school, but I found over the years that I could only truly express myself in the natural, "uneducated" dialect of my upbringing.

In a few striking cases, however, black fiction writers have extended the vernacular to narrative text. One of the earliest examples is "Tell Martha Not to Moan," a short story written in 1967 by Sherley Anne Williams (b. 1944), which begins:

> My mamma is a big woman, tall and stout, and men like her cause she soft and fluffy-looking. When she round them it all smiles and dimples and her mouth be looking like it couldn't never be fixed to say nothing but darling and honey.

Close on Williams's heels, June Jordan, whose essays have recorded her high regard for Black English, wrote the first novel entirely in the black vernacular (*His Own Where*, 1971). As in most twentieth-century writing, the effect is carried by the grammar, including unmarked present- and past-tense verbs, and invariant *be* (see chapters 6 and 7 for discussion of linguistic terms that appear in this chapter):

> First time they come, he simply say, "Come on." He tell her they are going not too far away. She go along not worrying about the heelstrap pinching at her skin, but worrying about the conversation. Long walks take some talking. Otherwise it be embarrassing just side by side embarrassing.

Jordan was criticized by some for her extensive use of the vernacular in this novel, especially since it was intended for young readers. But *His Own Where* won her a National Book Award nomination. As Paul Stoller noted, "Jordan shows us that stigmatized varieties of Black English can be poetic, artistic, and moving in a work of fiction."

The autobiographical *Brothers and Keepers* (1984), by John Edgar Wideman (b. 1941), also employs African American English in the narrative text. But the best-known black novel written entirely in the vernacular is *The Color Purple* (1982), which earned its author, Alice Walker (b. 1944), a Pulitzer Prize. As in the works by Williams, Jordan, and Wideman, the vernacular effect is carried by the grammar, including omitted *is* (*My mama dead*), unmarked past tense (*die, scream*), double negatives (*don't say nothing*) and invariant *be:*

> My mama dead. She die screaming and cussing. She scream at me. She cuss at me. I'm big. I can't move fast enough. By time I git back from the well, the water be warm. By time I git the tray ready the food be cold. By time I git all the children ready for school it be dinner time. He don't say nothing. He set there by the bed holding her hand an cryin, talking bout don't leave me, don't go. She ast me bout the first one. Whose it is? I say God's. I don't know no other man or what else to say.

The virtually uninterrupted vernacular flow in this novel (found in letters the protagonist, Celie, writes to God and a sister) is particularly effective. By letting Celie recount her experiences in what Stephen Henderson called the "language of feeling," Walker allows her black readers in particular to develop an emotional kinship with the testimony. Walker might have reasoned correctly that they who speak dialect think and dream dialect, too. This rule holds firm in Ntozake Shange's (b. 1948) *for colored girls who have considered suicide / when the rainbow is enuf* (1975), a "choreopoem" in which the artist's stream-of-consciousness technique gets a boost from the lexicon, the unique words, of African American English:

i got drunk & cdnt figure out
whose hand waz on my thigh / but it didn't matter
cuz these cousins martin eddie sammy jerome & bobby
waz my sweethearts alternately since the seventh grade
& everybody knew i always started cryin if somebody actually
tried to take advantage of me
    at jacqui's
ulinda mason was stickin her mouth all out
while we tumbled out the buick
eddie jones waz her lickin stick
but i knew how to dance
    it got soo hot
vincent ramos puked all in the punch
& harly jumped all in tico's face
cuz he was leavin for the navy in the mornin
hadda kick ass so we'd all remember how bad he waz
seems like sheila and marguerite waz fraid
to get their hair turnin back
so they laid up against the wall
lookin almost sexy
didn't wanna sweat
but me & my fellas
      we waz dancin . . .

In this excerpt from Shange's prose poem turned play, the most obvious evidence of audience is vocabulary. References to a *lickin stick* (a dance partner), *jumped all in tico's face* (confronted him), *their hair turnin back* (the wilting and frizzing of black women's straightened hair as their flattened natural coil reacts to the shock of dampness), all expose Shange's desire to engage a specific in-group. There is also some "eye dialect"—spellings such as *cdn't* and *waz*, which don't convey pronunciations different from "couldn't" and "was," but contribute to the impression of vernacular usage. The parlance of black teenagers relays the narrator's experiences effectively. But we must not overlook the *connotation* of the language; the expressed slickness of the joint and the youth trying to be "down" with the scene and the sexual tension and the violent possibility. These ideas don't always translate directly into the language of the white prom going on across town.

Authenticity

Authenticity in African American art and life is paramount. Within hip-hop circles, the mantra is "keep it real," but the same notion exists wherever black people meet. For a people who have been imitated and crossed over and sold out so relentlessly, authenticity is the highly valued sense of what is genuine. It is a question of privilege and access, the password uttered at the door to all that is soulful. And it poses an especially daunting challenge for the black writer. If members of the African American community are to consider a narrative legitimately homespun, they must recognize its origins. Here again, the vernacular can be an invaluable commodity.

It has been observed that the artist creates most poignantly when tapping the wellspring of his or her most intimate memories. Relics from the "oral world" of the African or African American child—phrases, axioms, toasts, boasts, tall tales, prayers—become ore in the imagination of the grown-up author. When the author bores into this source, what often issues forth is the most organic language, the language the author's mother used when scolding or cooing. So Zora Neale Hurston (1891–1960), born in the black township of Eatonville, Florida, must have enjoyed a knowing chuckle when she typed expressions such as these into the pages of her novel *Their Eyes Were Watching God* (1937):

> Ah yeah, she's too smart tuh stay round heah. She figgers we'se jus' uh bunch uh dumb niggers so she think she'll grow horns. But dat's uh lie. She'll die butt-headed.

Such colloquialisms might have swirled about Hurston in the household of her girlhood. Once grown, the accomplished folklorist and anthropologist draped her dialogue with the peculiarities and syntax of black small-town southern living. As Henry Louis Gates Jr. has noted about Hurston and Sterling Brown, "two of the truly great minds of 'the race,'" their

> reverence for the black vernacular and their use of it as the touchstone for rhetorical excellence provide critical models that I have tried to imitate, even if the critical language that I employ might seem to be a different language.

Elsewhere in *Their Eyes,* Hurston's sprite heroine, Janie—ever refusing to live under the heels of men—returns with a wicked tongue an insult her partner, Joe Starks, has hurled at her:

> Naw, Ah ain't no young gal no mo' but den Ah ain't no old woman neither. Ah reckon Ah looks mah age too. But Ah'm uh woman every inch of me, and Ah know it. Dat's a whole lot more'n *you* kin say. You big-bellies round here and put out a lot of brag, but 'tain't nothin' to

it but yo' big voice. Humph! Talkin' 'bout *me* lookin' old! When you pull down yo' britches, you look lak de change uh life.

Besides its deftly timed delivery of Spoken Soul—conveyed primarily through pronunciation spellings (*mo* for "more" and *Ah* for "I") and eye dialect (*uh* for "a")—what makes this passage so convincing is its nod to that ancient African American ritual of putdown swapping known variously as sounding, signifying, capping, snapping, or "playing the dozens." To play, opponents try to outdo each other in a lavishly styled, highly social, lightning-quick display of verbal prowess and improvisation. Hurston's characters observe such rituals again and again as they travel from page to page, lending an authoritative voice to the plot and revealing the author's familiarity with black rhetorical and speech-event traditions.

Hurston's love affair with black speech extended to a passion for black folktales. In many respects the precursors to African American literature, black folktales have always achieved their most memorable recital (and conveyed their most profound message) when delivered with the dramatic inflections of dialect. Daryl Cumber Dance, a leading authority on black folklore, observed as much in the introduction to her anthology of black folklore:

> It is important to note that practically all the jokes included here were delivered in dialect. Even the most sophisticated joke tellers usually revert to dialect in close company. Indeed the tales lose much of their flavor in standard English. As Chapman J. Milling aptly averred, "a Negro story not told in Negro dialect is about as successful as a honeymoon shared by the mother-in-law."

Passed on through generations from elders—descendants of African griots who held the wisdom of nations on their tongues—to youngsters, the various genres of African American folklore serve both to entertain and educate. Decidedly in the entertainment category is this "lie," or tall tale, narrated in 1970 by Walter Simmons, a Baptist deacon from Daufuskie Island, South Carolina, whose powerful prayer is featured in chapter 3. The Gullah roots of the tale are evident in his Creole pronunciations, and in many grammatical features, including the use of *dem* for "those" ("*dem* road," "*dem* wedge"), the occasional use of *um* for "it" ("keep *um* from rollin down"), the use of unstressed *been* for "was" or "were" ("dey *been* bout five thousan people *been* dere"), and the fact that virtually every past-tense verb apart from *was* and *had* is unmarked (*see, grow, roll*):

> I see a man raise a watermelon once. Dis watermelon was on a hill, was on de side of a hill, you know, an dey had—just like you gone up on de mountain an had dem road, road on de side of de mountain—it was on de hill, like dat. An dat watermelon grow so large until dey—he roll it up on de side dere in a low place, an been usin it fuh a BRIDGE! People useta come by from everywhere to look at dat watermelon. It was growin so large, until it grow so high until cars couldn't even much go OVUH de bridge! An dey had to—every two or three days dey had to put another wedge on de side of um to keep um from rollin down, you know. An dey been bout five thousan people been dere been lookin at dat melon dat Friday aftanoon. An one of dem wedge slip out, an dat melon start down de hill. An when it strike itself in front of dem rock, it break in half, an de water come out of um drowned over five hundred head o' people.

Walter Simmons is obviously taken with his story, displaying an acute enjoyment in the telling, in the setting up of the drama, and in the satisfying culmination. Note that although this "lie" deals with a watermelon, it has nothing to do with watermelon eating, the ubiquitous black stereotype. The watermelon is, in fact, merely a stage prop for the storyteller's clever exaggerations, piled one on top of another in his deadpan vernacular as his audience expresses mock amazement and rolls with laughter.

Intrinsic to the authenticity of many folk-tale genres is the dialogue between two or more characters, usually rendered in the vernacular. A compelling example of this is children's jump-rope rhymes, which often have the call-and-response structure prevalent in the African American church, in African American music, and in many other aspects of African American performance. The following passage from a jump-rope rhyme, "Aunt Dinah Died," was recorded in Alcoa, Tennessee. Note the use of unmarked *die* for "died," *wear* for "wears," and the omission of *is* in *where she living* and elsewhere:

CALL: Aunt Dinah died.

RESPONSE: How she die?

CALL: Oh, she die like this. (*Does expression and gesture.*)

RESPONSE: Oh, she die like this!

CALL: (*excited*) Aunt Dinah's living!

RESPONSE: Where she living?

ALL: (*fast*) Oh, she living in a place called Tennessee.
         She wear short, short dresses up above her knees.
         She gon' shake that shimmy wherever she go.

Of course, drama is the genre in which dialogue reigns, and plays involving African American characters seem almost to demand authenticity in the form of black vernacular conversation. James Baldwin (1924–1987), one of the most clairvoyant American writers of the twentieth century, penned the essays in *The Fire Next Time* (1963) in artful, incisive Standard English. But to render the dialogue of African Americans in his novels, short stories, and plays, he often chose artful, incisive Black English. This is from his 1964 play *Blues for Mister Charlie:*

PETE: Old Papa D. got something on everybody, don't he?

JUANITA: You better believe it.

RICHARD: He's kind of a Tom, ain't he?

PETE: Yeah. He *talks* about Mister Charlie and he *says* he's with us—us kids—but he ain't going to do nothing to offend him. You know, he's still trading with Lyle Britten?

RICHARD: Who's Lyle Britten?

PETE: Peckerwood, owns a store nearby. And, man, you ain't *seen* a peckerwood until you've seen Lyle Britten. Niggers been trading in his store for years, man, I wouldn't be surprised but if the cat was rich—but that man still expects you to step off the sidewalk when he comes along. So we been getting people to stop buying there.

JUANITA: He shot a colored man a few years back, shot him dead, and wasn't nothing never said, much less done, about it.

In a 1997 article about the Ebonics controversy, Christopher Hitchens, recalling an essay Baldwin wrote in praise of Black English, contended that the writer had defended a "language he didn't speak," as "a duty paid to history." But the Standard English that Baldwin commanded in speech and in prose may well have deceived Hitchens. After all, what's to say Baldwin didn't demonstrate an equally impressive command of the vernacular when he was hanging with his peers? Indeed, given the fact that Baldwin grew up a poor, black Harlemite, it's a safe bet that he could probably deploy some pretty bad jive. Not even nine years in France (1948–1957) could have eroded that competence, which is evident in the vocabulary of the passage (*got* for "has"; *Tom* for "black sellout"; *Mister Charlie* and *peckerwood* for "white man") as well as its grammar. Notice, in addition to linguistic features such as *ain't* and *been* (used here as an equivalent to "have been") and the double negative ("he *ain't* going to do *nothing*"), Baldwin's use of the inverted double negative in "*wasn't nothing* never said" (versus "nothing wasn't never said").

The vernacular also runs throughout the play *A Raisin in the Sun*, by Lorraine Hansberry (1930–1965). This masterpiece, awarded the New York Drama Critics Circle Award for Best Play of 1959, ran for 538 performances on Broadway, and was the longest-running Broadway production by an African American in its time. The opening sentence of the following passage rings as true to the voice of the vernacular today as it did forty years ago, and the grammatical features after it (including *ain't,* and the absence of *are* in *We just plain working folks*) further reinforce this timbre:

MAMA: Now don't you start, child. It's too early in the morning to be talking about money. It ain't Christian.

RUTH: It's just that he got his heart set on that store—

MAMA: You mean that liquor store that Willie Harris want him to invest in?

RUTH: Yes—

MAMA: We ain't no business people, Ruth. We just plain working folks.

RUTH: Ain't nobody business people till they go into business. . . .

August Wilson (b. 1945), whose 1986 play *Fences* won four Tony Awards and a Pulitzer Prize, has provided some of the most credible depictions of black characters in American drama. Wilson deploys a battery of grammatical vernacular features, including completive *done* ("they *done* trumped") and habitual *be* ("he *be* making out"):

BONO: I told Brownie if the man come and ask him any questions . . . just tell the truth! It ain't nothing but something they done trumped up on you 'cause you filed a complaint on them.

TROY: Brownie don't understand nothing. All I want them to do is change the job description. Give everybody a chance to drive the truck. Brownie can't see that. He ain't got that much sense.

BONO: How you figure he be making out with that gal be up at Taylor's all the time . . . that Alberta gal?

In an interview with John Rickford, Wilson explained that while he "values and respects the way that black people talk," when he first tried to write plays, in the early 1980s, he thought that "in order to create art out of it you have to change it." So he would put high-flown language in the mouths of his characters: "Terror hangs over the night like a hawk." In a 1996 article in *People,* he was quoted as saying, "Back then I didn't value and respect the way blacks talked—the everyday poetry of the people I'd grown up with." But then, as he testified in 1999, his feelings changed:

> I was reading a pamphlet by Sekou Touré called "The Artisans and Not the Political Leaders are Representative of the Culture." In that pamphlet he says, "Language describes the ideas of the one who speaks it." It's a very simple and profound statement. Stayed with me, and I began to think about it and analyze it: "Language describes the ideas of the one who speaks it." So there's really nothing wrong with the way that people talk. That is their language and it's describing their ideas. Language describing the ideas is a thought process also; you talk how you think. Once I put those two things together, I said, "Oh, I see, art is within the language of the people. You don't have to change it." . . . Before, [when] I'd try to write, the characters wouldn't sound right. It was stilted, it was stiff, it didn't work. 'Cause I was trying to change it instead of letting it be its own thing. Once I decided to just let it be its own thing, then the characters started talking, and I was writing it down, couldn't shut 'em up. Whereas before, I had trouble writing a dialogue, now it was easy, it flowed because I accepted it.

When asked whether the soulful speech patterns in his plays were relics from his childhood in Pittsburgh, or gems picked up later from observation and listening, Wilson went on to say that the language

> was just in the air. All the people in the neighborhood where I grew up, that's the way they talked. [In Pittsburgh] I spent a large amount of time in a cigar store where the elderly men from the neighborhood would congregate. And they'd sit around there and they'd talk all kinds of stuff and I'd stand there and listen to 'em. There's a lot of this, that's the way they talk: "Yes, I come up, yeah, I come ta Pittsburgh in 'forty-two. Come on da B&O Railroad." "No you ain't!" "You gon tell me . . . ?" "Yeah, hell, yeah, I'm gon tell you, too, 'cause B&O railroad didn' stop in Pittsburgh! B&O Railroad had four stops an' it ain't through heah!" So everybody that came in: "Ey, ey, ey ey, Joe, ey, Fillmore, come on, man. Man talkin', talkin' 'bout how he come up on the B&O Railroad in 'forty-two. Stopped at so-an'-so an' so-an'-so an' so-an'-so." This stuff could go on for two weeks. I found it fascinating.

Wilson's remarks reveal not only that he has a keen ear, but also that he enjoys the vibrant give-and-take of colloquial conversation. His ability to re-create and evoke the beauty, poetry, and wisdom of everyday black speech is a key element in his plays' authenticity and power.

Attitude

Wilson's deployment of Spoken Soul reveals his love for it, and his respect for its speakers. But not every work that employs the vernacular conveys equally positive attitudes, In fact, to trace the origins of some of the widespread condemnation Ebonics received during the 1990s, particularly among African Americans, we must go back more than a century, to the minstrel tradition that was popular in the United States between about 1840 and 1900. As Sylvia Wallace Holton, a professor of English, has noted:

> The minstrel show may have originated on the plantation, first as a means of entertainment by the slaves for themselves and later as a more stylized performance for their masters and their guests. . . . Whatever its origin, it developed rapidly into a ritualized three-part form performed by white men in black face [using grease or burnt cork] to burlesque the black. The image of the black man that grew out of the minstrel show, which became confused with reality in the minds of many Americans, was of a carefree entertainer who could sing about jumping Jim Crow. . . .

The minstrel tradition was infamous for reinforcing demeaning stereotypes of African Americans—as comical, childlike, gullible, lazy, and in the words of Nathan Huggins, "unrestrained in enthusiasm for music—for athletic and rhythmical dance" and "insatiable in . . . bodily appetite." These stereotypes were conveyed in part by a highly conventionalized "Negro dialect" used by the minstrel performers, as in this example in which *am* is used instead of "is"—a peculiarity one didn't hear in black speech of the time, and doesn't hear today:

END: Mr. Cleveland, a fellow was trying to stuff me dat when it am
       day here it am night in China.

MID: Well, James, that is true.

END: What makes it true?

MID: It is caused by the earth rotating on its axis, but—

END: What am an axis?

Zora Neale Hurston complained in 1934 about the inaccuracy of the dialect in minstrel shows and dialect literature ("If we are to believe the majority of writers of Negro dialect and the burnt-cork artists, Negro speech is a weird thing, full of 'ams' and 'Ises.' . . . Nowhere can be found the Negro who asks 'am it?' nor yet his brother who announces 'Ise uh gwinter' "). Black lawyer, poet, and novelist James Weldon Johnson (1871–1938) voiced in 1933 a more fundamental objection to it, as an instrument so fused to stereotype that it had become a limiting, insurmountable mold:

> I got a sudden realization of the artificiality of conventionalized Negro dialect poetry; of its exaggerated geniality, childish optimism, forced comicality, and mawkish sentiment; of its limitation as an instrument of expression to but two emotions, pathos and humor, thereby making every poem either only sad or funny. I saw that not even Dunbar had been able to break the mold in which dialect poetry had, long before him, been set by representations made of the Negro on the minstrel stage. I saw that he had cut away much of what was coarse and "nigger-ish," and added a deeper tenderness, a higher polish, a more delicate finish; but also I saw that, nevertheless, practically all of his work in dialect fitted into the traditional mold.

African Americans who resented the prominence bestowed on Ebonics by the 1996 Oakland resolution may have feared a resurrection of some of the vile stereotypes of the minstrel show and the "Negro dialect" tradition of a century before. Ebonics humor (see chapter 11) showed us that such fears were not entirely unfounded.

A century ago, James Weldon Johnson noted perceptibly that the writer working in the dialect conventions of the time was dominated by his white audience, and that "when he wrote he was expressing what often bore little relation at all, to actual Negro life; that he was really expressing only certain conceptions about Negro life that his audience was willing to accept and ready to enjoy." He contrasted this "outside group" orientation with the inward orientations of folk artists: "The latter, although working in the dialect, sought only to express themselves for themselves, and to their *own group*" (emphasis in original).

Not only were nineteenth-century minstrel shows and books containing black dialect intended mainly for white audiences, they also were dominated by white performers and writers. Indeed, the grand-daddies of vernacular literature—Joel Chandler Harris and Thomas Nelson Page—were white. Harris, who "played minstrelsy" in his youth, concocted the popular Uncle Remus (*Uncle Remus: His Songs and His Sayings,* 1880), a character who held up all the old stereotypes and who was enormously popular with whites, including President Theodore Roosevelt. Uncle Remus became the star of Walt Disney's Oscar-winning 1946 movie *Song of the South,* a box-office hit until it was withdrawn in the 1960s amid criticism that it perpetuated black stereotypes. Remus, a benign plantation figure, recited tales from the African American tradition for the amusement of a seven-year-old white boy. The first tale in the book, "Uncle Remus Initiates the Little Boy," opens as follows:

> One evening recently, the lady whom Uncle Remus calls "Miss Sally" missed her seven-year-old. Making search for him through the house and through the yard, she heard the sound of voices in the old man's cabin, and looking through the window, saw the child sitting by Uncle Remus. His head rested against the old man's arm, and he was gazing with an expression of the most intense interest into the rough, weather-beaten face, that beamed so kindly upon him. This is what "Miss Sally" heard:
>
> "Bimeby, one day, arter Brer Fox bin doin' all dat he could fer ter ketch Brer Rabbit, en Brer Rabbit bin doin' all he could fer ter keep 'im fum it, Brer Fox say to hisse'f dat he'd put up a game on Brer Rabbit, en he ain't mo'n got de wuds out'n his mouf twel Brer Rabbit come a lopin' up de big road, lookin' des ez plump, en ez fat, en ez sassy ez a Moggin hoss in a barley-patch.
>
> "'Hol' on dar, Brer Rabbit,' sez Brer Fox, sezee. . . ."

Harris has been praised by several generations of scholars for the accuracy of the copiously represented middle Georgia dialect spoken by Uncle Remus. The author has also been credited for his folkloric recording of the Brer Rabbit genre of African American folklore, with its roots in the African trickster tradition, and its invaluable survival lessons for slaves and ex-slaves. But he has also been criticized for his portrayal of Uncle Remus as a doddling, genial throwback to a romanticized period in which whites owned slaves and plantations prospered. As critic Robert Hemenway has noted, linking the Remus stereotype and his language:

> Uncle Remus, an "old time Negro," reminds Southerners of what was "good" about slavery, becoming a wish-fulfillment fantasy for a populace forced to deal each day with black people considerably less docile than the plantation darky. Remus's dialect especially supports this fantasy. The Standard English used by the author to frame the tales contrasts with the vivid dialect in the stories themselves, suggesting that black language is colorful but ignorant, that black people are picturesque but intellectually limited.

Thomas Nelson Page published his collection of dialect stories *In Ole Virginia* in 1887, seven years after Uncle Remus first appeared.

Page is usually hailed as an able chronicler of contemporary eastern Virginia black dialect. But as Sylvia Wallace Horton has noted, Page's representation "is similar to much nineteenth-century dialect writing in that it seems to be bent on representing black speech as 'special' and on suggesting the 'illiteracy' of the black speaker—on eliciting from the reader a patronizing attitude rather than one of empathy." Page's stories generally depicted slaves who were content with their lot and happy to serve their white masters. In this passage from "Marse Chan," Sam, an old black man, bemoans the good old planta-tion days:

> "Well, when Marse Chan wuz born, dey wuz de grettes' doin's at home you ever did see. De folks all hed holiday, jes' like in de Chris'mas. Ole marster . . . his face fyar shine wid pleasure, and all de folks wuz mighty glad, too, 'cause dey loved ole marster. . . ."

The Clansman (1905), by white novelist Thomas Dixon Jr. (1864–1946), shored up the stereotype Page and other dialect writers had constructed. In one scene of the book, which was billed as an "histor-ical romance of the Ku Klux Klan," a former slave reacts violently to a white northerner's suggestion that he turn on his "ole marster," ex-claiming: "Den take dat f'um yo' equal, d—m you! . . . I'll show you how to treat my ole marster, you low-down slue-footed devil!"

As the early decades of the twentieth century clanged to life, black intellectuals increasingly expressed intolerance for such por-trayals, and began to prod their own writers to combat old-school im-ages with a new breed of unapologetic, nationalist rhetoric (laid down in Standard English). Black philosopher and critic Alain Locke (1886–1954), a helmsman of the movement, called in the 1920s for African Americans to shed the worn, sentimental skin they had been assigned in the South and subscribe to the boldly independent and refined black spirit then developing in northern cities. He christened the creature produced by this metamorphosis the New Negro. For Locke, whose influence among black intellectuals cannot be overstated, the peddling of dialect by black authors signaled a backslide to the think-ing of yesteryear: a return, essentially, to the sensibilities of the Old Negro beloved by Harris, Page, and Dixon. Locke once observed that "the soul of the Negro will be discovered in a characteristic way of thinking and in a homely philosophy rather than in a jingling and juggling of broken English," using words clearly reminiscent of Dun-bar's famous lament about dialect poetry, "The Poet."

But other black writers refused to shun the speech of the black masses just because outsiders had misrepresented it. Ever vivacious and perhaps even scandalously outspoken for a woman of her time, Zora Neale Hurston was disgusted by the mere idea, which she said had sprung from the snobbish Negroes she tauntingly dubbed the "Niggerati." She and Langston Hughes, a contemporary and onetime friend, believed that the dialect best signified the black proletariat, the common folk whose stories they endeavored to tell truthfully. In his 1940 autobiography, *The Big Sea,* Hughes squared off with renowned black critics such as Benjamin Brawley and prominent newspaper reviewers who had skewered his second collection of poetry, *Fine Clothes to the Jew,* as "a disgrace to the race, a return to the dialect tradition, and a parading of all our racial defects before the public." Hughes seemed surprised and hurt by the whipping the publication received at the hands of black scholars. After all, weren't the verses true to the roustabouts and the down-and-out blacks who thronged New York City's Lenox Avenue? To those who would have had him stick to upscale Standard English, which he labeled an "un-Negro tongue," Hughes offered this defense:

> Anyway, I didn't know the upper class Negroes well enough to write much about them. I knew only the people I had grown up with, and they weren't people whose shoes were always shined, who had been to Harvard, or who had heard of Bach. But they seemed to me good people, too.

Nevertheless, Hughes acknowledged the minstrel legacy. He understood why black intellectuals, as he put it, wanted to extend to society the race's "politely polished and cultural foot" and parade "not-funny Negroes" before white spectators. But it was a compromise he would not make. Hughes believed that if the Harlem Renaissance was to be a true incubator for self-examination, for rooting out that which was organically African American, for establishing an aesthetic apart from the whims and history of Europeans, then language—the ultimate conduit of culture—had to be given its due.

He had allies. In 1928, the Jamaican-born poet and novelist Claude McKay (1889–1948) published *Home to Harlem,* the first best-selling book by an African American. McKay is often remembered for his sonnets, such as the militant "If We Must Die" (1919), which Winston Churchill later used to rouse England's wartime patriotism. That often quoted poem was delivered in Standard English. But *Home to Harlem*—whose title suggests a return to familial and domestic conventions—was loaded with vernacular dialogue. This was true as well of *The Walls of Jericho,* published also in 1928, by the black physician, fiction writer, and musical arranger Rudolph Fisher (1897–1934). Fisher's book included a ten-page glossary of "Contemporary Harlemese," with terms such as *Boogy* ("Negro. A contraction of Booker T., used only of and by members of the race") and *Mr. Charlie* ("Nonspecific designation of 'swell' whites").

Even before Hughes and Hurston, McKay and Fisher, however, Paul Laurence Dunbar (1872–1906), the first African American poet of national prominence and the dean of the early black-dialect writers, had been taking on genuine African American themes in this medium. In "When Malindy Sings" (1895), for instance, the poet chides his master's "missus," whose croak cannot match his mother's croon:

> G'way an' quit dat noise, Miss Lucy—
> Put dat music book away;
> What's de use to keep on tryin'?
> Ef you practise twell you're gray,
> You cain't sta't no notes a-flyin'
> Lak de ones dat rants and rings
> F'om de kitchen to de big woods
> When Malindy sings.

Dunbar received stinging criticism in his time for calling up nostalgic images of slavery in some of his poems (such as "The Deserted Plantation," in which a former slave laments the ruin of a glorious plantation). But "When Malindy Sings" does have undercurrents of political awareness. Though its mood is light, its motive is the poet's admiration for the charms of his mother over those of his missus. In praising his mother, he testifies not only to her superior singing voice, but also to her superior graces. The black woman, regarded by whites during slavery as an animal for breeding and portrayed as indelicate and unattractive long after emancipation, is thus elevated over a white woman, the mythical creature blacks had been programmed to worship as the archetype of femininity and beauty.

Dunbar's relationship with dialect was a complex affair, though. He was the master of the dialect genre, and stretched to his colossal stature on the shoulders of the idiom. As he told his contemporary and disciple James Weldon Johnson, he wrote black dialect "as well [as], if not better than, anybody else." Johnson agreed, noting that Dunbar "had carried dialect poetry as far as and as high as it could go," and "had brought it to the fullest measure of charm, tenderness, and beauty it could hold." At the same time, Dunbar was frustrated that while the dialect poetry gained him a hearing, "now they don't want me to write anything but dialect." He was especially frustrated that the many fine poems he wrote in Standard English (among them "Sympathy" and "We Wear the Mask") were not accorded the same recognition by white audiences and the literary world as his dialect pieces. In "The Poet," he expressed this frustration, deploying the word ("jingle") that would be used by other black writers (Locke and Johnson, for instance) to disparage dialect poetry.

> He sang of life, serenely sweet,
>> With, now and then, a deeper note.
>> From some high peak, nigh yet remote,
> He voiced the world's absorbing heat.
>
> He sang of love when earth was young,
>> And Love, itself, was in his lays.
>> But ah, the world, it turned to praise
> A jingle in a broken tongue.

Dunbar was only one of many black writers and laymen to display an attraction-repulsion relationship with the black vernacular. James Weldon Johnson, whose works include the black national anthem "Lift Every Voice and Sing" (1900) and *The Autobiography of an Ex-Coloured Man* (1912), began by writing dialect poems "after the style of Dunbar," such as the mournful "Sence You Went Away" (1900), with which he opened a section entitled "Jingles and Croons":

> Seems lak to me de stars don't shine so bright,
> Seems lak to me de sun done loss his light,
> Seems lak to me der's nothin' goin' right,
>> Sence you went away.

In his preface to the first edition of *The Book of American Negro Poetry* (1922), Johnson not only praised Dunbar's dialect poetry, but said more generally:

> It would be a distinct loss if the American Negro poets threw away this quaint and musical folk speech as a medium of expression. . . . They are trying to break away from, not Negro dialect itself, but the limitations on Negro dialect imposed by the fixing effects of long convention.

Here he struck a hopeful note for the future of dialect poetry, drawing a conscious distinction between the merits of the vernacular and the curse placed on it by the nineteenth-century minstrel and literary tradition. But in the anthology's revised 1931 edition, Johnson not only nixed a dialect section entitled "Jingles and Croons" (according to Sterling Brown), but was extremely pessimistic about the potential of dialect poetry, observing that "it is now realized both by the poets and by their public that as an instrument for poetry the dialect has only two main stops, humor and pathos." In the preface to *God's Trombones* (1927), a collection of "Negro folk sermons in verse," Johnson explained why he had once again favored Standard English over the vernacular:

> At first thought, Negro dialect would appear to be the precise medium for these old-time sermons: however, as the reader will see, the poems are not written in dialect. . . . although the dialect is the exact instrument for voicing certain traditional phases of Negro life, it is, and perhaps by that very exactness, a quite limited instrument.

Dialect, it seems, was a creature with which Johnson grappled or danced. One moment he would embrace it, unleashing its talents, allowing its cadence to guide his hand. The next moment he would try to hold it at bay, albeit grudgingly, conceding pats of admiration all the while. An ambivalent love affair, to be sure.

But if Johnson was locked in a push-pull relationship with the dialect, he was not alone. Seventy years later, Maya Angelou betrayed the same ambivalence. The renowned African American poet-novelist came across as a vehement foe of vernacular use after the Ebonics controversy erupted in December 1996, saying that she was "incensed" by the Oakland decision. (In fairness to her, she appeared to think, like most people, that Oakland was preparing to teach Ebonics and do away with Standard English instruction). But in applying the art of the vernacular, she had proven herself just as guilty (or as deft) as Dunbar. As many of today's most visible black writers have done, Angelou has distinguished herself in both Standard and vernacular African American English. Her poem "The Pusher" begins:

> He bad
> O he bad
> He make a honky
> poot. . . .

While "The Thirteens (Black)" ends:

> . . . Your cousin's taking smack,
> Your Uncle's in the joint,
> Your buddy's in the gutter,
> Shooting for his point,
> The thirteens. Right On.
>
> And you, you make me sorry,
> You out here by yourself,
> I'd call you something dirty,
> But there just ain't nothing left,
> cept
> The thirteens. Right On.

In both cases, Angelou effectively uses both vernacular vocabulary (*bad, honky, poot, smack*) and grammar (*He bad, there just ain't nothing left*) to convey some of the hard realities of urban life.

Does dialect literature limit or liberate? The question has framed a central conflict among black literati for decades. It is an issue that lives today, still poking a tender spot in the African American psyche. Although many writers seemed unable to hide the profound self-consciousness they felt with respect to Spoken Soul, those sampled above called on it not merely to serve as a curious adornment but also to capture essential elements of the African American experience, an experience that from day to day involves far more than merely pathos or humor. As we have observed, there was (and is) an array of practical and artistic motives behind the use of the idiom. But the most accomplished writers in the vernacular have understood two rudimentary principles: That message cannot be separated from language, and that Spoken Soul often thrives when and where Standard English is left mute. Those who were tormented by that reality swore up and down that they were limited and offended by the vernacular, but they couldn't fully divorce themselves from it either, making spirited use of it in their social interactions as well as in the literature they bequeathed to posterity.

3

Preachers and Pray-ers

But when God speaks, who can but prophesy? (Amen.) *The word of God is upon me like fire shut up in my bones* (Yes. That's right.), *and when God's word gets upon me, I've got to tell it all over everywhere. [Shouting.]* (Yes.)

—The Reverend Martin Luther King Jr. (1966)

I can kick up a little bit of dust sometimes if I got somebody to start de fire for me, an' kind of warm me up, ya' know what I mean? It'll make yuh rub yuh eye, anyhow.

—Deacon Walter Simmons (1972)

With their repertoire of styles and their passion for pageantry and dramatics, black preachers in the traditional black church don't merely deliver sermons. They hold court. When they testify for "King Jesus" in the tradition of the ancestors, the approach is eloquent, compelling, and certain to kick up dust. For the black church, which must reward the suffering of the stepped-upon and ward off despair in hard times, necessitates men and women who are on fire with the Lord, and who ain't too proud to perspire when delivering the Word. Ministers who can "take a text" from the Bible and "break it down" to the level of everyday people are adored. Intensity and fervor are almost always desired; "dead bones" preachers need not apply. In the many incarnations of the black church, the Living Word tends to be sung, shouted, clapped, hummed, stomped, and testified to in a majestic way that moves and moves and moves.

But black preaching is not just a romp. Many young African American ministers strain to perfect that lavish delivery, to tap an old-school tradition of oral performance that will help them upright toppled souls and earn the respect of the most demanding congregations. But first they must learn to conduct the elaborate exchanges between pulpit and pews that galvanize the black church. To keep members of the flock pressing toward that "mansion in the sky," even to hold their attention fully on a Sunday morning, the black preacher must become a maestro of style, appealing not only to the people's circumstances but to their sense of timing, elegance, tragedy, and humor as well.

So the way in which a sermon is presented becomes almost as crucial as its content. Worshippers must be cued to stand or clap or sway or say "Amen" or wave their palms in testimony through a variety of rhetorical strategies that work them up and draw them in, including innovative metaphors and similes; apt narratives and quotations; appropriate variation in voice quality, gesture, pace, pitch, and volume; and skillful deployment of alliteration, improvisation, humor, repetition, and rhyme. With this mélange, souls on both sides of the altar can be satisfied. As the Bible is "made plain" and the faithful are swept up in the grandeur of the worship experience, the preacher displays an intimate relationship with Christ and struts his or her own verbal panache.

With so many dishes to keep spinning, black preachers cannot forsake Spoken Soul. And many do use the vernacular purposely, effectively, and frequently. In fact, some preach almost entirely in dialect (whether or not they would acknowledge as much if challenged on the matter). Around 1950, a man of the cloth in Macon County, Georgia, described a biblical tragedy as follows:

> Ah, the world swolled up 'gainst man; the seven seas swolled up 'gainst man. Lawd! Telephone wire done come off the post—torn down. Lawd! Gonna make one day—it—Last mountain, Mount Calvery. Man had no salvation. I kin see 'im goin', "I must go to Calvery." Ah, Lord! "Captain's been waiting for me; Captain been looking for me; Captain have been waiting for me—four thousand years ago." Ohhhhhhh, Glory!

Most African American preachers, however, use primarily Standard English in their sermons, making deliberate or not so deliberate excursions into the black vernacular from time to time. So when we talk about Spoken Soul in preaching, we're talking less about a vernacular spree and more about a rhetorical style, an aggregation of vocal and body techniques that overlaps class, geographical region, and denomination.

Blindfold anyone who has ever heard the Reverend Jesse Jackson or Minister Louis Farrakhan preach, march that person into virtually any African American church from New York to Los Angeles, and without hearing a single "ain't" or "sho' nuff," the person will probably be able to identify the minister's race immediately. The Reverend Jackson is Baptist, Minister Farrakhan is Muslim, and both overwhelmingly choose Standard English in their sermons and speeches. But they share an unmistakable and undeniably soulful approach to "running down" the gospel that is reminiscent of the Reverend Martin Luther King Jr. and countless other black ministers and deacons.

Of course, there are many varieties of black churches, and many styles within the black preaching rubric. You may come across a Pentecostal or Holiness minister in Chicago who sings or screams his sermons, and witness a very different tradition in Catholic churches in Philadelphia or New Orleans. Yet it is remarkable that a visit to almost *any* African American church—particularly those in the Baptist and Pentecostal traditions—will yield at least some elements of the soulful preaching tradition, regardless of the educational background of the preacher and the extent to which he or she uses the vernacular itself.

With its quavering falsettos and sonorous baritones, purposeful stuttering, fetching snarls and whispers, singsong melody, rhymes and half-rhymes, interjected exclamations of "hunh," and other trademarks, black preaching is hard to miss and impossible to dismiss. When we examine its themes, functions, and form, we gain precious insight into the souls of black folk, and draw closer to understanding why many of their churches rock like Jericho.

Kickin' Up Dust: Themes and Virtuosity of Black Worship

One Sunday evening in 1970, on a tiny Sea Island off the coast of South Carolina and Georgia, a small group of black Baptists gathered in their praise-house. The Gullah people of Daufuskie Island (which had an almost all-black population of about 110 and—then as now—could be reached solely by boat) were so isolated that only rarely did an ordained preacher from the mainland come to call. Instead of formal church services, the islanders held weekly prayer meetings led by a handful of elders or deacons. That particular morning, Brother Walter "Plummy" Simmons, a subsistence farmer in his sixties, ran the ceremony with the soulful support of his wife, Sister Agnes. After offering the disclaimer "I ain't no preacher—I can't preach," he launched into the prayer that appears below in abridged form. (With the exception of the loss of the final *r*, we have tried to represent faithfully the pronunciation of the original, as well as its grammar.)

Walter Simmons	*Agnes Simmons*
Let us praise God.	*Mmm-hmm*
De day is past an gone.	*Lord, have mercy*
An de evenin shall appear.	*Mmm-hmm*
Oh, may we all remember well	
When de night of death draw nigh.	
We-we'll lay our garment by	
And upon our bed to res.	
An soon, death will corrode us all,	*Lord, have mercy*
An what we have possessed.	
Dis day, dis day, our Father,	*Lord Jesus*
Here is a few, of your own han made.	
We 'semble ourselves together, our Father,	
Not because we could 'semble here,	
Neither to be seen by man.	*Mmm-hmmm*
But, our Father, I ask you please,	
Oh please, our Father, while you ridin,	*Oh, please*
On de route one ridin on to Jericho,	*Have mercy*
Please, stop by dis house dis day, our Father,	
'Cause I want to give you thanks, our Father,	
For how las night's sleep has not found me dead.	
Here our early rise dis mornin	
Hasn' found us to dead man's bed.	*Oooh, yes*
Den, den, den, our Father,	
You lay me down las night,	
An you sen your angel	
An you guard me allll night long.	*Lord, have mercy*
An sooon dis mornin, our Father,	
You wake us up. Our Father,	
We are clothed, in our right mind.	*Lord, have mercy*
An our Father, we want to	
Give you another thanks,	
Our Father, dat when you	
Wake us up dis mornin,	
We found here a coool worl,	*Mmm-hmm*
Where yo prayers can be ascendin	

An your sins can be forgiven.
An den, den, den, our Father,
We—we got some boys,
An we got some girls,
Walkin up an down wid a
Stiff neck an a rebellious heart.
Pleeaase, oh pleeaaase, my Father,   *Oh, please God*
Call dem, my Father, an tell em
Dat de wages of sin is Death,
An de gift of God is Eternal Life.   *Mmm-hmm*
Tell dem, our Father, dat
De train dey ridin on
Is full of dead man's bones.
Make dem know, our Father,
Dat de house is on fire,
An de roof is what burnin down.   *Lord, have mercy*
Make dem know, our Father,
Dat you is de God,
An beside you is no other.
Make dem know, our Father,
Dat you can defen,
An you will destroy.
An our Father,
Make dem know, our Father,   *Mmmmmmmmm*
Dat when you thunder in de eas,   *Mmmmmmmmm*
No man can thunder in the west   *Mmmmmmmmm*
After you.   *Mmmmmmmmm*

Brother Simmons's prayer was not so much spoken as chanted and performed, and there is no way to represent its resplendent quality fully on paper. The chanting of the phrases, the rich modulation of the voice, the variations in volume and tempo, the metrical beat, and the stress patterns and intonations must be heard to be appreciated. While his pronunciation reflects the Gullah background of most (especially older) African Americans on the islands, his grammar, with the exception of a few zero copulas ("you ridin"; see the explanation of zero copulas in chapter 7) and unmarked pasts (*lay, sen, guard, wake;* "You wake us up"), is relatively standard. His word choice is rather ornate and his sentence structure rhetorically balanced: note the parallelism in such phrases as "You can defen' / An you will destroy," and "when you thunder in the eas / no man can thunder in the west." In these respects, Brother Simmons's prayer is similar to those in the devotional phase of Afro-Baptist churches elsewhere in the United States, as was observed in Walter Pitts's 1993 study of a Texas church.

The vocalizations and phrases Sister Simmons uttered and intoned in the background were organic to the prayer, accenting the deacon's especially plaintive or prophetic remarks—and letting him know when he was really cookin'. Toward the end of the prayer, her accompaniment was marked by a soft, continuous humming that gradually swelled into song ("Mmm . . . Oh, sinner, what you doin' 'bout the Lord? Sinner, what you doin' down there? . . . "). Worship among black folk is often characterized by expressiveness rather than solemnity (though not necessarily *unrestrained* expressiveness). Thus Sister Simmons's song both articulated and released the spirit that had been building inside her during her husband's recitation. Yet only the most evocative of words and phrases stir such spirits. Only images and metaphors consistent with the ideologies and experiences of the culture they serve are intimate enough to conjure the Holy Ghost.

Brother Simmons knew this. Without the benefit of divinity studies or a theology degree, he had an impressive awareness of black Baptist themes and how they might be used to dazzle his peers and hitch them emotionally to the prayer. He appealed, for instance, to "our Father, while you ridin'," summoning the image of a supreme warrior who journeys in his fiery chariot as if "on to Jericho," the biblical city of sin whose walls tumbled at the sound of the horns of the righteous (Joshua 2 and 6). A hymn heard in black churches similarly entreats, "O my Good Lord, show me the way—enter the chariot, travel along." And one of the most recognized spirituals calls for deliverance from the miseries of slavery with the refrain "Swing low, sweet chariot, coming for to carry me home."

Two classic African American prayer motifs are combined in Brother Simmons's allusion to a train brimming with "dead man's bones." One is the train, which appears within both sacred and secular categories of African American life. Think of the notion of the "freedom train," whether manifested by the underground railroad that escaped slaves "rode" to liberation, or by the railcars that during the early twentieth century hauled legions of southern blacks toward the promise of greater tolerance and opportunity "up North." Then there is the religious idea of the train, mentioned in the introduction to James Weldon Johnson's book of "old-time Negro sermons," *God's Trombones:* "Both God and the devil were pictured as running trains, one loaded with saints, that pulled up in heaven, and the other with sinners, that dumped its load in hell."

Brother Simmons opened his prayer (in the grand tradition of black preachers) by praising God for another morning that had found the dearly assembled not stretched upon "dead man's bed," but "clothed in our right mind." Extravagant thanksgiving in the black church is often in order if, during the previous night, "our sleeping couch was not our cooling board" and "our cover was not our winding sheet." One of the prayers that the late linguist Walter Pitts recorded at St. John Progressive Church in Austin, Texas, in the 1980s, included virtually the same phrasing as Brother Simmons's: "We thank Thee, our Heavenly Father, early this morning. / For waking up us, Oh Heavenly Father, clothed in our right mind." As Pitts notes, prayers recorded in Tennessee during the 1920s and in Texas during the 1930s employed very similar language. Brother Simmons's prayer, like others, followed the topical structure that anthropologist Patricia Jones-Jackson found on the South Carolina Sea Islands: formal opening, proem (expression of humility), thanksgiving, appeals, and peroration (including references to the end of life).

Like the most enduring folktales, the themes of Brother Simmons's prayer conformed to a cultural tradition. The deacon, a subsistence farmer, was able to lace together metaphors and biblical themes (for instance, the train brimming with "dead man's bones") that his fellow worshippers could easily internalize. And though his prayer borrowed its framework and some of its phrases from the black Baptist tradition, his genius for metaphor, delivery, and improvisation clearly helped elicit his wife's "Lord have mercy's" and nudge his listeners toward spiritual rhapsody. Brother Simmons was not a preacher. Still, he exhibited all the poetry, majesty, and virtuosity of black preaching and praying. That's how deeply and universally this tradition of ornately rendering words is entrenched in black culture.

In terms of education and fame, Dr. Martin Luther King Jr.—a reverend, a scholar, and a prodigy of Southern Baptist preaching—existed in a stratosphere well above Brother Simmons. But he was similar insofar as he "delighted in euphony, the sweet sound of words and rhythms." The public today tends to think of Dr. King as a dreamer, and to remember him primarily in terms of the constantly recycled conclusion of his "I Have a Dream" speech. Few recall the philosopher, the social engineer, and the Christian warrior who was King. Even fewer still acknowledge the preaching phenomenon who was reared in the black church and who relied on, even perfected, the rhetorical strategies of the black preaching tradition.

One such strategy is repetition, evident in this passage from one of Dr. King's sermons:

> Sir, we would see Jesus, the light of the world.
> We know about Plato, but we want to see Jesus.
> We know about Aristotle, but we want to see Jesus.
> We know about Homer, but we want to see Jesus.

As his biographer Richard Lischer has pointed out, Dr. King's "voice stabs at the first syllable of Pla-to and Ho-mer and drops at the end of each sentence to a gravelly and intimate Jee-sus." As this book was being written (and surely long after its publication), the same pronunciation of "Jesus" was and will be heard in black churches across the country. And yet people don't recognize the jewels of Spoken Soul that fell from Dr. King's lips. Many might indeed consider it blasphemy to suggest that the martyr even dabbled in down-home talk. But Dr. King probably could not have become such a trusted national spokesman for the black masses, and might not have been able to lead garbagemen and porters and church mothers as effectively as he did, if he had not had control over not only Standard English, but also the pauses, inflections, cadences, and other devices of the black rhetorical and preaching tradition—the same devices that put the swing in Brother Simmons's prayer.

Alliteration is another "sweet sound" rolling down from the black pulpit. Addressing visitors to a Baptist church in Palo Alto, California, in 1992, the Reverend Emil Thomas said:

> We want you to know that you are *w*elcome and you are *w*anted at Jerusalem Baptist Church. If you're looking for a church home, you might find some churches that are *b*igger, but you won't find any that is *b*etter. And you can make it straight to heaven from Jerusalem, if you *b*een *b*orn again! (All right! Amen!) So, as you worship with us today, we hope that you will *p*rayerfully *p*onder the *p*ossibility of joining with us on this *p*ilgrimage from time to eternity.

Alliteration is not an isolated trick. The genius of black preachers lies in their ability to use many tools of language simultaneously. Linguist Geneva Smitherman praised such displays of dexterity, calling them a function of "tonal semantics":

> Tonal semantics . . . refers to the use of voice rhythm and vocal inflection to convey meaning in black communication. In using the semantics of tone, the voice is employed like a musical instrument with improvisation, riffs, and . . . playing between the notes. This rhythmic pattern becomes a kind of acoustical phonetic alphabet and gives black speech its songified or musical quality.

Contributing to the songlike lilt of the black sermon is the "hunh" many preachers use at the end of chanted breath groups as an energizing punctuation, as in this extract:

> You got to persevere . . . hunh?
> You got to give yo' all . . . hunh?
> You got to be long-suffering . . . hunh?
> You got to *do* right!

As she circled the pulpit with microphone in hand, speaking first to the choir, then to the Amen corner, a pastor at a Pentecostal church in Berkeley, California, used a variation on this "hunh" to cap her most ecstatic phrases. Every pause she took was occupied by the peals of an organ, and the result was a delightful conversation between human voice and musical instrument:

> You wouldn't be here today, hunh-hunh-hunh,
> Hadn't God comforted you, hunh-hunh-hunh,
> Hadn't God had understanding for you, hunh-hunh-hunh,
> Hadn't God had love for you.
> Whoooooa, Lawd! Thankya, Jesus!
> When He receeeived you, hunh-hunh-hunh,
> Some o' you were prostitutes, hunh-hunh-hunh,
> Some o' you were dope addicts, hunh-hunh-hunh.
> When He receeeived ya, hunh-hunh-hunh,
> Some o' you were layin' with men, hunh-hunh-hunh.
> When He receeeived ya, hunh-hunh-hunh,
> Some o' you were bar-hoppers, hunh-hunh-hunh.
> When He receeeived ya, hunh-hunh-hunh,
> Some o' you were backsliders. Ooohhhh, Lawd!

Other calling cards of the traditional black preaching style include deliberate stuttering or the manipulation of voice texture and inflection to produce a grating, gravelly, or mellifluous tone. There are often abrupt starts and stops, bursts of acceleration that disrupt an otherwise plodding pace, and wild fluctuations in volume that come without warning. There is the exploitation of rhyme ("God don't bless mess") and the elongation of syllables, as in Dr. King's last great speech, in which, his pitch soaring as if to reach the providential summit he was envisioning, chanted, "I've *been* to the moun-tain-top."

Grace Sims Holt dedicated an essay to the black preacher's gift for "stylin' outta the pulpit." By "stylin'" she meant the process of strutting back and forth behind the pulpit with hand on hip or on the small of the back, or firing up a congregation by "stomping out the devil" with a polished wingtip heel, or "tearing down the gates of hell" with a violent kick. Even when a sermon is presented largely or entirely in Standard English, the signature of black preaching remains, as in James Weldon Johnson's poem "The Creation," based on the sermon of an old-time black preacher who originally spoke in dialect. The rich metaphors linked to the local environment ("Blacker than a hundred midnights / Down in a cypress swamp"), the direct speech quotations, the repetitions within a simple sentence structure ("And the light broke, / And the darkness rolled up") conjure the sense of being in the presence of the traditional black preacher, and one hears the words with the stretched-out vowels the preacher would give them ("And faaaaaar as the eye of God could see . . . "):

And God stepped out on space,
And he looked around and said:
I'm lonely—
I'll make me a world.
And far as the eye of God could see
Darkness covered everything,
Blacker than a hundred midnights
Down in a cypress swamp.

Then God smiled,
And the light broke,
And the darkness rolled up on one side,
And the light stood shining on the other,
And God said: That's good!

Then God reached out and took the light in his hands,
And God rolled the light around in his hands
Until he made the sun;
And he set that sun a-blazing in the heavens.

And the light that was left from making the sun
God gathered it up in a shining ball
And flung it against the darkness,
Spangling the night with the moon and stars.
Then down between
The darkness and the light
He hurled the world;
And God said: That's good!

The Worship Spiral

Few rituals in the black church are sedentary. Instead, they whirl and surge and ebb as if choreographed at sea. The service may begin slowly and sedately, with a deacon droning on about the upcoming Bible training classes or church picnic, with prayers and devotions being offered by the deacons and other church members, with the pastor scolding worshippers for falling short of their tithing and offertory duties, and dispensing with routine duties such as baptism. But as the morning wears on, often even before the sermon has begun, fans flutter, bodies sway, tambourines shiver, hands clap in response to "Onward, Christian Soldiers," "I Love the Lord," or another hymn, and a symphony of movement sets the rafters jumping.

Women generally initiate the hand-clapping that accompanies a hymn, and are usually the first to exhibit that they have caught the spirit—dancing, swooning, or (in Pentecostal churches) talking in tongues as ushers encircle them for their own safety and the protection of others. Later in the service, members of the congregation—again, women in particular—may stand and offer personal testimonies. Testifying is an impromptu act sometimes solicited by elders or deacons who set aside a section of the service for "moments of meditation and praise" and "ministry in music." But testifying can be just as lavish and stylized as any prepared portion of the service. The ritual consists of congregants' making short statements about how Jesus saved their soul from a life of gangs, drugs, alcohol, gambling, infidelity, or any of the devil's other works, or about how Jesus' hand guided them when they were laid off from work and their daughter was sick, or how He turned their face toward the rays of Everlasting Life when they didn't deserve salvation in the first place.

As the service intensifies, men, too, may shed whatever macho inhibitions they may have walked in with, stand up stiffly, stomp and shout, or wave at the preacher in an encouraging gesture that may seem dismissive to an outsider. There is at least a twofold explanation for such displays. First, in the tradition of the ring shout, each member of the black church is expected to fuel the worship experience through emotional investment and participation in the call-and-response ritual; second, the Holy Ghost is believed to inhabit the body at the height of spiritual ecstasy.

On a Sunday morning at Mount Calvary Baptist Church in Washington, D.C., a choirboy overcome by the crescendo of a rousing service leaped from his seat behind the minister, made his way to the front pews, and proceeded with a quick jog around them. Black denominations shaped by such a tendency to submit to the physically possessing properties of the Holy Spirit include the African Methodist Episcopal, African Methodist Episcopal Zion, Christian Methodist Episcopal, the various Baptist affiliations, the Church of God in Christ, and other Pentecostal, Holiness, and Sanctified churches.

Even in the many black churches where no shouting or speaking in tongues is heard, and no one is seen convulsing or weeping after receiving the Holy Spirit, congregations and preachers alike are governed by a spiral of conventionalized social cues—both spoken and acted out—within the worship service. The minister sets this spiral in motion by using one or more of the evocative rhetorical tools available, or by overtly seeking feedback from the congregation ("Can I get a witness?"). Worshippers receive the message and respond (by standing, clapping, testifying, waving, stomping, nodding their heads, clucking their tongues, or letting loose a "Hallelujah!").

The original message is thus amplified, and the minister is encouraged to continue while the spirit escalates, passed around the sanctuary by the choir, the congregation, the deacons, and others in the church. If the spiral peaks during the sermon and is sustained through the benediction, the pastor may remark that the spirit of the Lord "has taken hold" of the church. But do not be misled. No gesture from pews or pulpit is ever superfluous, or made for sport. A subtle order exists, even amid the apparent frenzy. It is always understood, for example, that the preacher's fundamental role is to explicate the Bible, while the congregation's fundamental role is to back up and build up the preacher. Such unwritten rules of behavior are learned over time as children are raised in the church, watching their mothers testify and their fathers say "Amen."

Anyone who has worshipped in an African American church knows that the most exhilarating exchanges evolve unrehearsed as the morning proceeds, and that some of the most prodigious preaching comes after the minister has folded up notes. Improvisation, a cornerstone of black preaching, was critical to the Daufuskie faithful, as chapelgoers could stand up at virtually any time in the fellowship—if the spirit so moved them—to offer testimony or song. Indeed, if the vibrations of worship are to reach a divine pitch (and this tends to hold true in large urban African American churches as well), some improvisation must occur.

Consider the sermon "When You Fail in Your Trying," delivered in 1998 at Chicago's Trinity United Church of Christ. The pastor, the Reverend Dr. Jeremiah Wright, amped up the congregation that morning with a footloose style steeped in spontaneity and informality. Drawing from Genesis 29, the Reverend Wright preached about the shortcomings of Leah, the misguided figure who slept with Jacob and bore him sons in a vain attempt to wrest his affections from her beautiful sister Rachel. The Reverend Wright used a conversational tone (and, as the sermon went on, more and more vernacular) to depict the Old Testament characters as everyday folk one might imagine hanging in one's own 'hood.

At one point, the reverend asked his congregation a question:

Do you all know any Jacobs? Sleeping with a woman that he does not love. Having sex with a woman that he does not love. And Dr. Weems reminded us on Monday night one ain't got nothing to do with the other. You missed that: Having sex with a woman ain't got nothing to do with loving a woman!

Black preachers are famous for demanding answers to rhetorical questions. When the Reverend Wright asked, "Do you all know any Jacobs?" he paused to allow the congregation to chorus, "Yessir." Church folk will supply speedy responses to such inquiries; they are obliged to do so for reciprocity's sake (hence the worship spiral). Proper etiquette dictates that when the "Rev" calls for support one must "get his back" and demonstrate that one is following along with the lesson. Black preachers demand participation from their congregations. If they so much as sense a lull, they will not hesitate to ask, "I'm not boring y'all, am I?" or "How much time I got left?" To which the only proper response, of course, is a hearty "No sir!" or "Take your time, Preach!" If an even more enthusiastic response is desired, or if the preacher arrives at a particularly transcendental point in the sermon, he or she will drop a hint: "Somebody ought to say 'Amen,'" or "Let the church say 'Amen.'" Using a similar strategy, the Reverend Wright, when preparing to broach a delicate topic, instructed his congregants to "turn to your neighbor and tell them, 'He's going there.'" Then he directed them to "turn to the other side and say, 'I wish he wouldn't.' "

Strategies for encouraging participation are common, for in the black church, sluggishness is tantamount to spiritual hibernation. As Grace Sims Holt observed:

> The preacher's beginning is slow-moving (funky) to get the audience physically involved. The preacher walks, body swaying from side to side, slightly bent, from one side of the pulpit to the other, or from one end of the platform to the other. He waits until he gets to one side, stands up straight, and makes a statement about sin. If a husband "ain't acting right," if he's running around with another woman, or gambling, and not bringing his money home to his wife and children, the preacher must "get on his case" with a strong use of melody and rhythm.

When they are about to introduce a crucial point, many black preachers alert their congregations. "Watch this," they'll say, or "Follow me close, now." Notice how the Reverend Wright warned the Trinity members, "You missed that," before echoing the sentiment that sex "ain't got nothing to do with loving."

Beyond embellishing the sermon and delivering the gospel, a black preacher is expected to display a keen cultural understanding of the congregants. The preacher must be intimately familiar with their ways and weaknesses in order to be taken seriously when coaxing them down a righteous path. A preacher must be able to relate, and at the very least must have the capacity to talk congregants' plain talk. When he began to dig into the meat of his sermon, the Reverend Wright changed Leah's speech from the biblical to the colloquial:

> And on the third baby, she said, "This time I got him. He can't go nowhere. Now he is joined to me. He's mine." Y'all know Leah, don't you? [Congregation: "Yes!"]

At that moment Leah stood transformed. Suddenly she was a sister who talked as many of the congregants did in their most informal moments. Suddenly it was much easier for them to relate to her circumstances. "I think somebody here knows what street Leah lives on," the

Reverend Wright said. "I think somebody here still living on that street." To this, a man in the pews cried out "Preach-uh!" The Reverend Wright continued.

> Leah conceived again and bore a son and said, "*This* time—I made a mistake once. I was too blind to see the second time. And I was a fool for you, baby, on the third time. But *this* time, I finally woke up. *This* time, I see my mistake. *This* time, I ain't falling for it, babycakes. *This* time, me and the Lord got this thing going on."

By now, secular references had crept into the sacred context. One might in fact expect to find such phrases as "I was a fool for you, baby," and "got this thing going on" on the pop charts. The informal flavor had at least two obvious benefits: it perked up the congregation, and it prompted laughter. Austere members of the church might have turned to one another and remarked that the Reverend Wright "sure is cuttin' up," but they were paying attention to the lesson, despite themselves.

The most accomplished black preachers—like the best black comedians—use levity to wade into sensitive discussions. In his sermon, the Reverend Wright used two very informal expressions for sex: "C'mon baby, we gon tear the roof off the sucka tonight," and "You got to give it up, tonight" (to which members of the church responded with hoots, laughter, and exclamations of "Wellll!"). Blurring the line between the sacred and the secular is permissible, as long as the preacher stays within the guidelines of the Bible, as long as the goal is to increase participation in the service and understanding of the Scriptures, and as long as the congregation is convinced that the preacher knows the deal.

In his book *Black Preaching,* Henry Mitchell observed that "black preaching requires the use of black language." Certainly the idea of a sentence like "We gon tear the roof off the sucka tonight" echoing in the house of the Lord may shock some critics. But in many black churches, as the emotions of congregants are stirred and the accoutrements of the starched work week are shed, use of the black vernacular peaks. Richard L. Wright demonstrated this in a 1976 study of five Afro-Baptist preachers. He showed that deletion of *is* and *are,* double negatives, and other markers of Spoken Soul in the speech of preachers occurred four times more frequently during the sermonic climax than during earlier portions of the service, such as the devotional.

Walter Pitts, replicating this analysis in 1993, found that preachers' use of black vernacular features during the sermonic climax was twice as high as in their conversational speech earlier in the service.

P. K. McCrary was perhaps conscious of this when she introduced her "black Bible series," which translated the Scriptures into Spoken Soul. Intended for young people who have trouble relating to or decoding the King James Version, the series featured distinctive black vocabulary and grammar, as in this extract from the Gospel of Matthew:

> And when these things go down like Daniel of a long time ago talked about, ya'll better run to them hills. Those on top of the house should stay put and those who are out in the field, don't worry 'bout packing a suitcase. . . . Folks will be stabbing you in the back and calling you names. Worse, they'll want to waste you for what you believe.

The Rev. Ervin Green, pastor of Brick Baptist Church on St. Helena Island, South Carolina, and a collaborator on the Gullah version of the Gospel According to Luke (*De Good Nyews Bout Jedus Christ wa Luke Write*), reports that a parishioner who'd read it told him excitedly, "Rev, dis de firs' time God talk to me de way I talk!"

Few of black America's most sought-after preachers and pray-ers have abandoned black preaching traditions, even if they speak (inside and outside the church) with the gloss of Standard English. Nation of Islam helmsman Minister Louis Farrakhan, speaking on the unwieldy subject of a "black agenda" in 1988, offered a good example of this double-consciousness:

> I saw in the newspaper this morning . . . they said we have got to find a way to accommodate Reverend Jackson and pacify his constituency. There it is! There it is! Do we need accommodation? [Audience: "No!"] And moral pacification? [Audience: "No!"] Tell me how accommodation feeds the hungry? And gives jobs to those who have no employment? And gives housing to those who are homeless? Tell me how does accommodation and pacification give justice to those who cry out for justice? [Audience: "Go 'head, brother, go 'head! Yessuh! Talk to the people, Brother Minister!"]

When Minister Farrakhan exclaimed, "There it is! There it is!" it was for the same reasons that the Reverend Wright proclaimed, "You missed that"—as a signal that a significant statement had just been made or was about to follow. A beguiling rhetorician, Minister Farrakhan knows that not even he can secure the optimal feedback from a black audience unless he is perceived, fundamentally, as a people's preacher. So the Muslim leader kept the rhythms of a black church's Amen corner in mind. Once again, the widest range of expression is the highest goal. Speaking before a younger audience of New York college students, Minister Farrakhan selected an even more overt vernacular style:

> When I was comin' up as a youngsta I used to smoke reefer. What? Well, wait a minute . . . I don't want you to think I came down from heaven. I-I-I-I came up from hell jus' like everybody else. But I knew where the reefers were. Anytime I wanted some I knew where to go. Don't you know where to go? You know where the coke is. You know where the man is that got the good stuff. You know where the man is that waters it down.

When Minister Farrakhan was fishing for feedback, he asked, "Are y'all all right?" or "Do I have a few more minutes?" just as the Reverend Wright did when he felt Trinity's members growing restless. Minister Farrakhan was able to swivel between the street and the standard in order to narrow the gap between himself and his audience, using commonalities of the culture.

Black preaching's rhetorical style—including its tendency toward repetition—also bled through the Reverend Jesse Jackson's speech before a mainstream audience during the 1988 Democratic National Convention:

> They work hard every day. I know. I live amongst them. I'm one of them. I know they work! I'm a witness; they catch the early bus. They work every day! They raise other people's children. They work every day. They clean the streets. They work every day. They drive dangerous cabs, they work every day. They changed the beds you slept in in these hotels last night, and can't get a union contract. They work every day!

Jackson tends to avoid heavy black vernacular grammar and syntax, particularly when speaking before mixed or predominantly white audiences. Yet he evidently "sermonizes" his speeches, drawing on the inflection, cadence, and rhyme of the same preaching tradition that produced his colleague the Reverend Martin Luther King Jr.

Because black preachers tend to seek as broad a verbal and stylistic range as possible, the vernacular is an empowering element of their craft. As we have seen, it isn't the only element. In the end, black preachers are expected to be graceful and versatile wordsmiths capable of wielding the language of prestige—Standard English. However, one rule is true of almost all black churches, working-class or middle-class, rural or urban: The preacher who uses Standard English exclusively, without any of the motifs, rhythms, and gestures of the soulful preaching style (as rare as he or she would be to come across) is in serious risk of appearing detached or "uppity," and thereby of losing the interest of a good portion of the congregation. When the Reverend Jeremiah A. Wright Jr. went on his dialect jaunts, he was not out to sound ignorant. And he didn't: He was strutting. It was a testament to his preaching virtuosity that he could switch so effortlessly between the diction of the evening news and the lingo of Chicago's South Side.

4

Comedians and Actors

The black comedian of today uses the language of the streets, and in doing his characterizations, he speaks the same way.

—Redd Foxx (1979)

Even the most sophisticated joke tellers usually revert to dialect in closed company. Indeed the tales lose much of their flavor in standard English.

—Daryl Cumber Dance (1978)

One of the surest indications that Spoken Soul is alive and deeply cherished, despite assertions to the contrary, is its pervasive and vibrant use among black comedians. To these performers, and their appreciative audiences, Spoken Soul is a mechanism for slipping the fetters of polite convention, and a source of intense pleasure.

Ground-breaking humorists such as Bert Williams, Sammy Davis Jr., Dewey "Pigmeat" Markham, Dick Gregory, Redd Foxx, Jackie "Moms" Mabley, and Richard Pryor should all be regarded as connoisseurs of the tongue, and contemporaries such as Adele Givens, Whoopi Goldberg, Steve Harvey, Eddie Murphy, and Chris Rock have proven themselves equally comfortable in mainstream English and black talk. These and other black comedians have mined Spoken Soul to enrich their comic routines, and sometimes have talked frankly about the critical role the vernacular has played in their comedy, especially through its dramatic contrast with mainstream English.

Bert Williams, one of the earliest black comedians to make a name for himself, did so as part of a comedy team with George Walker (the Two Real Coons) that began playing in San Francisco in 1893 and

moved to New York in 1896. The duo had a string of successes there
in the early 1900s, including the 1906 hit *Abyssinia,* in which Williams
sang the amusing but poignant song "Nobody," built around a series
of multiple negatives:

> I ain't never done nothin' to nobody,
> And I ain't never got nothin' from nobody,
> And until I get somethin' from somebody,
> Sometime . . .
> I ain't never gonna do nothin' for nobody,
> No time.

In the 1920s, with segregation still firmly entrenched, a series of
black comedians performed in black theaters throughout the Midwest and the South under the auspices of the Theatre Owners' Book-
ing Association, or TOBA; their tours were known as the Toby circuit.
Pigmeat Markham, Ethel Walters ("Sweet Mama Stringbean"), Bill
Robinson, and a number of other black performers became famous
on the circuit. Especially relevant to our topic is Sammy Davis Jr., who
started out on the circuit in blackface at the age of four as part of his
uncle's act, passed off (to circumvent child labor laws) as a forty-four-
year-old midget. In an interview with Redd Foxx, Davis was explicit
about the role of dialect in the humor of the day:

> Comedy at that time was done by the great dialecticians of that era.
> The black style of comedy was the same for the black man as for the
> white man. You had the Jewish comics who wore baggy pants, the
> Dutch comedians who had accents that were so strong you could cut
> them with a knife, and then there was the Irish comic. All of the com-
> edy in those days was ethnic. . . .
>   My concept of black humor is very nonracial in a way, until it
> reaches the punch line. At that time I color it with typical black sounds.
> For instance, I pretend that I'm walking up to a desk clerk and, in a
> very white-style voice, I'll say, "Good evening, my good man. My name
> is Sammy Davis, Jr. Do you have my reservation?" The desk clerk would
> answer, "I don't have your reservation and I don't know you." My an-
> swer, which would be the punch line, would be a switch to a typical
> black voice, "Whatcha mean ya don't know me!" It's not the words that
> are funny, it's when I switch voices and become colored that is funny.

In 1975, decades after the TOBA circuit, Richard Pryor embodied
this same principle—that humor lay in the swapping of voices—in his
routine of a black minister delivering a eulogy. Note the omission of
the plural *s* ending ("In other word") and the *is* copula ("the nigger

dead"; see chapter 7 for a discussion of copula), and the introduction of *been* and *ain't* as the minister switches registers:

> We are gathered here today, on dis so[rrow]fu[l] occasion, to say goodbye to the dearly departed. He was dearly, and he has departed. Thus, tha's why we call him the dearly departed. In other word, the nigger dead! [Laughter.] As you can see him laying here—I been here three days, the boy ain't move a muscle. So I know the nigger dead!

Leap forward to the 1990s—when black comedians' live performances before largely black audiences reached vast interracial and international populations through BET's *Comic View* and other television broadcasts—and you can still see the principle in effect. In her irreverent "Fake Bitch" bit, Adele Givens recalls how her mother used to switch from vernacular to straight English, depending upon who was on the telephone:

> Because everybody here, when you were little, you could tell who yo' mama—who she was talking to on the phone. . . . You just heard the "fake bitch" when she took over, didn't you?
>
> 'Cause when her friends call it's like, "Hello . . . ? Oh, hey, how you doin', girl? I ain't doin' nothin'. . . . Cookin' these beans! Yeah, I know we had them yesterday, but beans taste better the second day, ya know? Girl, I can't hardly hear nothin' you sayin', these kids with all that damn noise. Yah, yah. Hold on. Let me— Y'all kids stop all that damn noise! People think I ain't taught you nothing."
>
> That's how she talk to her friends. But you let the principal . . . or the insurance man . . . or somebody white calling: "Hello. Oh, hi, Mr. Kennedy, how are you? Gee, you haven't received it yet? I mailed it out on Tuesday. Well, don't you worry. I've got the account number. I'm gonna track it down. Can you hold on for just a second, Mr. Kennedy? I can barely hear you. Children, Mommy's on the phone now!"
>
> Get to know me, white people, so I can relax and just talk to you like I talk to everybody else. . . .

The last sentence explicitly associates the vernacular with speaking in a relaxed and natural mode, a mode Givens obviously values. But note, too, apropos of the theme of cultural duality in this book, that after this passage she adds the disclaimer that she doesn't "bash" the "fake bitch" and her change to Standard English, because "she the one got your ass where you at today!" After this, she tilts back toward the genuine and the vernacular, exemplifying Du Bois's push-pull dialectic: "But sometimes you got to reel her in. 'Cause sometimes she come out when it's unnecessary!"

A more extended example of how the contrast between black and white styles of speech are exploited for humorous effect comes from a live 1997 performance by Steve Harvey, broadcast on national television. Harvey, wisecracking emcee for years on the program *It's Showtime at the Apollo,* had his own weekly sitcom, but he displayed his linguistic and comic versatility fully in solo performances. The routine we'll examine involves two ill-fated workers, one white, one black, who are about to be fired by their white boss, Tom.

Harvey gets into the character of Tom, clenching his rear end and striding stiff-backed across the stage as if making his way out of a private office and into the cubicle of a low-level white drone, Bob, who is asked to enter the boss's office. Harvey also impersonates the doomed employee, who trots after his supervisor.

> TOM: Ya know, Bob, at the end of the board meeting this past week, and after going over the board, we were kinda looking at your evaluation. And well, to tell you the truth, you're just not cutting it.
>
> BOB: Tom, what're you saying? [Harvey slips out of character and speaks to the mostly black audience: "You know good and hell well what he sayin'. Yo ass is almos' outta here. You see what da hell's goin' on. But *denial.*"]
>
> TOM: Listen to me. You're making this so difficult. I know you're going to have a tough time explaining this to Becky, but we're going to have to let you go.
>
> BOB: Oh! Oh, Jesus! Oh Tom, what am I going to do? What about the mortgage? What about the children's college fund? Oh, Father God!

To mimic, or "mark" (see below), the white characters Tom and Bob, Harvey puts on an outlandish nasal voice and keeps their speech close to Standard English (vernacular features such as zero copula, *r* deletion, and *s* deletion are absent from their speech, but resurface in his aside to the black audience: "what he sayin' "; *Yo; almos'*). The white characters' speech comes across as stilted and, in Bob's case, corny ("Oh, Father God!"), accommodating, and hopelessly submissive.

When Tom tries to fire the black employee—brotha Willie—in the same manner, the employee's attitude and language change dramatically. Willie lets off sparks of defiance from the jump ("What da hell" replaces "Oh Father God"), and the pronunciation (*fo'; goin'; da; sompn*) and grammar ("we goin'"; *ain't*) of Spoken Soul emerge. Harvey's commentary to the audience—who absolutely delight in it—is also rife with vernacular features, including zero third-singular-present *-s* ("He know"), immediate future tense *fitna* ("Sompn *fitna* go down!"), and a series of black colloquialisms (*show his whole ass; act a damn fool*):

> TOM: Willie, can I see you in my office for a moment, please?
>
> WILLIE: What fo'? What da hell we goin' in da office fo', Tom? You got sompn to tell me, you tell me right here. I got a desk right here. I ain't goin' in da office. You got sompn to tell Willie, you tell Willie right here! [To audience: "Now . . . Tom know he got a problem. He know he got to get this altercation behind closed doors right now. 'Cause he know Willie fitna show his whole ass! Awww—Willie fitna act a damn fool out here! Willie fitna tear up all these cubicles in this office. Sompn fitna go down!"]

Even after Tom coaxes the black employee into his office, things don't go much smoother:

> TOM: Ya know, Willie, we were at the board meeting the other week. We were going over your evaluation. . . .
>
> WILLIE: What 'valuation? I ain't see no goddamn 'valuation! When did you have the 'valuation? I didn't—I wadn't dere fo' it. Did ya pos' it on da board in da cafeteria las' week? I ain't seen nothin'. I ain't signin' shit!

The audience roars at that one. But what is it that makes the routine so funny? The crowd of course recognizes the cultural contrast between Bob and Willie. One can easily differentiate between the rhetorical styles and dispositions of the two characters. Willie has much more bass to his voice, and his street demeanor and suspicious attitude run contrary to Bob's sprightly naiveté and accommodation. Willie is boorish, but he's also savvier than Bob, and more confrontational in his defense. The portrayal of blacks as more astute than whites and more capable of vigorous self-defensive or self-assertive talk is recurrent in black folk humor, and provides psychic rebuttal to the dominant society's stereotype that blacks are less sharp or less articulate. Two genres in which this is well represented are jokes about outsmarting the master, or "puttin' on ole massa," in the days of slavery and stories about blacks "shuckin" and "jivin" their way out of confrontations with police in modern times.

In Harvey's skit, the audience associates Willie's speech with expressiveness and spunk, and Bob's with detachment and restraint. Communications consultant Thomas Kochman has suggested that this may be true more generally:

> The modes of behavior that blacks and whites consider appropriate for engaging in public debate on an issue differ in their stance and level of spiritual intensity. The black mode—that of black community people—is high-keyed: animated, interpersonal, and confrontational. The white mode—that of the middle class—is relatively low-keyed: dispassionate, impersonal, and non-challenging. The first is characteristic of involvement; it is heated, loud, and generates affect. The second is characteristic of detachment and is cool, quiet, and without affect.

Whether this characterization is valid in all real-life cases is open to debate, but it does hold true in the Harvey piece. The cultural difference is familiar, and that hint of familiarity is entertainment enough for the ladies and gentlemen of the audience, who have paid to laugh not at a comedian but at themselves. Laughter, we must remember, is often nothing more than that fleeting and reflective moment when one lays aside pretension and peers into the shadowy corners of one's own self-image.

Even as Harvey mocks white speech and white mannerisms (with Bob's stilted walk), he pokes fun at his own folk (with Willie's emotional eruptions). There's no question that this self-chiding instinct is a cornerstone of black humor, a long-standing strategy for taking the edge off slanderous caricatures of the race established by outsiders. But the most compelling aspect of Harvey's skit is the clash of black and white styles themselves. And the most fundamental conveyor of those styles is the manner in which the characters talk, a fact the audience acknowledges and delights in.

To set up the contrast that really lends the scene humor, Harvey must master the linguistic extremes of both cultures. From his verbal repertoire, he must be able to produce the diction and delivery of not just a Bob but a Willie, too. He must capture the absurdity of Bob's feeble reaction to the news that his "ass is almos' outta here," as well as the novelty of Willie's theatrics in the middle of the office. And he must do so mainly with language. The routine demonstrates that Harvey, like many other black people in this country who deal with whites on a daily basis, is able to switch effortlessly between the most proper

"whitese" and the most exaggerated "soulspeak." This talent for playing dialect hopscotch, at least to the degree we see here, is not as ex-
ercised in mainstream culture. Few white comedians, for example,
can parrot the black vernacular as convincingly as Givens or Harvey.
Of course, one source of increasing concern today is that many black
youngsters seem unable or unwilling to shift into Standard English
when the social or educational environment seems to require it. But
it remains true that many blacks—ordinary people as well as celebrated comedians like Harvey—control a broad range of linguistic
registers, and flex them in everyday life and in their narratives and
jokes about everyday life.

In the routine, Harvey is "marking" his characters, using a narrative technique that anthropologist Claudia Mitchell-Kernan has described as follows:

> A common black narrative tactic in the folk tale genre and in accounts
> of actual events is the individuation of characters through the use of
> direct quotation. When in addition, in reproducing the words of indi-
> vidual actors, a narrator affects the voice and mannerisms of the
> speakers, he is using the style referred to as marking (clearly related
> to standard English "mocking"). Marking is essentially a mode of char-
> acterization. The marker attempts to report not only what was said but
> the way it was said, in order to offer explicit comment on the speaker's
> background, personality, or intent.

Mitchell-Kernan offers an instructive example in which the "marker"
(S2 in the dialogue below) conveys the Uncle Tom character of a
black company man by transforming his words at a corporation meeting (reported by S4) into the drawling speech of a "handkerchief
head":

S1: What did he say?

S2: [Drawling] He said, "Ah'm so-o-o happy to be here today. First of
all, ah want to thank all you good white folks for creatin so many
opportunities for us niggers and ya'll can be sho that as soon as
we can git ourselves qualified we gon be filin our applications. . . ."

S1: Did he really say that?

S3: Um hm, yes he said it. Girl, where have you been? [Putdown by
intimating S1 was being literal.]

S1: Yeah, I understand, but what did he really say?

S4: He said, "This is a moment of great personal pride for me. My very
presence here is a tribute to the civil rights movement. We now

have ample evidence of the good faith of the company and we must now begin to prepare ourselves to handle more responsible positions. . . ."

In a sense, all comedians and dramatists—and where the use of Spoken Soul is concerned, black comedians especially—are markers. Chris Rock, who is relatively standard in many of his routines, deploys the vernacular for an affectionate marking of his father in this bit:

> I [was] supposed to go on tour with Run DMC? Tol' my father, say, "Dad, I'm goin' on tour with Run DMC—they gon let me open up for dem, make a lot o' money!"
>
> "Dem boys ign'ant [ignorant]! Dem boys are ign'ant! Why dey got dem hats on dey head? Dey ain't Jewish! An' what's that thing around dey neck?"
>
> "A rope chain, dad."
>
> "I tol' you dem boys ign'ant! What nigger in his right mind wants a rope aroun' his neck?!"
>
> . . . Father was nuts, man.

Ironically, or perhaps predictably, Bill Cosby, caustic critic of Black English in the seventies (see below) and Ebonics in the nineties (see chapter 1), unspooled the vernacular (italicized segments below) to represent himself and his mother in his 1972 routine "The Lower Tract":

> My wife is from the South. Now, I'm from Pennsylvania. I *don' eat no—no* chitlins. My mother loves chitlins. . . . You say, "Somebody is *cookin'* chitlins!" she'll get in the car *an'* drive, man! She noses in: "Hi, *you havin' chitlins?* I'll be right in." *An' jus'* sit down, and eat *'em.* I can't eat *'em,* man. *Firs'* time she ever brought *'em* to me, I looked at *'em,* I *say,* "What is this?" They *was* all in the plate, like that. [Laughter.]
>
> She said, "Chitlins."
>
> I *say,* "What?"
>
> She *say,* "Chitlins."
>
> I *say,* "I *don' want none.* What is chitlin?"
>
> She *say,* "Well, it's the intestines of the pig."
>
> I *say,* "Noooo, I *don' want none* o' that! [Laughter.] Nooo, *'cause* if I know anything about anatomy, you know, you got the lower tract in there, *ain't* you? [Loud laughter.] *An' ain't no* food down in that area! Matter of fact, I think you better check it out—somebody misspelled a word! [Laughter and applause.]

This seems a far cry from the comedian whose position on Black English in the 1970s was represented by author Ronald Smith as follows:

> [Cosby's] conservative viewpoints seemed out of touch with the times. Guys like [Richard] Pryor were putting on the toughest of street-jive dialects, while Cosby took a dim view of black English: "We're lighting a fire that has no use, a fire that doesn't warm anybody, where you're going to make up your own language, your own mathematics and sciences. That's just an easy way out. We need black people in space and science programs and in many other areas. While these hoodlum packs are out roaming the streets and saying 'what it is, what it is' and 'right on' and giving handshakes and challenging each other over a piece of cement that the city owns, there are some very bright ones . . . who could contribute something to society."

As "The Lower Tract" and other Cosby skits showed, the funnyman did have a use for the black vernacular, drawing on it to re-create warmly the natural conversation among black friends and family. While the contrast between his statements about black talk and his use of Black English might be rationalized on a number of grounds (the derogatory statements quoted by Smith occur in an educational "future of the race" context, for instance, and they seem to focus on contemporary slang rather than grammar), it is ultimately a reflection of the larger love-hate relationship with Spoken Soul that has provided this book with both its subtitle and subtext.

Lest we leave the impression that black comedians use Spoken Soul only for routines about home and family, and reserve Standard English for more "lofty" themes such as civil rights and politics, we should remember that icons including Moms Mabley and Redd Foxx all possessed an unrestrained mystique, a self-issued license to say just about whatever they pleased, however they wished to say it. Because they were so wickedly funny, they got away with confronting even the most politically hot-wired or taboo topics head-on—poverty, crime, sex, homosexuality, drugs, and race, race, race. Vernacular simply reinforced their footloose styles, adding, for instance, to the wry flavor of Gregory's political remarks:

> I spent six months, once, sitting at an Alabama lunch counter. And when they finally served me, they didn't have what I wanted! . . . My brother is so sure he isn't going to get waited on, he don't even take no money with him. . . . Wouldn't it be funny if they finally decided to serve him? If they was ready, and he wasn't?

Mabley was equally incalculable. The "chitlin circuit" darling addressed topics such as the fall of President Nixon with homespun wisdom and a demeanor as deceivingly innocuous as the housecoat she always wore:

> Even old Moms couldn't do nothin' for that man 'cept give him a few licks upside the head . . . he was just too far gone. Only thing I got to say about him is, your sins will find you out. Like old Joe Louis says, you can run, but you can't hide.

Redd Foxx, popular for his stand-up comedy performances and recordings long before his starring role in the 1970s TV series *Sanford and Son,* reflected on the civil rights movement with similar down-home pragmatism:

> And when the civil rights marchers was parading through Selma and getting it from the white-sheet wearers, I used to say, "I ain't gonna do no marching nonviolently. Ain't no way I'm gonna let a cracker go upside my head with a stick and I do nothing but hum 'We Shall Overcome.' I'm going to cut him. I'm from St. Louis, and we wake up buck-naked with our knife on."

Redd Foxx not only exploited the language of the black community in his routines, but talked explicitly about doing so:

> The black comedian of today uses the language of the streets, and in doing his characterizations, he speaks the same way. . . . There is no doubt that black street language has spilled over to every walk of life in our society today, thus making the American English language that much more (if you'll pardon the expression) colorful.

This comment in fact closes a seven-page exposition, "Black Language," that concludes *The Redd Foxx Encyclopedia of Black Humor.* It includes a discussion of the history of black language, explanations of various slang terms, and recollections of how the vernacular was used by various entertainers. Foxx's delight in the vernacular is obvious. But in the immediately preceding chapter, it was the same man who wrote:

> When I first started out in the business, the blackface comedian was something I resented strongly. I used to see this in St. Louis and Chicago where I grew up and couldn't figure out why a man being black had to black up his face. I just couldn't see no reason for it.
>
> Even the dialect I resented. When Slappy White and I first began to work together back in 1948, the first thing I did was to take the de's and dem's and doe's out of his mouth. We were not going to talk like that. I knew I didn't need no dialect to be funny, so I never used it.

To understand the conflict between Foxx's expressed resentment for "the dialect" and his demonstrated affinity for "black street language," we need to remember that the dialect to which he objected was that stereotyped and tired characterization of late-nineteenth- and early-twentieth-century minstrelsy and the blackface performances that succeeded it. In this respect Foxx echoed James Weldon Johnson, who in 1933 took exception to the use of "conventionalized dialect" in poetry, rooted as it was in a despised minstrel tradition. In fact, the language in which Foxx reveled during his stand-up routines also included *des*, *dems*, and *doses*, and some of the vernacular features found in the blackface comic tradition, though not the shuffling, self-demeaning characterizations most endemic to that tradition. So Foxx, like Cosby and Givens, exemplified the same oscillating relationship with black language that such writers as Johnson and Dunbar and Angelou did, and that still has Americans of all stripes eating their words, as it were.

As we have emphasized throughout this book so far, the variously named vernacular of African Americans does have a remarkable capacity to elicit denial and shame from blacks (not to mention others). But if comedy is what happens when folks relax, "get down," and "let it all hang out," then one would expect to find vernacular—the variety of informality—where there is laughter. Indeed, the "dialect" of black jokesters—professionals or the sidewalk variety—is more than a prop for the burlesque (it remains vastly more essential than, say, Richard Pryor's casually dangled cigarette). It is organic to the culture of the man and woman of words, organic to the signifying tradition, and organic even to the types of scenarios African Americans consider funny.

In the 1990 movie *House Party,* which became something of a cult hit among black youth of the time, Robin Harris's character Pop comes off as comical and irreverent because he uses the vernacular, but also because he uses the "trash-talking," insult-trading style that is a mainstay of everyday humor within the black community. In one scene, the stern working-class father confronts two teenagers after showing up at a house party in search of his wayward son, who is supposed to be home as punishment:

POP: Bilaal, whateva yo name is. Sounds like something you catch under yo feet. You see my boy?

BILAAL: Nah, I haven't seen him, sir.

POP: You sure?

BOY: Yo, why don't you go home and watch the late show, Pops?

POP: Why don't you jus' go home? Test-tube baby. Wha's yo name?

BOY: Clinton.

POP: Clinton what?

BOY: Clinton, ahm, X.

POP: Clinton X, huh?

BOY: Yeah, Clinton X. Ahm a Muslim.

POP: Well, go home and bring me back two bean pies and a poke chop sandwich, li'l trout-mouf heathen. (*Turns to face another partygoer.*) Ohh, how you doin'? I shoulda known you was in here. I saw the drip in front of da driveway. You know som'n, wit dat Jheri Curl you got on yo head you betta not eva do a crime. Ain't no problem findin you—follow da drip, follow da drip.

The scene is not just cinema. Almost every African American has a father or an uncle or a grandmother or a cousin or a friend who "talks trash" relentlessly. In fact, the art of "clowning," "dissing," "busting caps" (or "snaps"), or "playin the dozens" by ritually insulting an individual and his kin (especially his or her mother, although some people draw the line there) is traditional and widespread in Soulsville. The following snaps were recorded among sixth-graders on a basketball court in East Palo Alto, California:

Went to yo house, I ask where the bathroom was, she said two bushes to the left.

I can tell by that neck, you bin in a helluva wreck.

Bobby, yo nose so big, you can go skiin' in it.

Yo granny got three teeth—one in her mouth, two in her back pocket.

Yo motha got a wooden eye, every time she blink she get a splinter.

Yo mama so fat, instead of usin a beeper, she use a VCR.

As James Percelay, Monteria Ivey, and Stephan Dweck observe in their book *Snaps:*

The dozens is the blues of comedy. It is a ritual that crosses generational, regional and class boundaries. The dozens illustrates the force of the spoken word, and is the ultimate expression of fighting with your wits, not your fists. This oral tradition is another example of the originality and verbal innovation that distinguish . . . African American culture.

Their compilation includes more than four hundred fifty snaps, of which the following represent only a small sample (we have skipped the popular but "dirty" snaps):

> Your mother is so fat, she broke her arm and gravy poured out.
> (From the movie *White Men Can't Jump*)

> Your mother is so fat, she puts on high-heel shoes in the morning, and by the end of the day, they're flats.

> Your sister is so fat, they had to baptize her at Sea World. (From the TV show *In Living Color*)

> If ugliness was a crime, you'd get the electric chair.

> Your brother is so ugly, when he sits in the sand the cat tries to bury him.

> Your family is so poor, the last time you had a hot meal was when your house was on fire.

Potent vernacular use on the schoolyard and stage notwithstanding, Black English in comedy has often been linked with some of the most crippling and one-dimensional portrayals of African Americans. In the 1950s, the television show *Amos 'n' Andy* raised the ire of the NAACP and other groups who contended that its slapstick humor and its characters' antics depicted blacks as inept and foolish. Two decades later, the myth that black life is rife with capers and jovial misadventure was still being pandered to on the tube (though to a lesser degree). *Good Times* (1974–1979) chronicled happenings in the life of a black working-class family living in a public housing development. The sitcom's premise was that despite insecure employment, paltry wages, pitiful health care, the specter of crime, a corrupt police force, and other circumstances of poverty, black people still manage to smile, hum, and exclaim in Pollyanna fashion, "Ain't we glad we got 'em . . . good times!" Although it represented one of television's first authentic portrayals of Spoken Soul, the program's content soon disappointed some blacks. In one typical family crisis, J.J. (the show's most memorable character) was jailed on bogus robbery charges. Unable to come up with the $500 he needed to make bail, his parents, Florida and James, spent the night at the police station. Friend Willona and brother Michael showed up the following morning:

FLORIDA: James? James!

WOMAN: You betta answer, cuz I ain't no James!

JAMES: I'm sorry, baby, I—I musta been dreamin'.

FLORIDA: Yeah, yo' dream musta been in a dance hall, cuz you changed partners.

WOMAN: People ain't safe no place. You even get molested in a po-lice station.

JAMES: I'm sorry, baby.

FLORIDA: Ah, that's awright, honey, I was dreamin' too. . . . I dream we was home and everything was awright. . . . You know, James, I was thinkin' dis experience might teach J.J. not to make a joke outta findin' things.

WILLONA: Good morning, y'all.

MICHAEL: Hi Ma, hi Dad.

JAMES: Hey, Michael. What choo got dere?

MICHAEL: I made a picket sign: "The fuzz unfair to brothers especially mine."

WILLONA: You think that one's bad, you shoulda seen the one he was gonna bring.

FLORIDA: What we gonna do with this boy?

JAMES: I don't know what choo gonna do, babe, but I'm 'onna get him some more cardboard so he can keep on makin' these signs.

MICHAEL: Right on, Dad.

Two years before *Good Times* premiered, *Superfly,* one of the most successful blaxploitation movies (with a reported gross of $6.4 million), arrived in theaters. The film, which glares like a Polaroid flash from a time when black men were painted as rifle-toting pimps and pushers who lorded it over urban streets, featured Ron O'Neal as the shadowy cocaine peddler named Priest. In an opening sequence, two huddled junkies prepare to rob Priest for his dope loot:

JUNKIE NO. 1: Did you get the money?

JUNKIE NO. 2: I ain't got nothin'. She wouldn't give it to me.

JUNKIE NO. 1: Wastin' all this goddamned time. We do it my way.

Fed up with such narrow big-screen roles, comic Robert Townsend lampooned the film industry's portrayals of blacks in his 1987 movie *Hollywood Shuffle.* The opening scene finds Townsend, who plays an aspiring actor looking for his first gig, rehearsing the part of a gangster in the bathroom mirror as his amused little brother looks on:

TOWNSEND: Tommy. Tommy. You kill-ded mah bro-tha. He was mah only bro-tha. I love-ded dis dude, babee. An you gonna pay, jive sucka. You done messed wit da wrong dude, babee. Ahm gon be on yo' ass like a pair of Fruit-of-the-Looms. Ahm gon' bounce you harder than a canceled check. As soon as you get yo' foot off ma face, I'm gon hurt ya, man. I'm gon hurt chyoo. Dis be ma turf, babee. Ah owns da East Side. Listen . . . listen . . . Oh! You tough now! Oh, you tough now! Becuzin' you be got yo' gang. You be got yo' gang. But when ma gang finds out . . . Oh. Oh! Why you gotta pull a knife, man? Why you gotta pull a knife? (*Slips out of character and addresses younger brother:*) What's the line?

BROTHER: I ain't be got no weapon.

The spoof is hilarious, of course, because of Townsend's outrageous, whiny inflection, and because some of the dialogue ("kill-ded," "love-ded"; "Becuzin' you be got yo' gang"; "I ain't be got no weapon") is contrived gibberish, involving a fracturing of some of Spoken Soul's genuine rules. In fact, this is how African American Vernacular English might sound if, as countless black and white columnists, policy makers, and pundits have maintained, it followed no hard-and-fast rules. Townsend uses the absurd script to illustrate Hollywood's apparent ignorance about black life and its penchant for churning out the most stereotypical of images. But he also pokes fun at a more widespread lack of awareness on the part of the larger culture about the nuances of black speech itself.

With the black vernacular so misunderstood, and so often placed in the mouths of jesters such as *Good Times*'s J.J. and criminals such as *Superfly*'s Priest, it's not surprising that many blacks let out a collective sigh when *The Cosby Show* came on the air in the 1980s. Clifford and Clair Huxtable, well-to-do professionals who spoke proper English and meted out textbook-perfect guidance and affection to their children, were redemptive in many ways. Once a week, like clockwork, black American families were ushered into that idyllic brownstone where Standard English and hundred-dollar sweaters—rather than jive and food stamps—were the norm. Now there are many such real-life households in black America. But there are many more black households in which neither parent holds an advanced degree—or any degree, for that matter. And in many of these homes, Black English is the lingua franca.

As Givens's and Harvey's routines imply, though, the black community's linguistic chameleons—and a chameleonlike existence remains an imperative of black life—probably have as much Bill Cosby coursing through their veins as they do Redd Foxx. In a very real sense, both are the result of cultural confluence. And black folk are better off for having them both around. For together they speak to both halves of the soul, allowing us to play doctor on the job and the dozens after quitting time.

5

Singers, Toasters, and Rappers

If the music of the Negro in America, in all its permutations, is subjected to a socio-anthropological as well as musical scrutiny, something about the essential nature of the Negro's existence in this country ought to be revealed, as well as something about the essential nature of this country, i.e., society as a whole.

—Leroi Jones (now Amiri Baraka; 1963)

In this present day, someone in Cairo is feelin' *Tupac's philosophy and graffing it on an ancient wall. They're doing the same in Tokyo. . . . In the last decade,* Black Street Speech *has become a planetary phenomenon, with global hip hop heads spittin' phrases like* da bomb! *and* you know what I'm saying?

—James Spady and H. Samy Alim (1999)

Some Americans embrace Spoken Soul (albeit subconsciously) only when it's delivered over the FM dial, crooned in a ballad, or draped atop the *thud-thud* of a funky baseline. Not that vernacular pronunciation and syntax are obscured when set to music, for they often take on an even grander flavor—becoming even more evocative and "in your face"—when jazzed up for twelve bars or worked over a catchy hook. It is then that Spoken Soul's aptness for expressing the exotic in the plainest of terms, for expressing the unremarkable with the greatest flamboyance, and occasionally, for expressing concepts that Standard English simply cannot becomes most obvious. Duke Ellington might have meant this, in part, when he observed in 1932 that "it don't mean a thing if it ain't got that swing." With that pronouncement, Ellington lent the era its jingle and proclaimed mainstream

America square. And she *was* square when compared with the dancing, jazzing culture then emerging from New York and other cities, a
culture in which black vernacular was the parlance of the hip.

Americans of all types tend to bad-talk soul talk, even though it is
the guts of the black music they so relish, and even though this would
be a much duller country without it. It is an absurd contradiction,
and as we observed on a drizzling May morning in 1997, one that often goes unnoticed.

It was commencement time at Howard University, the Washington, D.C., campus said to have placed the capstone on black education. African America appeared to have sent delegates from every city
block, cul-de-sac, and country lane, and black vernacular could be
heard everywhere among the crush of bodies. After the faculty pro-
cession, African American broadcast-news pioneer Carole Simpson
began her keynote speech, enunciating with broadcast-news diction.
She blurred through a medley of race matters, praising affirmative action and snubbing biracial blacks who had petitioned the federal government for a census classification other than "African American."
They threatened to undercut black political clout by denying a part of
their heritage that society would ascribe to them entirely anyway, she
suggested. The audience offered scattered Amens.

Then she turned to the matter of racism in America, some of
which, she said, was "the fault of white people, [but] not all. Some of
the negativism we bring on ourselves." Simpson offered two examples. The first was rap music, which, she maintained, cast black men
as "criminals, gun-toting gangsters, malt liquor–swilling, drug-taking
women-haters." She went on:

> You'll tell me it's about keeping it real—the beat, the rhyme, the mes-
> sage . . . *Please!* Most African Americans are like you—hardworking,
> law-abiding, family-loving, goal-oriented, patriotic people. You suffer—
> we *all* suffer—because white Americans think we are all the blacks
> portrayed in popular culture, which is produced by white people.

The second example, significantly enough, was the Oakland Ebonics
controversy, which had erupted six months earlier and was finally fad-
ing from the headlines:

> I was in Oakland, California, last week, the birthplace of Ebonics.
> [Scattered laughter from crowd.] I came in contact with many black
> people, and black children. I did not hear *one* person talking in
> Ebonics or Black English, or what when I was growing up we used

to simply call "street slang." What was Ebonics all about? . . . The story was distorted when it first came out, but to suggest that black children cannot speak good English makes me crazy. . . . Nobody is happier than I am that Ebonics has been stopped dead in its tracks!

After Simpson had finished, members of the Howard University Choir and Orchestra rose and offered their rendition of a spiritual. Their voices were buoyant, and Simpson and the crowd nodded and swayed approvingly:

Lord, I done done,
Lord, I done done,
Lord, I done done,
I done done whatcha tole me ta do.

It wasn't long before the final remarks were made, the last strains of "Pomp and Circumstance" subsided, and the graduates dashed down the hill with their extended families in tow. No one, evidently, had caught the contradiction. No one appeared to realize how odd the disdain for Ebonics (expressed by the keynote speaker and some—though not all—members of the crowd) seemed when paired with the obvious delight in such utterly idiomatic lyrics. This spiritual draws much of its poignancy and soul from the vernacular itself— note the completive *done* in "I *done* done," the dropping of the final consonant sound in *tole,* and other features—and from the image it conveys of an erstwhile slave or modern-day long-sufferer who has remained spiritually faithful despite the "trials of this world." But getting folks *consciously* to celebrate their ancestors' innovations on English—the living evidence of an African encounter with a socially and linguistically hostile New World—can be as exacerbating as getting them to confront the legacy of slavery itself. There will probably always be an astonishingly large number of blacks in this country who applaud the black vernacular only when they don't realize it is the black vernacular they're applauding.

Contemplate that audience's appreciation for the ebony phonics of the spiritual and the simultaneous distaste for "Ebonics" (again, this was taken to mean both the variety of speech and Oakland's public relations nightmare), and you may come to the following conclusion: Appreciating sung soul is one thing, but appreciating soul as it is spoken is something else entirely. It might well be said that music that draws heavily on non-Standard English (and by this we mean almost all popular music, including jazz, blues, rock and roll, soul, and rhythm and blues) has generally been embraced by the mainstream. Though its lexicon and sensibilities have seeped into mainstream talk for centuries, however, nonstandard English itself has generally been scorned or ridiculed by the dominant culture. In fact, middle America has quite often jeered those who speak "jive" in the same breath and with the same enthusiasm that it has grooved to black sounds à la Bessie Smith and Mahalia Jackson and Ray Charles and Lauryn Hill (all of whom were and are far less concerned with speaking "proper English" than with singing soulfully and unabashedly).

African Americans themselves pay tribute to those and other dialect-slingers precisely because of the abundance of their soul—that gift for articulating the most intimate spiritual and aesthetic selves of African America, with all its drama, irony, and poignancy. In fact, most blacks will acknowledge their own conventionally soulful characteristics (such as a fondness for certain foods, and distinction in a variety of musical genres including spirituals, jazz, the blues, and hip-hop), even if they denounce the soulful shadows of their most private speech. Many soul people feel at ease rooting for outsiders who ridicule or condemn Black English, but most would bristle if anyone dared to dismiss as primitive the notional attribute of soul itself, or suggest that it didn't even actually exist.

The idea of "soul" reached new heights in the 1960s (when blacks became "soul brothas and sistahs"), and found a champion in James Brown. Wrapped in bodysuits and capes, Brown would tattoo the stage with magical feet, slinging sweat and exchanging indecipherable calls and responses with his band. That sapsucker had him some soul—a fact that he articulated succinctly in his 1971 hit "Soul Power":

> I got something that makes me wanna shout,
> I got something that tell me what it's all about,
> I got *soul*, and I'm supa-bad.

When Brown did his "thang," he impressed even himself, and would exclaim, "Good God! I gotta jump back and kiss myself!" Such is the exuberance of soul power. And it sells, too: Brown had fifty-six R&B top-ten hits, eighteen number-ones and more than forty million-plus sellers. Americans of all colors went wild for the audacious, outrageous performer who dripped attitude and unleashed dialect. Now, imagine what those fans might have thought had they hustled to the music store for the latest James Brown album, and dashed home only to hear an announcer's broadcast-news diction pouring from their record players: "I have something that makes me want to shout, /

I have something that informs me what is happening, / I have soul, and I am super-good." Sure, that sort of syntax suits the evening news. Crisp broadcast talk has its place. But such language would not have gone over well with Brown's audiences. Feeling *hip, outta sight, cool, funky, bad,* or *fly* themselves, they prefer Spoken Soul, which, by virtue of the experience that produced it, conveys the intoxicating feel of *cool.*

The point was not lost on the Rolling Stones. Like other bands that emerged while rock and roll was young, they became famous by borrowing black styles and black talk, and often without attribution. Several of their hits can be loosely traced to black standards of the South; a few are plain knock-offs. When recording "You Gotta Move" in 1971, for instance, the band did nothing more than lay a grinding electric guitar behind old, old African American lyrics:

> You gotta move, you gotta move, child,
> Oh, when the Lord gets ready,
> You gotta move.

The original "I Gotta Move" was sung in black churches for years, particularly on the Carolina and Georgia Sea Islands and elsewhere in the South, and is likely still being sung there. It contains many of the classic characteristics of ring shouts, the praise sessions of slaves who rekindled faith and resisted misery by drawing themselves into animated worship circles. Ring shouts tended to carry simple messages through simple lyrics. It was their rendering that was adorned. The following version of "I Gotta Move," recorded in the 1960s during a live a cappella performance by a group of Georgia Sea Island women, began almost liltingly, with booming voices, syncopated claps, and stomps on a naked floor creating an orchestra without instruments. One woman alone introduced each line, but she was soon accompanied by the harmonizing wails of the others. A few bars into the plaintive melody, the footfalls sped up and the clapping went double-time. The resulting sound was layered and throbbing and sepulchral, as if it had wafted up from a sad netherworld:

> I got to move, we got to move,
> We got to move, we got to move,
> Oh, when the Lord, Lord get ready,
> You got to move. Oh,
>
> You may be rich, you may be poor,
> You may be high, you may be low,

But when the Lord get ready,
You got to move. Oh,

My brother move, my brother move,
My brother move, my brother move.
Oh, when the Lord get ready,
You got to move.

Sometime I'm up, sometime I'm down,
Sometime I'm almost to da groun'.
Oh, when the Lord get ready,
You got to move. . . .

There are layers of meaning here as well as of sound. You got to move when the spirit says move, the song suggests, as when the Holy Spirit winds you up on Sunday morning. But you've also got to move on home to Jesus when He says it's time to rest. And this is the great equalizer, for as is observed, the rich and high-ups must go before Him when He is ready, just as the poor and low-downs. Such a profound faith in the equal opportunity of mortality might have scraped a slaver's spine like an icy finger. Lord knows all men were created equal, the lyrics imply. And in the afterlife, you will be equal too.

But to understand fully the original song's character and intent, we must also scrutinize its language, which plainly shows its folk roots: *got to,* not "have to," *Sometime,* not "Sometimes," *groun'* not "ground," *the Lord get ready,* not "gets ready." Tense in particular must be considered at some length, because it forces us to wrestle with this question: When those Sea Island women sang, "My brother move," were they omitting the present-tense suffix ("My brother move*s*") or the past ("my brother move*d*")? In African American English, "he move" can denote either. Yet the significance of the song hinges in part on which of the verb's two forms was originally intended. Did the first soul to wail these lyrics mean to convey that his or her brother was moving at that moment—which would suggest that the sibling in question was still present—or that his or her brother had already "moved," and was, as the old folks say, "resting in the bosom of Jesus"?

Maybe both. Human capitulation to the will of the Lord is the song's main concern. But "I Got to Move" might also be viewed as a carry-over from the African faith system that tells us that departed kinfolk inhabit a dynamic spirit world, a realm from which they can participate in and guide the affairs of the living. If your brother had passed on, or even if he had escaped or been purchased by a plantation owner far away, you and he would still have been wrapped in a

quilt of co-dependency—a notion perhaps articulated by the haunt-
ing phrase "We got to move."

So the vernacular is a survival tool, encoding the culture's semantic dualism and expressing the "double consciousness" necessary to
negotiate the world as it is and envision it as it could be. Spoken Soul
can camouflage or elucidate. Its sleight of tongue can hide a message
from members of the larger culture, or feed it to them on the sly. It is,
necessarily, the language of double entendre:

> Steal away, steal away, steal away to Jesus,
> Steal away, steal away home,
> I ain't got long to stay here.
>
> My Lord, He calls me,
> He calls me by the thunder,
> The trumpet sounds within-a my soul,
> I ain't got long to stay here.
>
> Steal away, steal away, steal away to Jesus,
> Steal away, steal away home,
> I ain't got long to stay here.
>
> Green trees a-bending,
> Po' sinner stands a-trembling,
> The trumpet sounds within-a my soul,
> I ain't got long to stay here.
>
> Steal away, steal away, steal away to Jesus,
> Steal away, steal away home,
> I ain't got long to stay here.

The slaves who uttered those words were not just gazing longingly
into the firmament, but picturing a homecoming they intended to experience *during their lifetime*. The scene of redemption could have
been a free state in the northern United States, or it could have been
Canada or the continent of Africa. No matter where the jumping-off
point, the belief that the sons and daughters of Africa could "fly" out
of bondage manifested itself both in everyday oral abstractions and in
real designs to flee the plantation. Though many went barefoot in
North America, the old Negro wisdom reassured that "all God's children got traveling shoes." The implication perhaps being that some
fortunate Negroes were even going to get their running shoes here
on earth.

Many a slave master must have dismissed the ditties and dirges of
his bondmen and bondwomen as wishful thinking, as cryptic pleas for

the deliverance of death, or as quaint noise-making, never suspecting that his singing slaves were tacitly resisting psychological bondage, concealing subversive messages, possibly plotting uprisings or escape. Nevertheless, most spirituals can be linked to philosophies of liberation, and their genealogy traced to the first moment a kidnapped African paused from the labor imposed by the white man to observe the ancient custom of chanting one's discontent.

Makers of black music have always defined themselves, with the gloss of Spoken Soul, in terms of who they were to become once they had reached the Other Side. Whether the Other Side was seen as a trouble-free afterlife or an earthly life of liberation, a wistful paradise or a destination well worth holding on for (or throwing down for) in this world, black folk have always used their music to project themselves into a place where they are in control, where they do not have their humanity gouged out for their having been born black, where they overcome, or get even:

> Monday morning, gonna lay down my cross, get me a crown
> Late in the evenin'. Oh, I'm goin' home, live on high
> Soon as ma feet strike Zion, gonna lay down ma heavy burden
> I'm gonna put on ma robe in glory
> I'm goin' home one day an' tell ma story
> I've been comin' up hill and mountain
> Gon' drink from the Christian fountain.

Mahalia Jackson, often hailed as the world's greatest gospel singer, recorded "I Will Move On Up a Little Higher" in 1947. The song explores the exhilarating conviction that black folk will shed earthly constraints and be richly rewarded on that "great gittin'-up morning" when they see Christ and are reunited with long-gone kinfolk. An end to the toil of slavery and poverty is envisioned, and the spiritual metaphors of "goin' home," walking without weariness, and drinking from the fountain become sweet music for the thirsty, the dispossessed, the displaced and overworked. These are powerful Christian ideas, and Jackson expresses them with every ounce of her sanctified self. The phrase "get me a crown," for instance, conveys a sense of entitlement and self-righteousness that the Standard English translation ("I'm going to get a crown for myself") cannot.

But not all representations of the Other Side have been as pious. When blacks set out to articulate heartache and a vision for deliverance in secular terms, what came up was foot-thumpin', name-takin', raunchy, bad, and blissful. It was the blues:

Now when I was a young boy, at the age of five,
Ma mutha said I was gon be the greatest man alive.
But now I'm a mahn, way past twenty-one,
I wan choo ta believe me baby, I have lots of fun.
I'm a mah-yun!
I spell M, A child, N
That represent man! (Yeah)
No B (Whooo), O child, Y (Yeah)
That mean mannish boy!
I'm a mah-yun! (Yeah)
I'm a natural-born lover's man!
I'm a mah-yun!
I'm a rollin' stone!
I'm a mah-yun!
I'm a hoochie-coochie man.

When a black youngster is giving too much lip, showing out, acting up, or generally behaving "too grown" for his own good, his grandmother is likely to snap, "Quit actin' so mannish, boy!" So with this song's title, "Mannish Boy," Muddy Waters was playing on an expression organic to African American childhood. It's easy to hear this blues classic and attribute it just to braggadocio. But between the ecstatic cries from the audience heard on the original recording, beneath the gusto of the legendary voice and the virility with which Waters growls "I'm a mah-yun," a deeper message percolates. We must not forget that at the time of this recording (1955), black men were still being called "boy" well into their advanced years, an indignity that Waters—born the son of a Mississippi sharecropper in 1915—was no doubt all too familiar with. Stripped to its core, then, "Mannish Boy" is a rousing affirmation of black manhood, the unequivocal resolution to the slave plea: "Am I not a man and a brother?"

Of course, with boasts such as "The line I shoots, it will never miss— / when I make love to a woman, she cain't resis'," Waters also exemplifies the swagger typical of the "signifying" tradition. This ritualized wordplay, a highly stylized lying, joking, and carrying on with such virtuosity as to inject one's message with metaphor and eloquence while elevating one's social status and parodying one's interlocutors or their attitudes and behaviors, goes on every day in the backyards, poolrooms, and front porches of Soulsville. It's hard to attach a textbook definition to such an inclusive speech event, but anthropologist Claudia Mitchell-Kernan has suggested that it is "a way of encoding messages or meanings in natural conversations which involves, in most cases, an element of indirection."

> The black concept of *signifying* incorporates essentially a folk notion that dictionary entries for words are not always sufficient for interpreting meanings or messages, or that meaning goes beyond such interpretations. Complimentary remarks may be delivered in a left-handed fashion. A particular utterance may be an insult in one context and not in another. What pretends to be informative may intend to be persuasive. Superficially, self-abasing remarks are frequently self-praise. The hearer is thus constrained to attend to all potential meaning carrying symbolic systems in speech events—the total universe of discourse.

Signifying, then, is the verbal artistry you're likely to overhear whenever black folk get together in an informal forum, whether that is a fish fry or a barbershop. It's part of an appreciation for "rapping," for fluid speech that brings the speaker and the listener immeasurable pleasure. One of the signifying tradition's most outlandish genres—generally the province of adult (especially older) males—are "toasts," including "The Signifying Monkey," "Stagolee," and "Shine and the *Titanic.*" Linguist William Labov and his colleagues define toasts as "long oral epic poems." Folklorist Roger Abrahams, the first scholar to reprint and discuss toasts at length, offers this characterization:

> The toast is a narrative poem that is recited, often in a theatrical manner, and represents the greatest flowering of Negro verbal talent. Toasts are often long, lasting anywhere from two to ten minutes. They conform to a general but by no means binding framing pattern. This consists of some sort of picturesque or exciting introduction, action alternating with dialogue (because the action is some kind of struggle between two people or animals), and a twist ending of some sort, either a quip, an ironic comment, or a brag.

Toasts (which may be compared to the less-than-genteel "'Twas the Night Before Christmas" poem in chapter 11) often contain profanity, lawless capers, improbable sex romps, and exploits of heroes who, as Abrahams notes, fall into two main categories: tricksters and badmen. Into the trickster-hero category falls "The Signifying Monkey," perhaps the best-known toast, and one that forms the centerpiece for a theory of black literary criticism developed by Harvard Afro-American studies professor Henry Louis Gates Jr. One version of this toast begins:

Down in the jungle near a dried-up creek,
The signifying monkey hadn't slept for a week.
Remembering the ass-kicking he had got in the past
He had to find somebody to kick the lion's ass.
Said the signifying monkey to the lion that very same day,
"There's a bad motherfucker heading your way.
The way he talks about you, it can't be right,
And I know when you two meet there going to be a fight."

In the badman tradition is "The Great MacDaddy," whose hero defies the judge he faces two hours after he's picked up "on a lame rap." As in many toasts, characters speak in the vernacular:

Later on, 'bout ten past ten,
I was facing the judge and twelve other men.
He looked down on me, he said,
"You're the last of the bad.
Now Dillinger, Slick Willie Sutton, all them fellows is gone,
Left you, the Great MacDaddy, to carry on."
He said, "Now, we gonna send you up the way. Gonna send you up
    the river.
Fifteen to thirty, that's your retire."
I said, "Fifteen to thirty, that ain't no time.
I got a brother in Sing Sing doing ninety-nine."

Somewhat intermediate between the trickster and the badman traditions, as Abrahams pointed out, is Shine, a powerful, quick-witted, metaphorical black man who stoked the coals in the belly of that ill-fated cruise ship, the *Titanic,* and whose exploits are celebrated in a series of toasts of the same name. Shine is the first to notice the water coming in after the boat runs up against an iceberg, but his initial attempts to address the situation are all rebuffed by the captain, over-confident about his vessel and disdainful of this black boiler-room boat-hand. Eventually, Shine leaps overboard and begins to swim:

Shine took off his shirt, took a dive. He took one stroke
And the water pushed him like it pushed a motorboat.
The captain said, "Shine, Shine, save poor me,
I'll give you more money than any black man see."
Shine said, "Money is good on land or sea.
Take off your shirt and swim like me."

In almost every version of this toast, Shine also turns down the entreaties of both the captain's wife and his daughter, who, from the deck of the doomed ship, offer him their affections in return for salvation. Shine swims on, besting a shark in the open sea and making it to shore, where, it is said, he gets himself good and soused by the time the *Titanic* goes under.

Shine possesses the superhuman abilities typical of many toast protagonists. Similarly incredible traits are exhibited by Dolomite, a notorious character (often portrayed by entertainer Rudy Ray Moore) who was so bad that he kicked African lions "to stay in shape" and who conquered scores of women (almost always presented as loose and scurrilous). It was said of Dolomite:

> At the age of one he was drinkin' whiskey and gin,
> at the age of two he was eatin' the bottles it came in.
> Now Dolomite had an uncle called Sudden Death,
> killed a dozen bad men from the smell of his breath.
> When his uncle heard how Dolomite was treatin' his ma and his pa,
> he said, "Let me go and check on this bad rascal before he go too far."
> Now one cold, dark December night,
> his uncle broke in on Dolomite.
> Now Dolomite wasn't no more'n three or four,
> when his uncle come breakin' through the door.
> His uncle said, "Dolomite,
> I want you to straighten up and treat your brother right,
> 'cause if you keep on with your dirty mistreatin',
> I'm gonna whup your ass till your heart stop beatin'." . . .
> He led off with a right that made lightnin' flash,
> but Dolomite tore his leg off, he was that damned fast.

For black men, who have been physically and psychologically castrated during their North American internment, assertions of manhood—of strength, potency, and bravado—must be larger than life. The badmen of toasts thus represent irreverent heroes of redemptive proportions. They're immortal, and they're worth mentioning in a chapter on singers because they help us understand first, the continuum of oral dexterity that blurs the distinction between black speech and song, and second, the wicked self-aggrandizement found in the newest chapter in the African American book of folklore, hip-hop:

> When rap begin then I gotta join in and
> Before my rhyme is over, you know I'ma win
> Cool J has arrived so you better make way
> Ask anybody in the crowd they say the kid don't play

Sparring competition that's my hobby and job
I don't wear a disguise because I don't own the mob
Got a pinpoint rap that makes you feel trapped so many girls on my jock
I think my phone here is tapped

I'm bad
(Cool J)
(Cool J)
(Cool J)
(C-C-C-C-Cool J)
(C-C-C-C-C-C-C-Cool J J J J J)

I'm like Tyson icin', I'm a soldier at war
I'm makin' sure you don't try to battle me no more
Got concrete rhymes, been rappin' for ten years and
Even when I'm braggin' I'm bein' sincere

The precise origin of hip-hop is a matter of dispute, but the originators appear to have been New York City youths who, in the middle and late 1970s, with nothing more than turntables and their imagination, began mixing old-school jams by funk prophets such as James Brown and George Clinton. The parents of the hip-hoppers (who were themselves of the Dolomite generation) must have groused when their Ohio Players, Isley Brothers, O'Jays, and Sly and the Family Stone records were returned scratched. But by the time the Sugarhill Gang dropped "Rapper's Delight" ("I don't mean to brag, I don't mean to boast, / but we like hot butta on our breakfast toast") in 1979, and Grandmaster Flash and the Furious Five released "The Message" ("It's like a jungle sometimes, / it makes me wonder how I keep from going under") in 1982, rap culture was oozing from the streets of urban America.

Remember, no creation in the Spoken Soul universe emerges from a vacuum. LL Cool J, the MC responsible for the immodest lyrics above, is as much a son of Rudy Ray Moore as he is of Muddy Waters. The braggadocio of his 1987 ballad "I'm Bad" (in which the musical theme from the blaxploitation movie *Shaft* was sampled) in a sense represents the incarnation of a Dolomite chant, or the ranting of a "Mannish Boy" in the 1980s. And boasts delivered Gatling-gun style remain the bread and "butta" of rap. In much the same way that Muddy Waters had enumerated his hustling credentials ("I'm a rollin' stone! . . . I'm a natural-born lover's man . . . I'm a hoochie-coochie

man") four decades earlier, Smooth Da Hustler testified to his bad-
ness in a 1997 joint that earned him some underground acclaim:

> The money stasher, gun-blastin' razor slasher
> The human asthma breath-taker
> Body dump waster
> The Glock cocker, block locker, the rock chopper
> The shot popper, the jock cock Glocker
> The face splitter, human-disgrace getter

But the rap game wasn't all about getting "big ups" or "mad props"
(respect and acclaim). Hip-hop artists also inherited the struggle to
"get ovah" to the Other Side. Some, such as bawdy material girl Lil'
Kim, envision "Money, Power, Respect" as the keys to transcendence.
Others offer a more complex scenario. Nas's single "If I Ruled the
World" (1996) imagines the ghetto turned B-boy utopia, and blends
an appetite for luxury cars with a longing for liberated black minds:

> Brand-new whips to crash then we laugh in the iller path
> The Villa house is for the crew, how we do
> Trees for breakfast, dime sexes and Benz stretches
> So many years of depression make me envision
> The better livin', the type of place to raise kids in
> Open they eyes to the lies history's tole foul

Nas pictures *whips* (cars) and *dimes* (fine women) as playthings for
his *crew* (posse) on a track teeming with insider lingo. Slick lexicon is
hip-hop's Magna Carta, establishing the rights of its disciples to speak
loudly but privately, to tell America about herself in a language that
leaves her puzzled. This glossary is forever morphing, constantly rein-
venting itself, bumping off words that were considered tony just the
other day (but that have now been mainstreamed and co-opted by
Madison Avenue to hawk everything from cereal to soda pop). Many
of the more or less new hip-hop terms for, say, cash—including *bank,
bank roll, benjamins, cheddar, cheese, cream, dead presidents, dividends, ends,
g's, loot, mail, papers, papes,* and *scrilla*—are guaranteed to go stale soon,
maybe inside a few years.

Any MC who wishes to maintain street validity had better be able
to wield the most contemporary slang. For this, along with a raw, un-
slurred delivery, is what determines much of prowess when it comes
to freestyling, a ritual in which "hip-hop heads" form a circle and
"bust" improvised rhymes "off the top of the dome." Holding only a
slightly lower profile than slang in the rap game, of course, is bona
fide Black English, which encompasses vocabulary—and thus slang—

but is also composed of distinct grammatical and phonological elements. There is no question that black talk provides hip-hop's linguistic underpinnings, but manifested strikingly in "The Day After" (1995) by the ultraconscious Atlanta-based group Goodie Mob:

> I been this way since birth
> Heaven above sent a newborn to tell it like he see it
> No lies through the eyes of an angel suggest you don't table
> Every angle be obtuse, ain't no truce, it's war
> It won't stop, to compromise wouldn't stop the bloodsheddin'
> It's Armageddon in the streets of each inner city
> Ain't takin' no pity on the unjust callin' it trust
> I'm on the bus starin' out of a window
> Thankin' 'bout them happy days I had

Rap aficionados gush about this group's talent for flowing in the "cipher," the supercharged circuit of rap knowledge and creativity (something not dissimilar—in the vein of highly communal, responsive rituals—to the ring shout). What many hip-hop heads probably don't realize is that Goodie Mob owes plenty to Spoken Soul. Not just for sledgehammer lyrics and the style in which they're delivered, but for its coveted, noncommercial status within the industry. After all, the Mob is regarded as "real" and truthful because of its image of fierce nonconformity, and nothing thumbs its nose at conformity like the unrestrained African American vernacular. Although white suburban youngsters eat up hip-hop's edgy tales of money, sexual adventure, ghetto life, and racial injustice (and keep ghetto rhymes atop the pop charts), black urban youngsters are the genre's target audience. And black urban youngsters follow artists who roam the world implied by the neighborhood language of black urban youngsters. "Peep" (look at) rapper DMX's "How's It Going Down":

> What type of games is bein' played, how's it goin' down
> If it's on til it's gone, then I gots to know now
> Is you wit me or what, they gon try to give me a nut
> Just honeys wanna give me the butt, what

These lyrics reverberated from car speakers throughout 1998. It is a good example of hip-hop's allegiance to both slang and the grammar of Black English. But it's safe to say that of those who turned up their radios when "the jam bumped," few if any were contemplating hip-hop's ties to the blues, old-school toasts, or jazz, or even considering its developing role as the new conventional wisdom of pop culture, or as folklore transformed. Few hip-hop heads are inclined to trace their music culture to the fast-talking of Fats Waller and Cab Calloway, or even to the scatting of Louis Armstrong. But jazz is in the energetic nonsense words that kick off "Rapper's Delight":

> I said a hip hop the hippie the hippie to the hip hip hop
> a you don't stop a rockin' to the bang bang boogie
> said up jump the boogie to the rhythm of the boogie da beat.

It is a tribute to the resilience of a people who resisted annihilation for centuries, then came out swinging, bebopping, and now hip-hopping, that they are able, with each new generation, to reinvent themselves artfully using the same essential mortar.

The Howard University crowd that found itself swept away by a spiritual's sentiment unwittingly paid homage to the language of "soul power." Members of that audience who experienced a flash of recognition, a starburst of emotion from their communal experience, should acknowledge that the disposition, the very organization of the phrase "I done done" helped trigger those feelings. And if the students in that audience had listened, really listened, to their *own* music, perhaps they would have discovered not only the lingering growl of Muddy Waters and wail of Mahalia Jackson, but the talk of the spirituals as well. Consider 1999 Grammy Award winner Lauryn Hill's "Lost Ones," a hybrid hip-hop-and-reggae tune that did some serious radio rotation in 1998:

> You might win some but you really lost one
> You just lost one, it so silly how come
> When it's all done did you really gain from
> What you *done done*, it so silly how come [Emphasis added.]

As Hill herself submits, there is "not a game new under the sun." Her use of Spoken Soul features such as the completive ("done done") and the deletion of the contracted *s* ("*it so* silly") are natural, accepted, even appreciated elements of a linguistic convention that has sustained the soul. There are many black singers, including Nat King Cole and Sam Cooke, who produced exhilarating, beloved music in "mainstream" English. But if the Rolling Stones flattered the language of our black ancestors with constant imitation, why must the direct heirs to that language disparage it on the street? Why indeed, when the next hip-hop generation busies itself sampling and resampling James Brown, and the parlance of soul still crowns the pop charts?

Part Three

The Living Language

6

Vocabulary and Pronunciation

Ebonics has no dictionary, no text books, no grammar, no rules. It is rebellious and outside rule-based language.
> —America Online contributor (December 23, 1996)

You are 100% incorrect that "Ebonics" has no rules, structure, or dictionary. Africanized English has a consistent structure and rules. . . . Please do not confuse street slang with Africanized English.
> —America Online contributor (December 23, 1996)

For most people, languages and dialects are distinguished primarily by their words and expressions. French speakers say *"Bonjour,"* English speakers "Hello." The British say "lorry" where Americans say "truck." Bostonians use "tonic" for what other northeasterners refer to as "soda" and midwesterners call "pop." And so on. Similarly, for most casual commentators, what sets black talk apart is its distinctive word usage, particularly the informal and usually short-lived "slang" expressions known primarily to adolescents and young adults. The only examples of Black English in James Baldwin's 1979 tribute to the vernacular ("If Black English Isn't a Language, Then Tell Me, What Is?") are expressions, especially slang, that have crossed over into general American use, such as *jazz, sock it to me, let it all hang out, right on, uptight,* and *get down.* And for nine out of ten people who contributed to the America Online discussion of Ebonics in December 1996, Ebonics was "just a bunch of slang."

But Spoken Soul, like any other language variety, is much more than slang, and much more than the sum of its words. For linguists, the scientists who study human language, two other aspects of any language variety are as important as vocabulary, if not more so: its rules for pronouncing words, or pronunciation patterns, and its grammar—including its rules for modifying or combining words to express different meanings and to form larger phrases or sentences. African American vernacular has, for instance, a rule of grammar that allows speakers to move negative helping verbs such as *ain't* and *can't* to the front of a sentence to make the sentence more emphatic, so that "Nobody ain't going" can become "Ain't nobody going!" (This is an emphatic utterance, not a question, and usually such a phrase has the falling intonation of a statement or exclamation.) The verb can be moved to the front only if the subject of the sentence is a negative quantifier such as *nobody* or *nothing*. If the subject is not a negative quantifier—say, *John* or *the boy*—the rule does not apply. You can't convert "John ain't going" into "Ain't John going," at least not as an emphatic statement. (With rising intonation, of course, "Ain't John going?" would be an acceptable question.)

From this example, it should be clear that by "rules" we don't mean regulations that are prescribed in grammar books or consciously memorized. Nobody sits a kid down at the age of six and says, "Okay, time to learn the negative fronting, or inversion, rule." But through exposure and experimentation, children in every speech community around the world learn the conventional and systematic ways of pronouncing, modifying, and combining words that are characteristic of their community's language variety (or varieties). It is these conventional and systematic ways of using language that we refer to as rules.

Every human language and dialect studied to date—whether loved or hated, prestigious or not—has regularities or rules of this type. A moment's reflection would show why this is so. Without regularities, a language variety could not be successfully acquired or used in everyday life, and this applies to Spoken Soul, or Ebonics, as much as to the "Received Pronunciation," or "BBC English," of the British upper crust. Characterizations of the former as careless or lazy, and of the latter as careful or refined, are subjective social and political evaluations that reflect prejudices and preconceptions about the people who usually speak each variety. In contrast, linguists try, as objectively as possible, to understand and reveal the systematic regularities that every language inevitably possesses. That is our goal in this chapter and the next, beginning with the vocabulary and pronunciation of Spoken Soul, and then considering its grammar. Whereas pronunciation and grammar vary less than vocabulary from one region to another, they tend to vary more by social class. And because of their impact on verbal expression and literacy, they loom large when we consider the education of African American children.

Vocabulary

The claim that Ebonics has no dictionary (see the first comment at the beginning of this chapter) is incorrect. Since 1994 there have been two authoritative guides: Clarence Major's 548-page *Juba to Jive: A Dictionary of African American Slang* (a revised, expanded version of his 1970 *Dictionary of Afro-American Slang*), and Geneva Smitherman's 243-page *Black Talk: Words and Phrases from the Hood to the Amen Corner* (a revised and expanded edition of which will appear in 2000). There has also been no dearth of shorter, more informal glossaries, from "Introduction to Contemporary Harlemese" in Rudolph Fisher's 1928 novel *The Walls of Jericho,* through *The New Cab Calloway's Hep-ster's Dictionary* (1944), to more recent word and phrase books such as *A 2 Z: The Book of Rap and Hip-Hop Slang* (1995). Add to this dozens of scholarly articles and a number of book-length studies, including J. L. Dillard's *Lexicon of Black English* (1970) and Edith Folb's *runnin' down some lines* (1980), and it's clear that there is substantial information on the vocabulary of Spoken Soul, past and present.

Since vocabulary, especially slang, is always changing, new studies will always be needed. And a full-fledged Ebonics dictionary with pronunciation, etymologies, and historical attestations, to parallel the *Oxford English Dictionary* or *Webster's Third,* remains to be written. But we know enough from existing studies to make a number of generalizations.

One of the many fascinating features of black vocabulary is how sharply it can divide blacks and whites, and how solidly it can connect blacks from different social classes. In 1992, sociologist Teresa Labov published a study that examined the extent to which adolescents used and understood eighty-nine slang terms. Of all the social variables she considered, race turned out to be the most significant factor, with blacks much more familiar with terms like *bougie* ("an uppity-acting African American"), *busting out* ("looking good"), and *fresh* (for "cool"), and whites much more familiar with terms like *schlep* (for "to drag along") and *bombed* or *smashed* (as a synonym for "drunk"). That the black respondents knew the black terms is significant: they were college students at predominantly white institutions. Although "bloods

from the 'hood" and those from the hills certainly differ in the range
and kinds of black slang they use (see the comments quoted by Edith
Folb later in this section), familiarity with distinctive black vocabulary
is one of the ways in which virtually every African American can be
said to speak some form of Ebonics, or Spoken Soul.

In 1972, Robert L. Williams, the psychologist who coined the term
"Ebonics," created the so-called BITCH test, which, like Teresa Labov's
study, highlighted differences in black and white vocabulary and experience. Williams's aggressive acronym stood for "Black Intelligence
Test of Cultural Homogeneity," which was designed to give blacks an
advantage, unlike the usual intelligence tests that privileged the experience of whites. The test included one hundred multiple-choice
questions, most of them requiring the test-taker to select the right
gloss for words and expressions "from the black experience." Test
items (with Williams's glosses) included: *blood,* "a brother of color"; *to
hot-comb,* "to press [one's hair]"; *HNIC,* "head nigger in charge"; and
playing the dozens, "insulting a person's parents."

What is revealing about Williams's test is that many of the terms
are not slang—relatively new and informal usages that are most common among teenagers, and likely not to last long—but words familiar
across all age groups in the African American community, and words
that have been around for a long time. As the preceding examples
show, many of these historically "black" words refer to unique aspects
of the black experience, including the physical attributes, social distinctions, and cultural practices and traditions of African Americans.
Other examples in this category include the following (definitions
are from Smitherman's *Black Talk*):

Ashy: The whitish or grayish appearance of skin due to exposure to
wind and cold; shows up more on African Americans due to Black
people's darker skin pigmentation.

Bad: Good, excellent, great, fine. [In] the Mandingo language in West
Africa, *a ka nyi ko-jugu* [is] literally "It is good badly," meaning "It is
very good."

Juneteenth: The day, usually in mid to late June, when African Americans celebrate emancipation from enslavement; originally June 19,
1865, the date enslaved Africans in Texas learned they had been freed.

Kitchen: Hair at the nape of the neck, inclined to be the most curly
(*kinky*) and thus the hardest part of *straightened* hair to keep from
going back.

Tom, Uncle Tom: A negative reference to a Black person, suggesting that he/she is a sell-out, not down with the black cause. Tom comes from the character Uncle Tom in Harriet Beecher Stowe's *Uncle Tom's Cabin,* who put his master's wishes and life before his own. . . . For women, *Aunt Thomasina, Aunt Jane.*

Yelluh, high yelluh: A very light-complexioned African American.

Many blacks don't realize that their use of many of these words differs from that of other Americans. (Of course, *bad* and *yelluh,* which have crossed over into general usage, differ in this regard from other words on the list.) When a group of African American college students was told recently that *ashy* in the sense of "dry skin" was not standard English usage—you wouldn't find it with that meaning in standard American dictionaries, much less British ones—they were bowled over. It's often only when a questionnaire survey is conducted that the impact of race on word usage becomes clear. In 1976, for example, a survey of thirty-five blacks and thirty-five whites revealed that blacks were far more familiar with *cut-eye* and *suck-teeth,* words for visual and oral gestures, respectively, that express annoyance or anger at the person to whom they are directed. Thirty-three of the blacks (94 percent) but only four of the whites (11 percent) were familiar with *cut-eye;* twenty-four of the blacks (69 percent) were familiar with *suck-teeth,* but only one of the whites (3 percent) was.

When the multivolume *Dictionary of American Regional English* (DARE) was being prepared in the 1970s, an even larger survey was conducted in which 2,777 American informants—representing various races, age groups, and education levels—participated. One result was a comprehensive picture of which terms were used "among Black speakers" (e.g., *ace-boon-coon,* "a very close friend") or "chiefly among Blacks" (e.g., *bid whist,* "a variation of the card game whist in which players bid to name trump"), and which were "especially common among Blacks" (e.g., *bubba,* "term of address for a brother"). Some of the terms DARE identified as black were compounds involving body parts, such as *bad-eye* ("the evil eye: a curse or threatening glance"), *bad-mouth* ("to speak ill of someone"), and *big-eye* ("greedy, covetous"). Like *suck-teeth,* these are translations into English of literal and metaphorical expressions in West African languages (e.g., Mandingo *da-jugu* and Hausa *mugum-baki* for *bad-mouth,* and Igbo *íma osò,* Yoruba *kpóšé,* Hausa *tsaki,* Efik *asiama,* Kikongo *tsiona,* and Wolof *cipu* for *suck-teeth* sound).

The mention of African languages raises a larger question about the major sources and domains of black vocabulary. Besides African languages, these include music, especially the blues (*jazz, gig, funky, hep, boogie*); religion and the church (*shout, Amen corner*); sex and lovemaking (*grind, johnson, mack*); superstition and conjure (*obeah, voodoo, mojo*); street life, including prostitution, drugs, gangs, fights, and cars (*trick, pimp walk, numbers, cracked out, bus a cap, hog*); people (*cuz, posse, saddity/seddity, the Man*); abbreviations (*CP time, HNIC, on the DL*); and slang or youth culture (*fresh, phat, bustin out*).

When it comes to slang, which overlaps to some extent with the other categories (e.g., sex and lovemaking), variation by region and social class is widespread, as is rapid change over time. Edith Folb's two-decade-old study of the language of black teenagers in Los Angeles documents how slang use there varied according to age, gender, region, social class, and life-style. Her comments on class differences are worth quoting, if only to counteract the impression one might otherwise get that all blacks are hip to exactly the same range of black slang (if the slang sounds dated, it's because Folb's fieldwork was conducted in the late sixties and early seventies):

> There are ghetto realities that most middle-class teenagers simply have no contact with. As one politically active middle-class youth put it, "Sure, I know a lot of the words [in the lexicon], but I'm not livin' down there. It's different. Can't pretend it isn't. Some of those terms just not part of my life." His ghetto peer agrees: "Dig. The brothers up dere in dem Hollywood Hills, out dere at UCLA and all dem li'l ol' colleges, they okay—hear what I'm sayin'? They hip to some o' d' happ'nin's, they blood. But when dude come down here, better take it slow, 'cause gon' be lot shit he ain' got together. Some blood blow his mind, send 'im on a hombog. Run down some lines he done never heard!"

Although some slang words do hang around for a long time (*pad*, for instance, has been used for "apartment" or "home" since the 1800s), slang is *the* most rebellious and dynamic aspect of any language. As noted by Clarence Major:

> Black slang is a living, breathing form of expression that changes so quickly no researcher can keep up with it. A word or phrase can come into existence to mean one thing among a limited number of speakers in a particular neighborhood and a block away it might mean something else or be unknown entirely—at least for a while.

The regional and rapidly changing aspects of slang account for the variations in vocabulary that people notice between East Coast and West Coast (not to mention southern and midwestern) rap. In Philadelphia, "That's whassup" affirms a statement. In Washington, D.C., it's "I'm with it," and in New Orleans it's "I'm 'bout it." To learn the state of affairs, ask a New Yorker, "Yo, what the deal?" and a Chicago native, "What the demo?" Because the life span of slang verbiage is so short, many of the most contemporary terms cannot be found in the 1994 dictionaries of Major and Smitherman. Both dictionaries, for instance, include *player.* In Major, one of the definitions is "a lady's man; a sexually active male; male with more than one woman"; Smitherman has a similar gloss, but adds: "a flamboyant, flashy, popular man or woman, who may or may not have many women or men." But neither includes the more recently coined *player-hate* (pronounced *playa-hate*), "to be jealous of or to impede the success of a player or anyone who is doing well." Similarly, while they both include *short,* slang for "car" that goes back to the 1930s, neither has *shorty* (pronounced *shawty*), a newer term for "girlfriend" or "female" (as in "Shorty, what your name is?") popular on the East Coast and in the South. (However, both terms appear in the 2000 edition of *Black Talk.*)

Claude Brown confronted the changing nature of slang back in 1968:

> The expression "up-tight," which meant being in financial straits, appeared on the soul scene in the general vicinity of 1953. Junkies were very fond of the word and used it literally to describe what was a perpetual condition with them. The word was pictorial and pointed; therefore it caught on quickly in Soulsville across the country. In the early Sixties when "uptight" was on the move, a younger generation of people along the Eastern Seaboard regenerated it with a new meaning: "everything is cool, under control, going my way."

Clarence Major comments on the subsequent evolution of *uptight:* "Later, in the late sixties, early seventies, it was adapted by white teenagers to mean mental or emotional disorder."

Which brings us to another point. Quite apart from words such as *bubba, big daddy, grits,* and *chitlins/chitterlings*—which long ago diffused among southerners as a group (from black to white in the case of *bubba* and *big daddy,* from white to black in the case of *grits* and *chitlins*)— black slang has been spreading to teenagers of other ethnic groups more generally (primarily through music), and thence to mainstream

America, for quite some time. James Baldwin remarked on this in 1979:

> Now, I do not know what white Americans would sound like if there had never been any black people in the United States, but they would not sound the way they sound. *Jazz*, for example, is a very specific sexual term, as in *jazz me, baby,* but white people purified it into the Jazz Age. *Sock it to me,* which means roughly the same thing, has been adopted by Nathaniel Hawthorne's descendants with no qualms or hesitations at all, along with *let it all hang out* and *right on!*

And in 1998, Hampton University professor Margaret Lee listed more than sixty black expressions that had crossed over into mainstream newspaper use, including *chill out; threads; all that; boom-shaka-laka; main squeeze; you go, girl; high-five; homeboy; soulmate;* and *got game.*

Although many blacks complain about white and mainstream adoption of black slang, new slang terms that provide secrecy and reflect rebelliousness are constantly being created within the black community. Furthermore, as Clarence Major reminds us, the process of diffusion is not just normal, but unavoidable:

> This evolution from private to public is not only essential to the vitality at the crux of slang, but inevitable. By this I mean, African-American slang is not only a living language for black speakers but for the whole country, as evidenced by its popularity decade after decade since the beginning of American history. The most recent example of this popularity is rap and hip-hop during the 1980s and 1990s.

Pronunciation

Claude Brown, who paid homage to the "communicative and meaningful" sounds of Spoken Soul, insisted that it was such sounds ("soul vocalization"), rather than slang, that represented the distinctive identity of the black vernacular. As he noted:

> Spoken soul is distinguished from slang primarily by the fact that the former lends itself easily to conventional English, and the latter is diametrically opposed to adaptations within the realm of conventional English. Police (pronounced pō′ lice) is a soul term, whereas "The Man" is merely slang for the same thing.

Brown was not a linguist, and most of the 1968 article in which he wrote this was about slang. But he did realize that the system represented by black pronunciation was a more fundamental part of

Spoken Soul. As he observed, this system allowed virtually any word in "conventional English" to be converted to the sounds of a black vernacular:

> There are specific phonetic traits. To the soulless ear, the vast majority of these sounds are dismissed as incorrect usage of the English language . . . To those so blessed as to have had bestowed upon them at birth the lifetime gift of soul, these are the most communicative and meaningful sounds ever to fall upon human ears: the familiar "mah" instead of "my," "gonna" for "going to," "yo" for "your."

The first example he offered was the pronunciation of "my" as *mah*—to which one could add other examples: "I" as *Ah,* "side" as *sahd,* and so on. In these cases, what linguists call a diphthong (a two-vowel sequence) involving a glide from an *ah*-like vowel to an *ee*-like vowel, is produced as a long monophthong (a single vowel) without the glide to *ee.* Like many other pronunciation features of Spoken Soul, this monophthongal pronunciation is characteristic of southern white speech, as shown by the first entry in a popular little glossary entitled *How to Speak Southern:*

> **Ah:** The things you see with, and the personal pronoun denoting individuality. *"Ah* think *Ah*'ve got somethin' in mah *ah."* ["I think I've got something in my eye."]

Another instance in which Spoken Soul resembles southern white speech is in the similar pronunciation of *e* and *i* before nasals (sounds like *m, n,* and *ng,* which require air from the lungs to flow through the nose as well as the mouth), so that *pin* and *pen* sound like *pin,* and one might have to ask, "Do you mean a sticking *pin,* or a writing *pen?*"

That white southerners also say *mah* and *Ah* and merge *pin* and *pen* does not detract from the significance of these features as markers of Spoken Soul. For one thing, in the vast areas of the North, East, Midwest, and West where African Americans now live, *mah, Ah,* and the *pin/pen* merger are regularly used and interpreted as distinctive elements of "sounding black." In a recent study in Detroit, for instance, linguist Walter Edwards found that working-class blacks used monophthongal pronunciations like *mah* and *Ah* 60 percent of the time, while working-class whites used them only 12 percent of the time. It is possible that in these as in other cases (e.g., *r*-lessness, as in *yo* for "your"—an example that Brown also cites), white southerners adopted the feature from blacks rather than vice versa.

Recall that until the northern and western migrations of the early twentieth century, 90 percent of the country's black population was concentrated in the South. The fact that it is southern white speech that most resembles black speech is probably not an accident, and some observers have explicitly attributed the features of southern white speech to black influence, most recently linguists Erik R. Thomas and Guy Bailey:

> Campbell (1746), Barker (1855), Jackson and Davis (1908), and Cash (1941) all report that White children on plantations often adopted features from the slave children who were their playmates. Feagin (1990) uses such historical evidence as a basis for postulating that African American influence promulgated r-lessness among whites in the South. It is important to remember that on smaller plantations and farms (where the vast majority of slaveholders lived), the owner and his family often worked alongside slaves in the fields. Moreover, after the Civil War, Whites often fell victim to the system of tenancy so that in many cases Blacks and Whites worked alongside each other as tenant farmers.

In at least some cases, blacks who influenced southern white speech in the nineteenth and twentieth centuries might have been transmitting features their ancestors in turn had acquired from English, Irish, and Scots-Irish indentured servants and peasant settlers in the seventeenth and eighteenth centuries, better preserved by them for a variety of historical reasons. (Compare East Indians in Guyana, who acquired deep Guyanese Creole from the newly emancipated Africans when the former group first came to what was then British Guiana as indentured servants in the 1830s. Today, because East Indians are more heavily represented in the peasant farming areas where deep Creole speech thrives, they are statistically more likely to exemplify it than are the more urban descendants of the Africans.)

But despite mutual influence between blacks and whites, it would be a mistake to assume that black and white pronunciations are identical, even in the South. Thomas and Bailey in fact point to two other features of vowel pronunciation distinguishing blacks and whites, even those from the same area. One is the pronunciation of the *a* (phonetically [e] in *name, state, pay, say, baby, slaves,* and similar words) and the *o* (phonetically [o] in *go, so, no, home,* and similar words), as pure monophthongs, or words with little variation or change in sound from beginning to end. Ex-slaves born in the 1840s and 1850s had this feature, in common with older African Americans born before World War I and Caribbean English Creole speakers. White Americans born in the 1840s and 1850s did not have this feature, displaying a more diphthongal pronunciation, in which the tongue rises at the end. Younger African Americans follow their white counterparts in this respect, but in their pronunciation of the second feature, the [ɑ] onset of the [ɑu] diphthong in words like *down* and *house,* they differ from whites of all ages, and follow older African Americans and their Caribbean English Creole brethren in using nonfront pronunciations, more like the vowel of *father* than like the vowel of *cat.* In a recent study, nearly 70 percent of black Texans began the diphthong of *thousand* with a nonfront pronunciation, while less than 20 percent of white Texans did.

The issue of whether blacks can be distinguished from whites by the sound of their voices alone came to national attention during the O. J. Simpson murder trial in Los Angeles. On July 12, 1995, prosecutor Christopher Darden tried to have witness Robert Heidstra validate an earlier statement he had allegedly made that one of the two voices he heard near Nicole Brown Simpson's house on the night of her murder sounded like that of a black man. Defense attorney Johnnie Cochran objected immediately, and Judge Lance Ito sustained his objection. In a dramatic moment, the jury and the witness were asked to leave the courtroom, and Mr. Cochran angrily explained the basis of his objection:

> You can't tell by somebody's voice whether they sounded black. . . .
> I resent that [as] a racist statement. . . . This statement about whether
> he sounds black or white is racist and I resent it and that is why I
> stood and objected. And I think it is totally improper in America
> [that] at this time . . . we have to hear and endure this.

However, as linguist John McWhorter has noted in a recent book:

> In fact . . . Cochran got away with murder on that one. . . . Most
> Americans, and especially black ones, can almost always tell that a
> person is black even on the phone, and even when the speaker is
> using standard English sentences.

The evidence lies in more than a dozen studies that have been conducted over the past three decades showing that listeners are able to identify accurately the ethnicity of black and white speakers on the basis of tape-recorded samples of their speech, some less than 2.5 seconds long. The overall accuracy of identification is typically between 80 and 90 percent in these studies, and the pronunciation cues (in many cases the speakers are using identical Standard English grammar) include differences in vowel quality of the type described above, and other features. In a 1972 study by John Rickford, speakers uttering "Hey, what's happening" and other phrases were accurately identified as black or white 86 percent of the time, apparently on the basis of what listeners described as their "inflection," "variation in pitch and rhythm," "intonation," and "tone." Acoustic phonetic analysis revealed that the two black speakers did indeed show wider variation in pitch and intonation (with their voices rising higher and falling lower) than the whites, even when their pronunciation of individual consonants and vowels was more similar.

The speech of highly educated black speakers was identified much less accurately in early studies by researchers Richard Tucker and Wallace Lambert (around 50 percent), and Roger Shuy (8 to 18 percent). These results, along with a subsequent study by William Labov and his colleagues in which listeners were only moderately successful (30 to 66 percent correct) in identifying the ethnicity of "difficult cases"—whites who had been raised in the South or who otherwise showed strong black influence, and blacks who had been raised entirely in white communities—firmly established that "sounding black" (or "white") is not rooted in genetics or physiology, but influenced by society and culture. Cochran was right to resist the "racist" insinuation that *any* black person, regardless of education, cultural upbringing, and association, could be infallibly identified as black by the sound of his or her voice alone. Yet it was not "totally improper" for Darden and the prosecution to allege otherwise, for in the vast majority of cases, cultural and sociological factors have conspired to make blacks and whites sound different, and they do.

So far we have been talking about "soul vocalization" almost entirely in terms of vowels and intonation. But sometimes what's distinctive happens with syllables. Take, for instance, the fact that blacks place the stress on the first rather than the second syllable, as in *PO-lice* and *HO-tel*, or the fact that blacks (especially older ones) delete the unstressed initial and medial syllables in words like *(a)bout*, *(be)cause*, *(a)fraid*, and *sec(re)t(a)ry* more often than whites do.

Moreover, it is often the pronunciation of *consonants* that distinguishes the speech of blacks from the speech of other ethnic groups in the United States, quantitatively as well as qualitatively. Some black consonant pronunciations—such as *aks* (or *axe*) for "ask"—are shibboleths of vernacular black speech. In a March 1995 segment of *60*

Minutes, television news reporter Morley Safer asked Arch Whitehead, a well-suited African American who recruits corporate executives, what would happen if a black man applying for a Wall Street job were to say, "May I *aks* you a question?" versus "May I *ask* you a question?" Whitehead laughed and said, "He won't get to *aks* that very often, I'll tell ya," and the two men agreed that he wouldn't even "get a foot in the door."

But two things should be noted about this widely stereotyped and stigmatized pronunciation, which is often a focus of "speech improvement" classes taken by black students. The first is that it was widespread in British English in earlier times. In Old English for example, as the *Oxford English Dictionary* or *Webster's Third New International Dictionary* will tell you, *a-csian* alternated with *a-scian* as the word meaning "to ask." Even in Middle English, the spelling alternated between *axen* and *asken,* although the latter won out to become the Standard English pronunciation of modern times. Second, *aks* for "ask" is an example of metathesis—switching two consonants in a word, often to achieve an easier articulation. (An example from Standard English is "comfortable," where the *t* is sometimes pronounced before the *r,* even though it's spelled with *r* before *t.*) Another example in Spoken Soul is the pronunciation of "wasp" as *waps,* but that is much less common than *aks* for "ask."

Much more widespread in their effects are rules deleting *l* and *r* after vowels, as in *he'p* for "help," *afta* for "after," and *yo* for "your" (one of Claude Brown's examples of soul vocalization). These processes are found also in the speech of whites and other ethnic groups, but they tend to occur more often in black vernacular speech, and they sometimes affect *r* between vowels (as in *Ca[r]ol*), unlike other dialects. Note that the deletion of contracted *'ll* from *will* allows invariant *be* to function sometimes as a future marker, as in "He('ll) *be* here in a few minutes"—a point we'll return to in chapter 7.

Another pronunciation that is often described as deleting a consonant—the practice of dropping the final *g* in words like *walkin'* and *singin'*—does not actually involve deletion, but the replacement of one type of nasal (the *eng*-like velar nasal, as at the end of *thing,* formed with the back of the tongue raised toward the back of the mouth) with another (the *en*-like alveolar nasal, as at the end of *thin,* formed with the front of the tongue raised behind the upper teeth). Other examples of consonant replacement rather than deletion are the pronunciation of "street" as *skreet* and "stretch" as *skretch* (with *k* replacing *t* in *str* sequences, especially in the South), and the use of *b* for *v* (as in *hebben* for "heaven" and *nebba* for "never").

What all this talk about consonant deletions and replacements tends to miss is the fact that these processes are highly systematic, and not the careless or haphazard pronunciations that observers often mistake them for. (Recall the America Online contributor quoted at the beginning of this chapter who said that Ebonics has no rules, and the William Raspberry column, quoted in chapter 11, in which Ebonics is said to have "no consistent spellings or pronunciations and no discernible rules.") To appreciate this, let us consider two well-known features of Spoken Soul—the simplification of consonant clusters (by deletion of the final consonant) at the end of words, as in *tes'* for "test," *des'* for "desk," and *han'* for "hand," and the replacement of *th* by *t, f, d,* or *v,* as in *tin* for "thin," *Rufe* for "Ruth," *dem* for "them," and *bave* for "bathe." Not just any consonant cluster at the end of a word can be simplified; you can't simplify "jump" to *jum'* or "pant" to *pan'*, and the *th* in "Ruth" can't be replaced by *v* instead of *f*, nor can the *th* in "them" be replaced by *t* instead of *d*. In order to produce the correct vernacular pronunciations in each case, speakers of Spoken Soul have to attend to whether the corresponding Standard English pronunciations are voiced or voiceless.

Voiced or voiceless, you say? What you talkin' 'bout? We're referring to whether your vocal cords are held closely together, vibrating noisily (voiced), or whether they are spread apart and not vibrating (voiceless). The consonants *s* and *z* are identical sounds, except that *s* is voiceless and *z* is voiced. If you put your fingers in your ears and say a prolonged *s* followed by a prolonged *z*—*sssszzzz*—you'll hear the difference quite dramatically as voicing begins for *z* and the vibrations resonate from your throat through your entire head. The consonants *s, f, p, t,* and *k* (among others) are voiceless, and *z, v, b, d,* and *g* (among others) are voiced. Now, we'll bet your parents or teachers never taught you about voicing. But if you're a native speaker of English, it's something you've been attending to every day of your life, at least from the time you learned to form plurals. Although grammar books tell you that you simply add *s* or *es* to the end of a word to form a regular English plural, the rule holds true only for writing. In speech, it's slightly more complicated. If the word ends in a sibilant (a hissing sound like *ch* or *s*), the pronunciation becomes *uhz* or *ihz*, as in *rozuhz*, "roses," or *churchihz*, "churches." If the word ends in a vowel (all English vowels are voiced) or a voiced nonsibilant consonant, like *b* or *g,* you add a voiced *z,* as in *teaz,* "teas"; *cabz,* "cabs"; or *bidz,* "bids"; if the word ends in a voiceless nonsibilant sound like *p* or *t,* you add a voiceless *s,* as in *caps* or *bits.*

Let's return to Spoken Soul. The unconscious but very regular rule for simplifying consonant clusters by deleting the final consonant at the end of a word applies only if both (or all three) consonants are voiceless (as in *test*) or voiced (as in *hand*). If one of the consonants is voiced and the other is voiceless, as in *jump* and *pant,* you can't simplify them. Of course, all good rules have exceptions (compare *oxen* and *sheep* as English plurals). Spoken Soul is no exception, but even the exceptions are regular. Negatives like *can't, won't,* and *shouldn't* regularly lose their final voiceless *t* (as in *can', won', shouldn'*) even though it's preceded by a voiced *n.* Many colloquial dialects of English have similar rules for consonant cluster simplification, but Spoken Soul applies it more often than most. And for speakers who regularly simplify the final cluster in "test" to *tes',* the latter becomes the base form in their mental dictionary, and its plural becomes *tesses* (*tessuhz*) instead of "tests" (which ends in a triple consonant cluster) because of the rules for plural formation outlined in the preceding paragraph. (Compare also *desses* instead of "desks.")

In the case of *th,* voicing is relevant because English *th* comes in both a voiceless variety, as in "think," and a voiced variety, as in "them." English spelling masks the difference, but you can hear it by taking the initial voiced sound in "them" (more like a *dh* than a *th*) and substituting it for the initial sound of "think" (yielding something like *DHink,* which sounds funny), or taking the initial voiceless sound of "think" and substituting it for the initial sound of "them" (*THem,* which also sounds funny). The rules for replacing "th" in Spoken Soul depend crucially on voicing. Voiceless *th* can be replaced by voiceless *t* or *f* (the latter primarily at the end of words, as in *toof,* "tooth"; the former almost anywhere: *tink,* "think"; *nutten,* "nothing"; *toot,* "tooth"); voiced *th* can be replaced by voiced *d* or *v* (the latter in the middle or at the ends of words, as in *muvva,* "mother," and *bave,* "bathe"; the former anywhere: *dem,* "them"; *mudda,* "mother"; *bade,* "bathe"). The ways in which English *th* is pronounced in black vernacular therefore reveal in a very systematic way whether it is voiced or voiceless, even more so than English spelling does.

Finally, voicing is relevant to another pronunciation feature of Spoken Soul, which shares with many English-based creoles a rule deleting *b, d,* or *g* (all voiced "stops" when any one of them is the first consonant in tense-aspect markers or auxiliary verbs). Examples include the *d* of *don't* (*Ah 'on' know* = "I don't know") and *didn't* (*He ain't do it* = "He didn't do it") and the *g* of *gonna* (*ah ma do it* = "I'm gonna do it," with the *g* and most of *gonna* deleted). Among U.S. dialects, this rule is apparently unique to the black vernacular or very nearly so, and it provides one indication among others that Spoken Soul may have had Creole English ancestry or been influenced in its history by Creole speech. (See chapter 8.)

Variation in Pronunciation

As we have indicated, despite a certain cohesiveness of vocabulary use among blacks as opposed to whites, social class and other factors differentiate vocabulary even among blacks. This is more true of pronunciation. One of the most careful studies of social-class differences in black pronunciation, conducted in Detroit by linguist Walt Wolfram more than thirty years ago, showed that while upper-middle-class (professional) blacks simplified their consonant clusters quite often—an average of 51 percent of the time in their recorded speech—lower-working-class blacks (unskilled workers) did so even more frequently—an average of 84 percent of the time. Catherine Chappell's 1999 replication study in Oakland also showed lower-working-class blacks there simplifying their final consonant clusters 84 percent of the time. She had no upper-middle-class blacks in her study, but her lower-middle-class blacks simplified their clusters 72 percent of the time, similar to the 66 percent simplification figure for the lower-middle-class blacks in Detroit whom Wolfram wrote about in 1969. When it came to pronouncing the voiceless *th* of *tooth* as *t*, the class differences in Wolfram's study were even more dramatic, with working-class blacks using the *t* pronunciation 70 to 73 percent of the time, while the middle-class blacks did so only 23 to 25 percent of the time. The pronunciation features we've associated with Spoken Soul in this chapter are most characteristic of the working classes. This is why the middle-class blacks who serve as media spokespersons on Ebonics and other language-related matters are so sensitive about—even hostile toward—the suggestion that black people as a group speak "Black English" or have a distinctive vernacular.

But virtually all African Americans use some of the pronunciation features identified in this chapter at least some of the time, especially in their most informal moments. A recent study showed, for instance, that Oprah Winfrey, perhaps the country's most popular talk-show host, pronounced her *ay* diphthongs like monophthongs (*ah* for "I," *mah* for "my") significantly more often (38 percent of the time) when introducing or discussing someone black than when referring to someone who was not black (10 percent of the time). Arch White-head, the executive recruiter who on *60 Minutes* laughingly dismissed the prospect of blacks' getting or keeping executive jobs if they said *aks* instead of *ask,* went on to make these remarks:

> When I get home, I don't want to think about all that nice English. I wanna go back to my golden years, when I could say *dis* and *dat,* when I could say "How ya doin?" instead of "Hi, guys!" When I didn't have to belong and fit.

The significance of style in black pronunciation was illustrated in Walt Wolfram's 1969 Detroit study; black speakers of *every* class used the vernacular variants (e.g., *t* or *f* for voiceless *th*) less often when reading a text than when talking with the interviewer.

Other factors that were correlated with the extent to which speakers used black pronunciation in Wolfram's study included age (preadolescents and teenagers generally using the black vernacular variants more often than adults), gender (males using the vernacular variants more often than females), and racial isolation (blacks with predominantly black social contacts using the vernacular variants more often than blacks with predominantly white social contacts).

Interestingly, a replication study in Detroit by linguist Walter Edwards, published in 1992, showed similar correlations, but not always in the same way. Although age was a significant factor in the extent to which blacks used *ah* instead of [ay] in words like *find,* it was the oldest rather than the youngest age-groups who did this most often, and this was true also of *r* deletion after a vowel, as in *store.* However, Edwards's study did not include any teenagers below the age of eighteen, as Wolfram's study did, and, on the other side of the coin, Wolfram's study did not distinguish the four "adult" age groups that Edwards's did. Furthermore, in Edwards's study, gender was not significant overall, although females tended to use more of the vernacular variant than did males; the one exception was in the oldest (sixty-plus) age group, where men deleted *r* after a vowel more often (59 percent of the time) than the women did (46 percent of the time).

Edwards's 1992 study showed that individuals in Detroit who were relatively restricted to their inner-city neighborhoods and/or more positively oriented toward it used black vernacular pronunciations more often than individuals who had more interactions with people outside the neighborhood and/or more negative attitudes toward it. (More succinctly: If you stay in the 'hood and you're cozy there, you'll likely speak more soul than a neighbor who often roams beyond and/or tends to dis it.) In this respect, Edwards's study agreed more substantially with Wolfram's. Both concur with our own informal experiences and observations in reminding us that language use in the African American speech community, as in every other, is variable, influenced by such factors as social class, gender, social network, and style.

One factor in phonological variation that people who aren't linguists are less aware of is variation according to linguistic "environment"—where in a word a particular sound occurs, for instance, or what kind of word it is, and whether the following word begins with a consonant or vowel. We've referred to these sorts of factors throughout this chapter, when we talked about rules "deleting *l* and *r* after vowels*.*" The italicized qualification is necessary to rule out the deletion of *l* and *r* before vowels, as in **ed* for "red" or **ast* for "last"— something that doesn't happen in Spoken Soul or other varieties of English (hence the asterisks, indicating nonoccurring forms). The exception is a pronunciation like *tho* for "throw," where *r* follows *th* and precedes *o*. (Note that even for such exceptions, we have to specify the linguistic environment; in Spoken Soul, as in all other language varieties, language is not random but systematic.)

The effect of linguistic environment we want to close with here is not qualitative, as in these cases, but quantitative. Several studies have shown that consonant cluster simplification, as in *jus'* for "just," is more common before a word beginning with a consonant (as in "just *g*lad") than before a word beginning with a vowel (as in "just *e*nough"), and least common when the deleted consonant represents the past tense (as in "miss*ed*"—spelled *ed* but pronounced *t*). In their most informal group interactions, the New York City adults recorded by Labov and his colleagues deleted the final *t* in words like "just" 79 percent of the time before a consonant, and only 32 percent of the time before a vowel; in words like "missed," where the final *t* sound represents the past tense, they deleted it 30 percent of the time before a consonant, but never before a vowel. Wild, huh? This regular symphonic variation, it should be remembered, occurs far below the level of consciousness.

7

Grammar

In sentences like "An' so I comin' down an' she out there blabbin' her mouth told my sister I was playin' hookey from school" there are no words which are not in Standard English, and no word forms which white dialects do not have. . . . A syntactic analysis, however, reveals a greatly different system. Syntax, the focus of more modern linguistics, is the area in which the analysis of Black English is most revealing.

—J. L. Dillard (1972)

Linguistically speaking, the greatest differences between contemporary Black and White English are on the level of grammatical structure.

—Geneva Smitherman (1986)

The claim that Ebonics, or Spoken Soul, has no grammar is as bogus as the claim that it has no dictionary. If this is taken to mean, as it often is, that African American vernacular is unsystematic, without rules or regularities, then it is blatantly false, as we will show several times over in this chapter. If it is taken to mean that no one has studied or written about the rules and regularities of African American Vernacular English (AAVE)—the most popular name for Spoken Soul among linguists—then it's equally absurd. Since the 1960s, at least (there were occasional studies even earlier), scholars have produced detailed accounts of AAVE pronunciation and grammar. Two of the best-known, dealing with black speech in New York City and Detroit, were conducted in 1968 and 1969, respectively. Now, as is true of most languages and dialects, much remains to be discovered and published about the linguistic features or attributes of black vernacular. But linguists (who study the sounds, words, and grammar of languages and dialects) already know enough to present an informed picture of the system—the "systematicity," if you will—of the tongue.

When discussing grammar we'll use mostly snatches of actual conversations among blacks recorded by us and others in East Palo Alto, California; Philadelphia; the South Carolina Sea Islands; and elsewhere. These might be thought of as instances of Spoken Soul in spirited use by ordinary, everyday people—the folk who in some neighborhoods are said to "talk regular." Their usage extends the discussion of the spirited and pleasurable use that black writers, preachers, entertainers, and other men and women of words make of the vernacular that we explored in chapters 2 through 5.

Let's begin with a quotation from East Palo Alto's Foxy Boston, whom we have recorded periodically since 1968, when she was a teenager. (Here, as elsewhere, we'll use the symbol for zero, Ø, to show where the copula—usually *is* or *are*—is absent.)

> But *i's*—*i's* a lot of girls . . . it *seem* like, when I *be* driving, it *seem* like every corner I drive around, there *go* somebody you know pushing a baby. . . . Me and Teresa *and them be* like, "Tha's a shame, huh?" . . . I *be* like, "Dang, Teresa, she Ø in the same grade with me and she *have* three kids!"

Plural *s* and *dem*.   We must acknowledge from the start that AAVE shares an array of grammatical features with mainstream English and other dialects. In fact, as linguists Stefan Martin and Walt Wolfram point out in a recent article:

> The distinctiveness of AAVE does not particularly reside in the structure of its sentences. Basic utterance types—e.g. declarative, interrogative, and imperative sentences—are all formed in essentially the same way as they are in other dialects.

Plural formation is really an aspect of inflectional morphology—the different forms words take to show grammatical relationships—rather than of sentence structure, but it illustrates the same point. Take, for instance, the elementary rule that says you add *s* to most nouns to form the plural—that is, to refer to more than one person, place, or thing. AAVE speakers sometimes ditch the plural *s,* but not often (1 to 10 percent of the time, in studies to date). In the passage above, *girls* and *kids* hold fast to the final *s.*

AAVE has other ways of marking plurality, as with *dem*. One way is to use *an dem* after the name of a person, to refer to others associated with that person, as in *John an dem,* for "John and his friends." This associative plural, as some linguists call it, can be used also with definite nouns (i.e., preceded by "the") that refer to people, as in *the judge an dem,* for "the judge and people like him." In the Gullah of coastal South Carolina and Georgia, as in many Caribbean Creoles, the *an* may be left out, but this is less common in urban Spoken Soul. Another way of using *dem* to mark plurality is by putting this form before the noun, as in *dem books,* "those books." In this construction, the *dem* does not simply indicate that more than one book is being referred to; it also indicates that it is "those" and not "these" books, and the plural is simultaneously or redundantly marked by the *s* ending on *books.* In Gullah, as in the Caribbean Creoles, the plural marking function is clearer, because the construction can be used without plural *s,* as in *dem book,* meaning "those books."

Existential *it is*. The italicized portions of Foxy Boston's speech indicate points at which AAVE diverges from the English of the nightly news. Instead of "there is" or "there are," she uses the characteristic AAVE alternative, *it's* or *i's* (reduced forms of *it is*), which may be used with singular or plural nouns, as in:

i's a lot of girls (= there are a lot of girls)

Absence of third-person singular present-tense *s*. *Seem,* the next italicized word in Foxy's quotation, exemplifies another typical AAVE feature: "it *seem* like, when I be driving, it *seem* like every corner I drive around." Like *go* in the subsequent line, *seem* snubs the *s* that mainstream English requires, in "it seem," or "the man seems," or as a high school English teacher might put it, when you have a present-tense verb with a third-person-singular subject. To make it clearer, "third-person-singular subject" means that the subject refers to a single person, place, or thing, neither the speaker in a conversation (*I,* the first person), nor a person being addressed (*you,* the second person).

Standard English is somewhat fickle because it requires adding an *s* (or *es*) to verbs with third-person-singular subjects ("he go*es*") but requires the bare verb (the form with *to,* as in "to go") for all other subjects ("I go," "you go," "we go," "they go"). In getting rid of third-person *s,* you might think of AAVE as making the rules of English more regular, or as an advocate for equal opportunity: the verb doesn't have special endings with other subjects, so it shouldn't with third-person-singular subjects.

Since it lacks the Standard English *s* ending, *it seem* is a clear case of the AAVE rule, "Thou shalt not treat present-tense verbs with third-person-singular subjects any differently from verbs with other subjects." Somewhat less obviously, *she have* (instead of "she has") in the last line of Foxy's quote ("Dang, Teresa, she in the same grade with me and she *have* three kids!") also exemplifies this rule. In Standard English, *has* is the third-person-singular form of *have* in the present tense, as one can see by contrasting "he has" with "I have," "you have," "we have," and "they have." The use of *he do* and *he don't* instead of "he *does*" and "he *doesn't*" are yet other examples of the rules, beautifully illustrated (along with the absence of third person *-s* in Oprah's vernacular) in this *People* magazine account of an encounter between Oprah Winfrey and a man looking for her house: "He said, 'Hey, I was going down the road to see Oprah Winfrey's house. *Don't* she have a house down there?' " she recalls. The multimillionaire television star looked the stranded traveler deep in the eyes and said in her best down-home accent: "I believe she *do*."

This tendency of soul speakers to drop the third-person-singular *s* was evident in earlier studies of working-class folk in New York and Detroit, where *s* was absent from 56 to 76 percent of the time. For Foxy Boston and Tinky Gates, another East Palo Alto teenager we have recorded in multiple interviews, the rate was even higher—97 and 96 percent, respectively. In other words, in virtually every case, the girls used forms like "John *go*" instead of "John *goes*" and "John *have* a car" instead of "John *has* a car."

Absence of possessive *'s*. Although this particular feature doesn't show up in Foxy's quotation, it's worth mentioning while we're on the subject of Standard English *s* forms that get zapped in AAVE. For an example of a noun without the *'s* ending that Standard English relies on to indicate possession (as in "girl*'s* house"), we'll turn to Tinky:

This one day, Nito came over to that *girl* house.

In this case, AAVE indicates possession through the juxtaposition of the two nouns (*girl house*) rather than with an *'s* ending. As in many pidgin and creole languages—produced by fusing and simplifying two or more languages when their speakers come in contact (see chapter 8)—the possessor comes immediately before the thing possessed. We pointed out earlier that AAVE speakers rarely toss out the plural *s*. But it's quite common for them to chuck the *possessive 's*. A group of working-class teenagers in New York, for example, did so between 57 and 72 percent of the time. For Tinky and Foxy, the rate was 53 and 86 percent, respectively.

Invariant *be*. The verb *be* is one of the most celebrated features of Spoken Soul. Over the past thirty-five years, linguists have studied it to death—or nearly so, since it's still kicking, and every few years we discover something new about it. *Be* comes in two basic flavors: (1) conjugated, or inflected, which *varies* in form (*am, is, are, was, were,* and so on), depending on the subject (*I, you, he/she/it, we, they*) and whether it refers to present or past; and (2) invariant, which, as its name suggests, doesn't vary (although it occurs occasionally as *be's* or *bees*). One of the interesting things about the first *be* is that some of its forms (*is* and *are*) can disappear, yielding zero copula, about which we'll say more below. For now we want to focus on the second, invariant *be*.

There are a few different kinds of invariant *be* in AAVE. One—the kind that comes in imperatives ("*Be* good!"), in infinitives with *to* ("He tried to *be* good"), and after helping verbs like *can* and *must* ("He must *be* good")—is used much the same as in mainstream or Standard English. A second kind results from leaving out *will* or *would* (more accurately, their contracted forms *'ll* and *'d*) and produces sentences with future or hypothetical reference:

> Wait awhile. She *be* [= *'ll* be] right around. (Johnny Guitar, forty-four, Philadelphia)
>
> Well, if I be the winner, I *be* [= *'ll* be or *'d* be] glad. (thirteen-year-old, New York City)

The third and most distinctive kind (distinctive because it occurs rarely or not at all in white vernaculars) is the invariant habitual *be* that occurs twice in Foxy's passage: "when I *be* driving . . . Teresa and them *be* like . . ."

This invariant habitual *be* is probably the best-known but least understood of AAVE's grammatical signposts. Many outsiders to Spoken Soul believe that black folk replace Standard English *is* and *are* with invariant *be* all the time, as in, "He *be* talkin' to her right now." But AAVE is actually more discriminating. For one thing, invariant habitual *be* describes only an event that is performed regularly or habitually, as in "He *be* talkin' with his lady every day." Contrast this habitual sense with "He Ø talkin' to her right now"—which is what a speaker of Spoken Soul might say when describing an event taking place at the moment of speech, without any implication that it happens regularly.

Furthermore, unlike *ashy,* invariant habitual *be* is more than an isolated AAVE word; it is part of the grammatical system, an integral tile in the mosaic of the dialect. Each piece has its place and its purpose, and reacts predictably with other pieces to create the collage we call conversation. Indeed, we can prove that invariant *be* is not random, because it minds its grammatical manners. To form the negative version of a sentence in AAVE, you usually use *ain't* ("John isn't walking" becomes "John *ain't* walkin'"). But to form the negative with habitual *be,* you have to use *don't:* "John *don't be* walkin'." If you said, *"John ain't be walkin'" (as before, the linguistic convention is to put an asterisk before a sentence or form to show that it is a nonoccurring form or ungrammatical), not only would you be speaking improper Ebonics, you'd probably get some funny looks. Here is a grammatical example with *don't,* courtesy of Foxy:

An she *don't be* listenin'. So I be like, "Hey, I tried to tell you . . ."

Ebonics speakers also use *do* and *don't* to phrase questions with invariant *be,* as in "*Do* John be listenin'?" This is true also of so-called tag questions, in which the speaker assumes a positive response, as in "John *be* listenin', *don't* he?" or a negative response, as in "John *don't be* listenin', *do* he?"

When an AAVE speaker wants to intensify, or stress, the continuous, persistent nature of an action, he or she will sometimes hitch on a *steady,* as in this sentence made famous by John Baugh, the linguist who introduced us to *steady:* "Ricky Bell *be steady* steppin in dem number nines."

Zero copula (absence of *is* or *are*).   The last noteworthy AAVE feature in Foxy's quotation is known among linguists as zero copula—that is, the absence of *is* in "she Ø in the same grade." *Is* and *are* are called copulas because they couple, or join, a subject (in this case, "she") and a predicate (what's said *about* the subject—in this case, that she's in the same grade). Here's an example from a twenty-six-year-old Philadelphia woman who doesn't use the copula *are* in her first sentence but includes it when she repeats the sentence, with emphasis:

People Ø crazy! People *are* stone crazy!

Zero copula provides a clear demonstration that the grammar of Spoken Soul is systematic and rule-governed. To begin with, there are some copula forms that cannot be left out. You can't delete the past-tense copulas *was* and *were,* both of which are left intact in the following sentences from forty-four-year-old Johnny Guitar of Philadelphia, as they are in the speech of virtually all speakers of black vernacular:

> You *were* a thousand miles away.
> He been doin it since we *was* teenagers, and he Ø still doin it.

Even in the present tense, you can't delete *am*. "I am" is often contracted to *I'm* in AAVE, but the *'m* is not deleted. In Caribbean Creole English, you can delete *am* or *'m* ("I Ø cuttin off de heads," a young Barbadian fisherman explains, as he deftly slices up fish on a tray). But you can't do this in African American Vernacular English.

You can't delete infinitive *be* in AAVE, either (for instance, after *to, can, may, must, shall, should, would, will*), as this forty-six-year-old in East Palo Alto shows by retaining *be* in the first half of this sentence while deleting *are* in the second half: "You can *be* sitting up in class, an nex' thing you know, you Ø out of it."

The only copula forms you *can* leave out in Spoken Soul are *is* and *are*, but even so, there are restrictions. If *is* or *are* comes at the end of a sentence, or is stressed, it can't be deleted ("That's what he *is!*" but not *"That's what he Ø!"). When negative *is* or *are* becomes *ain't*, the *ain't* cannot be erased, either. The forms *what's, it's,* and *that's*—which contain contracted *is* and often lose their final *t* as well (*wha's, i's,* and *tha's*)—behave somewhat like *am*. That is, you can't delete the contracted form of the copula (in this case *'s*), except in some greetings, for instance, *Wa'apnin* as a variant of "What's happenin . . . ?" and *What up?* as a variant of "What's up?"

That's a pretty complex set of rules and restrictions. As with most rules of spoken language, no AAVE speaker has ever been taught these things formally, and few speakers could spell them out for you (unless, perhaps, they had learned them in a linguistics course). But AAVE speakers follow them, almost religiously, in their daily speech. In these animated words from fifteen-year-old Tinky Gates, the copulas that cannot be omitted are intact (and are shown in boldface), and the copulas that can be omitted have indeed been zapped (*are* and *is,* with Ø showing where they might have occurred):

> I**'m** gone! Maria **was** gone! She **was** up under a tree. She say, "Cops! Oh gosh, wha**'s** gon happen? How Ø we gon get home?"
> "Uh, uh," I said. "Oh gosh," I said. "My mama think we Ø at this shirt party havin a goo' time," and I said, "I **ain'** tellin her this, 'cause she **ain'** gon never let me go back!"

In allowing the deletion of present-tense *is* and *are* but not past-tense *was* and *were,* Spoken Soul differs from mainstream English but is similar to many other languages, including Arabic, Hungarian, Russian, and Swahili.

So far we've told you which copula forms speakers of Spoken Soul can and cannot delete. But there's more. Soul speakers from New York to Detroit to Atlanta to Los Angeles are remarkably similar in terms of *how often* they delete the forms of the copula that can be deleted (basically, unstressed *is* and *are*). For instance, AAVE speakers delete *are* ("They Ø happy") more often than *is* ("He Ø happy"). They delete both *is* and *are* more often when these copulas come after a pronoun ("They Ø happy") than when they come after a noun ("The boys Ø happy"). And they delete *is* and *are* least often before a noun ("He Ø a man"), more often before an adjective ("He Ø happy") and most often before *going to* or its reduced forms, *gonna* and *gon* ("He Ø gon tell Mama").

Want proof? See the chart below, which showed how often zero copula was observed in recordings with different groups of AAVE speakers across the country. For each group, copula deletion was least frequent before a noun, more frequent with a following adjective, and most frequent with a following *gon(na)*. In this respect, AAVE is similar to pidgin and Creole English elsewhere in the world—in Barbados, Jamaica, Guyana, Hawaii, and Liberia. That's a crucial commonality, and as we argue in chapter 8, it's strong evidence that AAVE may have had Creole roots and influences itself.

Copula form and AAVE group studied	Copula deletion before noun ("He Ø a man")	Copula deletion before adjective ("He Ø happy")	Copula deletion before *gon(na)* ("He Ø gon go")
is, New York City Thunderbirds (teenage gang)	23%	48%	88%
is + are, Detroit working class (all ages)	37%	47%	79%
are, Los Angeles (all ages)	.25	.35	.64
is + are, Texas youngsters	.12	.25	.89
is + are, East Palo Alto, California (all ages)	.27	.45	.83
is + are, ex-slaves (mainly from South, recorded 1930s)	12%	29%	100%

***Been*, BEEN, and Toni Morrison's "five present tenses."** Now that
we've gone through zero copula, *be,* and *steady,* we're almost ready to
exemplify the "five present tenses" that Toni Morrison was probably
referring to in the passage cited in chapter 1: "It's terrible to think
that a child with five different present tenses comes to school to be
faced with books that are less than his own language." We have to say
"probably" because the good sistah didn't give us any examples of
the different present tenses she was referring to when she praised
Spoken Soul, and because "five" might have simply been meant to indicate more present tenses than in Standard English, rather than a
precise number. And we have to say "almost ready," because we first
have to introduce *been* and BEEN (sometimes spelled *bin* and BIN, to indicate their pronunciation better).

Been is an unstressed form, lacking in the stress that speakers put
into BEEN. It's pretty much (but not completely) equivalent to "has
been" or "have been" in mainstream English, as shown by these sentences from thirty-nine-year-old "Bomb" Jones of Philadelphia and
her husband, Johnny Guitar.

> I *been* playing cards since I was four. (Bomb)
>
> He *been* doin it since we was teenagers, and he still doin it. (Johnny)

Sometimes *been* occurs with *has* or *have,* or their contracted forms *'s*
and *'ve:*

> 'Cause I*'ve been* through it. I*'ve been* through them changes. (Johnny)
>
> Here's a guy, live next door to him. He*'s been* a gangsta all his life.
>   (Johnny)

The differences between *been* in Black English and *has been* or *have
been* in Standard English are sometimes discernible in the kinds of
verbs and adverbs with which they can be linked. Johnny uses *been*
with *knowing* in the following sentence, where a speaker of Standard
English would use *have known:* "I *been* knowing her for a long time. I
been knowing her for twenty years." And in the following sentence,
Joe, a twenty-nine-year-old man who regularly hung out with Johnny
and Bomb, uses *been* to refer to a specific time where a mainstream
English speaker would use *was:* "About eleven or twelve o'clock he
been eating everything."

This phrasing resembles that of the Gullah, or "Geechee," variety
of black vernacular spoken on the Sea Islands off the South Carolina
and Georgia coasts (the setting for Julie Dash's movie *Daughters of the
Dust*). In the following Gullah example, a fifty-nine-year-old black man

from Daufuskie Island, South Carolina, alternates between *was* and *been*: "I don't know if dat snake *was* coil, or either *been* stretch out or what." Gullah, like Jamaican patois—its Creole English counterpart in the Caribbean—uses *been* before a verb stem (*thief* in the example below) to mark an action in the past:

> We *been see* [Gullah = saw] that man thief that man car. (Cited in Cunningham)
> Me *been know* [Jamaican Creole = knew] say him wouldn come. (Cited in Bailey)

You wouldn't hear this *been* much in mainland (especially northern) varieties of AAVE these days, although it may have been more frequent in earlier centuries. An example occurs in A. B. Lindsey's 1807 play *Love and Friendship:* "I tink dey *been like* [= liked] sich a man de bess."

What you're much more apt to come across, both on the Sea Islands and in Detroit, Philadelphia, New York, or Los Angeles, is stressed BEEN (with increased emphasis on the word). This exaggerated BEEN describes an action that took place or a state that came into being a long time ago, which is why stressed BEEN is often called a "remote time" marker:

> She ain't tell me that today, you know. She BEEN tell me that. (thirty-one-year-old woman, Sea Islands)
> He [the dentist] finish so quick. I ask him was he finished, and he say, "I BEEN finished!" (seventy-two-year-old black woman, Philadelphia)

One crucial point about BEEN: Unlike its milder twin, *been,* it can't be used with adverbial phrases that mark the passage of time. The contrast is clear in this sentence, in which Philadelphian Johnny Guitar alternates between the two forms:

> INTERVIEWER: I see your friend's doing good business.
>
> JOHNNY: Oh yeah—you mean the fruit seller? I BEEN know that guy. He's a numbers runner—*been* doing that *for years.*

Note, too, that when BEEN brings a state into being, that state remains in effect up to the moment of speech. When Johnny says he "BEEN know that guy," he means that he not only has known him for a long time, but still knows him. These nuances can be confusing to those who don't speak the vernacular. Some years ago, twenty-five whites and twenty-five blacks were asked whether "She BIN married" meant that the woman was still married or not. Twenty-three of the blacks said yes (the correct answer for AAVE), as compared with only eight of the whites. The vast majority of the whites thought that the person was not married—a misunderstanding that could lead to embarrassment, or worse.

Two final notes about BEEN. First, the "remoteness" of the time involved is a subjective matter. In many cases, people front, or pretend, that they've had a particular possession for quite a while, when in fact they just acquired it. You may have complimented someone on an outfit only to hear the person say dismissively, "Aw, man, I BEEN had this!" Second, stressed BEEN can be combined with *had, coulda, shoulda,* and other forms to create complex constructions in which the period designated by BEEN remains in effect until a time earlier than the moment of speech:

> We had BEEN married when this lil' one came along. (seventy-one-year-old Philadelphian; cited in Dayton)

> They coulda BEEN ended that war. (twenty-nine-year-old Philadelphian)

Now that we've seen the workings of *been* and BEEN, let's return to Toni Morrison's "five present tenses" of AAVE, which might look like this (the Standard English equivalent is given in parentheses):

1. He Ø runnin. (He is running.)
2. He *be* runnin. (He is usually running, or He will/would be running.)
3. He *be steady* runnin. (He is usually running in an intensive, sustained manner, or He will/would be running in an intensive, sustained manner.)
4. He *been* runnin. (He has been running—at some earlier point, but probably not now.)
5. He BEEN runnin. (He has been running for a long time, and still is.)

Pretty impressive, isn't it? As you can see from the glosses, you can't convey quite the same idea in Standard English without adding adverbs and lengthy explanations.

***Done, be done, finna, had,* and other tense-aspect markers.** By now you may have realized that the grammar of Spoken Soul is quite distinctive in its tense-aspect markers—forms such as *be, steady,* and BEEN that come just before or after the verb and tell when (tense) or how (aspect) something happened. The vernacular has other forms like these, which we'll go through quickly in this section.

Done, which emphasizes the completed nature of an action, and/ or its relevance to the present, is one of the best-known vernacular forms. As these examples show, it's often more or less equivalent to Standard English forms with *has* or *have* and *already:*

> I *done* had [= have had] enough. (Renee Blake, New Yorker in her thirties)
>
> They *done* tore [= have already torn] the school up. (Sue, sixteen, Philadelphian)
>
> Even though he *done* took [= has already taken] all the bullets out . . . he still may shoot me because I got a gun. (Calvin, forty-four, Alabama resident)

Done is not identical, however, to *has/have.* For one thing, soul speakers report that *done* feels and sounds more intense, more forceful. And there are subtle linguistic differences between the forms, including the fact that *has/have* can be used with negatives (e.g., "He *hasn't* gone"), while *done* cannot: *"He ain't done gone" is ungrammatical, and *"He donen't gone" is even worse.

Done can be hitched up with *be* to make matters more interesting. Since *be,* as noted above, can have future, conditional, or habitual meaning, *be done* sentences combine each of these meanings with the completive sense of *done,* as in:

> Another few weeks, the Puerto Ricans *be done* took [= will have taken] over. (Future completive; Joe G., thirty, Philadelphia)
>
> If she [= dog] wasn't spayed, she*'d be done* [= would have] got pregnant cause she gets out. (Conditional completive; Philadelphia speaker; cited in Dayton, p. 655)
>
> The children *be done* ate [= have usually eaten] by the time I get there. (Habitual completive; cited in Green, p. 43)

Be done is most common with the future completive or future perfect, and sometimes occurs with the future marker *will* or *'ll* before it, as in:

> I*'ll be done* bought my own CB waitin on him to buy me one. (Los Angeles speaker; cited in Baugh, p. 78)

This is a complex construction—the future perfect equivalent in mainstream English ("John will already have left by the time Mary arrives") is fairly rare—and it has developed a number of additional subtleties in Spoken Soul. See the notes for further reading on this.

Another striking tense/time marker in Spoken Soul is *finna,* which is used for immediate futures (events just about to happen), as in these sentences from Tinky Gates, the East Palo Alto, California, teenager. She is talking about the moment when she and her friend Ruth decide to leave a party because a fight has broken out and things are on the verge of "getting turned out"—becoming even more rowdy:

> I'm serious! I foun' Ruth an' I said, "Word." I said, "This thang *finna* get turned out, so y'all better get in yo' lil car an' . . . go home." Ruth said, "I'm *finna* get up out of here, 'cause i's gettin' rowdy." So I found her an' we left.

Finna is derived from *fixing to,* which both blacks and whites use for the immediate future throughout the South, as in "He is *fixin' to* go." But in vernacular black speech all over the United States, especially among teenagers, *is* or *are* is almost always dropped (but not *am, 'm, was,* or *were;* recall the rules for copula deletion outlined earlier), and *fixing to* is reduced to *finna, fidna* or *fitna.* Again, you can't use it for things in the distant future (e.g., you can't say, *"I'm finna get married five years from now"), but only for things that are just about to happen.

Somewhat different from *finna* is the use of stressed BE for states that exist now and are likely to continue for a long time in the future. Johnny Guitar's response in this sequence was recorded in Philadelphia some years ago:

> J: How long is your brother gonna be here?
>
> JOHNNY GUITAR: Oh, he gon BE here. I ain't seen him for a long time, so he's gon' BE here.

Although this use of stressed BE is rare—this is the only example we have in our files—it is a logical extension of stressed BIN, and was immediately understandable when it was used. That is, stressed BEEN can refer to a situation that exists now and began long ago in the past (*He BIN here* = "He is here now and has been for a long time"). Stressed BE, by analogy, refers to a situation that exists now and will continue long into the future. We aren't crystal-ball gazers, but we won't be surprised to record other examples, and to see stressed BE become even more common in the future.

One tense-aspect marker that does appear to have become more common over the past two decades is the use of *had* plus a past-tense verb to refer to narrative events that would usually be referred to just with a past-tense verb, as in this example:

> This is a story that happened to me Monday, not too long ago. I was on my way to school, and I *had* slipped and fell [compare "I slipped and fell"], and I ran back in the house to change my clothes.

The speaker here is Dafina, a twelve-year-old girl from East Palo Alto who, like other preadolescents from this area, uses *had* to refer to the high point of a story. In East Palo Alto, speakers seem to abandon this use of *had* over time; older teenagers including Foxy and Tinky showed no use of it (they use *had* in the pluperfect, as in Standard English "By the time I got there, he *had* already left"). In Texas and other parts of the country, however, examples of Dafina's *had* have been recorded among older teenagers and even among people in their twenties, so it might not be as age-restricted as we first thought.

One other thing we've said little about is the use of *come,* usually before a verb ending in *ing,* to express the speaker's indignation or anger about an event, as in this sentence:

> He *come* walkin in here like he owned the damn place!

This isn't a tense-aspect marker—it tells us not when the event occurred, or how it occurred, but how the speaker *felt* about the event that occurred (i.e., he didn't like it—was mad, angry, or resentful). In that sense, it's really more of a modal marker—representing the speaker's mood or feeling about an event. But we include it with forms like *finna* and *had* and BEEN because it's one of the rich set of "helping" verbs (or auxiliaries) that soul speakers use before other verbs to encode fine nuances of meaning about situations and events around them. Far from being deficient, Spoken Soul is very impressive in this regard.

Negative forms and constructions. The most common negative form in Spoken Soul—and the main feature some writers use to represent the vernacular—is *ain't.* As in other vernacular varieties in the United States, *ain't* can be used as the equivalent of Standard English *am not, isn't, aren't, don't, hasn't,* and *haven't:*

> I *ain't* [= am not] lyin'. (Bomb Jones, Philadelphia)
>
> He *ain't* [= is not] comin' in now. (John, Trenton, New Jersey)
>
> No you *ain't* [= are not]. (Bomb Jones)
>
> He thinks I *ain't* [= don't] got no more aces. (Bomb Jones)

He *ain't* never [= hasn't ever] had a job in his life. (Johnny Guitar, Philadelphia)

Contrary to most white vernaculars, however, *ain't* can be used as the equivalent of "didn't" in the African American vernacular, as in:

He *ain't* go no [= didn't go any] further than third or fourth grade. (Johnny Guitar)

This unique usage has historical implications for the origins of AAVE, as we explained in the pronunciation section of chapter 6.

One of the most commonly discussed features of the black vernacular—and other English vernaculars—is the double negative, in which a negative verb such as *ain't* or *don't* or *wasn't* is used with a negative noun or pronoun such as *no . . . lady, neither,* or *nothing* instead of Standard English equivalents "any . . . lady," "either," or "anything":

She *wadn't no* young lady, *neither.* (She wasn't any young lady, either—Larry, late sixties, outside Philadelphia)

I *don't* want *nothing nobody can't* enjoy. (I don't want anything nobody can enjoy—Dorothy, thirty-five, Philadelphia)

Contrary to what purists often allege, double negatives are virtually never interpreted as positives (as the logical "two negatives make a positive" rule would predict), even by Standard English speakers. That is, no one thinks that "She wasn't no young lady" means "She was a young lady"—any more than they thought this in Chaucer's or Shakespeare's time, when double negatives were used even in literary British English, as in:

Ther *nas no man nowher* so vertuous. (Chaucer, referring to the Friar)

I *cannot* go *no* further. (Shakespeare, *As You Like It,* act 2, scene 4)

Even in the second Spoken Soul sentence above, which is more complex because it joins two double negative sentences (*I don't want nothing* = "I don't want anything"; and *Nobody can't enjoy* = "Nobody can enjoy"), the meaning is crystal clear in context.

Less often discussed but more unusual among English dialects are Spoken Soul sentences like these that begin with a negative verb such as *ain't* or *can't,* followed by a negative noun or pronoun such as *nobody* or *nothing:*

Can't nobody beat 'em. (Cited in Labov et al., ex. 367)

Ain't nothin' went down. (Cited in Labov et al., ex. 359)

In these examples, the negative verb appears to have changed positions with the subject (i.e., *"Nobody can't* beat 'em → *Can't nobody* beat 'em"), and so linguists frequently describe this as negative inversion. But bear in mind that these are statements—often emphatic statements—not to be confused with Standard English questions, which also involve inversion ("Isn't John going?" from "John isn't going"). Bear in mind too that the uninverted order is sometimes impossible (e.g., "Ain't nothing I needed" comes not from *"Nothing ain't I needed" but from "There ain't nothing I needed" or "It ain't nothing I needed").

Questions, direct and indirect.   Inversion is curious in AAVE, because when it comes to questions, AAVE speakers appear to be doing exactly the opposite of what Standard English requires. In simple direct questions, AAVE speakers often do not invert the subject and the verb, as formal Standard English requires, but use rising intonation to signal that they are asking a question instead of making a statement (as, of course, do many Standard English speakers in their colloquial speech):

> This is a microphone, too? (Is this a microphone, too?—Arnold, ten, East Palo Alto, California)

Contrarily, where Standard English uses the noninverted word order with *if* or *whether* in embedded or indirect questions ("I asked him *if he could* come with me"), AAVE speakers typically use inverted word order without *if* or *whether* in such questions:

> I asked him *could he come* [if he could come] with me.

> Could you ask her *is she* [whether she is] Miss or Ms? (Dawn, sixties, Philadelphia)

In the 1960s, an experiment was done in which African American adolescent males in Harlem were asked to repeat sentences like "I asked Alvin *if he could* go." About half of the respondents would repeat the sentences as "I asked Alvin *could he* go," showing that while they understood the Standard English formulation with *if*, they preferred—in fact were almost wedded to—the inverted vernacular formulation without *if*. Similar results were obtained in experiments done in Baltimore and Washington, D.C.

    We can't do justice to all the features of the African American vernacular in a chapter of this length. But to help you understand them if you're a speaker of Spoken Soul, and to help you recognize them in speech or writing if you're not, we'll briefly discuss some other features of Spoken Soul under two headings: "Pronouns" and "Verbs Once More."

Pronouns.   In this category is the feature double subject, sometimes referred to more technically as pleonastic or appositive pronoun.

> *My mother, she* told me, "There's a song I want you to learn."
> (vs. "My mother told me"—Helen B., black gospel singer on radio, San Jose, California, 1999)
>
> *That man, he* walks to the store. (vs. "That man walks to the store.")

Here a pronoun corresponding to the subject noun is inserted after it, creating a second, or double, subject. Standard English sometimes does this for emphasis, or with very long noun phrases in which the subject is in danger of getting lost (as in "The little old man who lives down the street and who I was telling you about earlier, *he* walks to the store"), but in the African American vernacular it seems to occur more frequently, and even when the subject noun phrase consists of only one or two words, as in the examples above.

Another instance in which AAVE inserts a pronoun where Standard English does not or need not is in dative pronoun, or benefactive pronoun, constructions like this: "Ahma git *me* a gig" (I'm going to get [myself] a job). This usage is shared with white vernaculars. At the other extreme are cases in which AAVE deletes a relative pronoun (*that, who, whom, which*), as in:

> Alan saw the car [that] Charlie sold. (Martin and Wolfram)

Sentences like this, in which the deleted *that* refers to an object noun (*the car* is the object of the verb *sold*), are not uncommon in Standard English. Somewhat more distinctive is the fact that Spoken Soul allows you to delete relative pronouns that are the *subjects* of verbs, as in these sentences from recent work by linguists Stefan Martin and Walt Wolfram:

> He the man [that] got all the old records.
>
> Wally the teacher [who] wanna retire next year.

Verbs once more.   By now it should be clear that verbs (zero copula as well as tense-aspect markers) are where a lot of the action is in Spoken Soul, where much of what is distinctive and identity-affirming about the vernacular is marked out. One special construction that we haven't talked about is the use of double and sometimes triple modals (verbs such as *can, could, might,* and *should* that indicate ability, possibility, or obligation), as in these examples; this usage is found also in some white vernacular dialects, especially in the South:

> He *might could* do the work.
>
> She *may can* do the work.
>
> They *should oughta* go.
>
> They *might should oughta* do it.

AAVE speakers also sometimes use a singular verb with a plural or second-person-singular subject, as in *they is* instead of "they are" or *you was* instead of "you were." This is sometimes referred to as verb generalization or verb nonagreement. The former term (referring to the generalization of the singular form to the plural) is probably better, since the latter term suggests that AAVE speakers would just as readily use a singular verb form with a plural subject as they would a plural verb form with a singular subject. In fact, sentences like "I *were* happy" (instead of "was") are very rare; much more common is the generalization of the singular verb form to the plural (*we was, they is*).

Variation in Grammar

The kind of variation by *social class* that occurs with Spoken Soul pronunciation patterns is even more dramatic with its grammar. In Walt Wolfram's 1969 Detroit study cited in the last chapter, blacks from the lower working class (unskilled workers) and upper working class (skilled workers) used multiple negation, as in "He can't see nobody" on average 78 and 55 percent of the time, respectively. But blacks from the lower middle class (white-collar workers) used multiple negation only 12 percent of the time, and blacks from the upper middle class used it only 8 percent of the time. In short, this feature provided an example of what Wolfram called "sharp stratification," with a much clearer line between the middle and the working classes than seen in the case of consonant cluster simplification in the preceding chapter, which showed a more "gradient" stratification between the social classes. Other grammatical features of Spoken Soul showed even sharper stratification by social class. The deletion of the *s* suffix on third-person present-tense verbs, as in "He walk," occurred 71 percent of the time in the recorded speech of lower-working-class black speakers in Detroit, and 57 percent of the time among upper-working-class black speakers. But among lower-middle-class blacks, the feature fell to 10 percent, and among upper-middle-class blacks to only 1 percent.

Grammatical variation is influenced by *gender* as well. In Wolfram's Detroit study, lower-working-class black men deleted copulas (e.g., "He Ø walkin" and "She Ø nice") 66 percent of the time, while lower-working-class females did so less often, 48 percent of the time. This association of black vernacular speech with maleness and toughness was common in early studies, and it may still be true today. But many of the early studies were conducted by men, who did not get down with the sistahs as effectively as they did with the brothas. In more recent studies in the black community of East Palo Alto, California, a black woman, Faye McNair-Knox, who grew up in the same community, established a close rapport with her female interviewees; the teenage girls she recorded deleted their copulas a striking 81 to 90 percent of the time.

Of course, variation by *age* is also relevant. In virtually every study, younger people use vernacular grammar more often than older speakers do. In Wolfram's Detroit study, lower-working-class black teenagers (fourteen to seventeen years old) deleted their copulas (e.g., "He Ø happy") 68 percent of the time, almost twice as often as their lower-working-class adult counterparts (38 percent of the time), although the difference in copula deletion rates between teenagers and adults for the other social classes were much less significant (e.g., 30 and 27 percent for upper-working-class teenagers and adults, respectively). Among the East Palo Alto speakers recorded by McNair-Knox, fifteen-year-old Tinky Gates deleted her copulas 81 percent of the time, but her mother, Paula Gates, deleted her copulas only 35 percent of the time, and a seventy-six-year-old woman in the community, Penelope Johnson, deleted her copulas even less often—15 percent of the time. It isn't always true that younger people use the grammatical variants of Spoken Soul more often than their elders. For instance, Tinky Gates used unmarked past tenses (e.g., *he say* for "he said") 11 percent of the time, while senior citizen Penelope Johnson did so 14 percent of the time, and eighty-eight-year-old John Carbon did so even more often—20 percent of the time. But cases like these are more the exception than the rule.

In discussing copula deletion, we've already shown variation by linguistic environment (recall the table showing that zero copula was least common before a noun, as in "John Ø a man," and most common before *gon(na),* as in "He Ø gon do it"). It remains only to show how grammatical variation in Spoken Soul varies with speakers' styles. This was demonstrated quite dramatically in a recent detailed study of how often East Palo Alto teenager Foxy Boston deleted her copula in different contexts. In one interview conducted by a black person with whom she was familiar, Foxy was very comfortable, and used Spoken Soul more extensively, deleting her third-person-singular present-tense *s* inflections ("He walk") 73 percent of the time, and deleting her *is* and *are* copulas 70 percent of the time. But subsequently, with a white interviewer whom she didn't know, Foxy used the black vernacular less often, deleting the *s* inflections only 36 percent of the time and copulas only 40 percent of the time. Within each of the interviews, however, her use of these and other vernacular features varied by topic. When talking with the black interviewer about graduation and plans for college and career, Foxy's copula deletion rate fell to 43 percent, but when talking more animatedly about boy-girl relations, it rose to 86 percent.

Our overall point is that although it is common to think of Spoken Soul as a fixed entity, in everyday use it is dynamic and variable. Like dress and other kinds of social capital, speakers deploy it to greater or lesser extents to delineate identity, to mark differences of social class, gender, and age, and to express how comfortable they are with their audiences and topics. In short, it is a resource or commodity that speakers exploit or avoid, depending on their social backgrounds, relations, and attitudes, on what they want to achieve, and on how they want to come across in each interaction.

8

History

*Pupils were made to scoff at the Negro dialect as some peculiar possession
of the Negro which they should despise, rather than directed to study the
background of this language as a broken down African tongue.*

—Carter G. Woodson (1933)

*There is not a single sentence structure in Black English that is traceable
to West African languages. . . . We would die trying to find any African
language that worked anything like Black English. On the other hand,
if we went to England and took a train into the countryside, we would
find much of what we were looking for.*

—John McWhorter (1998)

While the issue of whether Spoken Soul is a dialect of English or a
separate language fascinates the public, other questions have kept
scholars arguing for the past thirty years: How did Spoken Soul come
to be the way it is, and where is it headed now?

Some scholars contend that the African American vernacular
bears the vivid imprint of the African languages spoken by slaves who
came to this country in waves from the seventeenth to the nineteenth
centuries. Others maintain that the devastating experience of slavery
wiped out most if not all African linguistic and cultural traditions, and
that the apparently distinctive features of Spoken Soul come from
English dialects spoken by white (British) peasants and indentured
servants whom Africans encountered in America. For many scholars,
the central question is not the "Africanness" of the black vernacular,
but its "creoleness"—whether it was ever as different from Standard

129

English as the "creole" varieties spoken today in such places as Jamaica, Trinidad, Guyana, and Barbados, or whether it was ever influenced by them.

The newest question, posed only over the past fifteen years, concerns whether African American English is currently diverging or veering farther from white vernacular and Standard English.

According to one hypothesis, some of the central linguistic features of Spoken Soul developed only in the twentieth century, as blacks migrated north and west to segregated inner cities and their English became less and less like that of whites. If so, the future portends an even greater rift between these varieties unless the separate continents of white and black America reverse their drift.

If we had a time machine equipped with tape recorders and videocameras, we could answer these questions about the development of Spoken Soul. Instead, we must seek the truth by considering evidence of various kinds:

- Sociohistorical information about how many blacks were in contact with how many whites, when, were, and how—which allows us to gauge whether conditions in the United States were similar to those in Caribbean countries where more African features were retained

- Samples of black speech from earlier times, which are unfortunately not as numerous or as old or as reliable as we would wish

- Comparisons of current Black English with West African languages

- Comparisons with Caribbean English

- Comparisons with white nonstandard dialects of English, especially in Britain, but also in the United States

- Evidence from the African American diaspora—e.g. Liberia, Samaná (in the Dominican Republic), and Nova Scotia, where African Americans emigrated in the eighteenth and nineteenth centuries and where their descendants remain in linguistic and cultural enclaves

- Comparisons of the speech of older, middle-aged, and younger African Americans—which give us some idea of how Spoken Soul is evolving today

A Thumbnail, Century-by-Century History of African Americans

Let's begin our search by taking a walk through the history of African Americans, concentrating on sociohistorical events potentially relevant to the development of Spoken Soul.

The seventeenth century. The earliest Africans brought to what is now the United States are believed to have been one hundred slaves who formed part of a Spanish colonizing expedition of six hundred that attempted to settle in Virginia in 1526. But as far as the development of African American English is concerned, the colonization of the American mainland by English settlers is more important. That did not begin until the seventeenth century, with the successful English settlement at Jamestown, Virginia, in 1607. A dozen years later, the Jamestown settlers acquired twenty Africans as indentured servants. Indenture, the arrangement under which most white servants and laborers came to America, involved contracted work for a period (often five to ten years), after which the laborer might receive land and would be free to work for himself or herself. As historians John Hope Franklin and Alfred A. Moss Jr. have noted:

> As late as 1651 some Negroes whose period of service had expired were being assigned land in much the same way that it was being assigned to whites who had completed their indenture.

By the end of the seventeenth century, twelve British colonies had been established on the North American mainland: the New England colonies of New Hampshire, Massachusetts, Rhode Island, and Connecticut; the Middle colonies of New Jersey, New York (acquired from the Dutch in 1664), Pennsylvania, and Delaware; and the Southern colonies of Virginia, Maryland, North Carolina, and South Carolina. Neighboring Georgia, the last of the original "thirteen colonies," was not settled until 1732.

Although Africans were present in each of these colonies in the seventeenth century, they generally did not constitute a large segment of the population. English, Irish, and other indentured servants were the main workers, and labor-intensive crops such as tobacco, rice, and cotton had not yet become the norm. (Virginia began tobacco cultivation in the 1620s, and until about 1680 most of its workers were white indentured servants.) In 1671 there were only some two thousand blacks in Virginia, 5 percent of a total population of forty thousand.

In most of the New England and Middle colonies blacks were even sparser. These low proportions have led observers to suggest that the newly arrived Africans might have acquired relatively quickly and successfully, although of course not instantly, the English of the indentured servants and other colonials they met in America. As in naturalistic, unschooled second-language learning everywhere, Africans arriving in America in the seventeenth century might have transferred words and other features from their native languages, and simplified or generalized features of the target language. But they were perhaps less likely than their Caribbean counterparts to have drastically restructured it.

By 1690, Africans in Jamaica constituted 75 percent of the population. By 1746, that percentage had climbed to 92 percent. In Suriname (Dutch Guiana), Africans represented 93 percent of the population in 1700. And in both places, new creole languages based on English had begun to emerge—Jamaican Creole in Jamaica and Sranan in Suriname. Linguist Derek Bickerton has suggested that creoles develop only when the language learners constitute at least 80 percent of the population in a contact situation. Creoles have arisen in Martinique and Haiti, where the language learners (in these cases Africans) were only 35 or 50 percent of the population in the first twenty-five years. But Bickerton's figure captures the reality that creoles emerge when language learners have limited opportunities for contact with target-language speakers, and essentially work out their own norms based on their native languages and universal principles of language.

What's a creole, you might ask. To understand that, you have to know what a pidgin is. When speakers of different languages come into contact with one another (e.g., slaves speaking Yoruba, Twi, Igbo, and Mende on a Jamaican plantation), they may develop a simplified variety of the socially dominant language (in this case English) to communicate with one another. Such a variety is called a *pidgin* language. In addition to being simpler than any of the contact languages, the pidgin is usually mixed, in the sense that it shows strong grammatical influences from the languages of the socially subordinate speakers who bear the primary burden of linguistic accommodation and play the central role in creating it. If that pidgin is acquired and used as a native language (for example by slave children born on the plantation), it is called a *creole.* Because they are used as native languages—to talk about everything—creoles usually develop more words and more complex grammars than pidgins, but they often remain simpler than their input languages in several respects.

The following Sranan version of the sentence "Dogs are walking under the house" reveals how radically English can be transformed by pidginization and creolization, and how much it can show grammatical influence from socially subordinate languages (in this case Ewe and the Niger-Congo family of languages from which it derives, especially the Kwa subgroup):

Sranan:	Dagu	e	waka	go na	oso	ondro
Ewe:	Avu	le	tsa	yi	xo	te
English:	Dog	are	walk	go at	house	under

Even if we accept that seventeenth-century Africans in America might not have arrived in sufficient numbers and with sufficient distance from English norms to create pidgin and creole varieties, such varieties might have found their way into America via slaves imported from the Caribbean, or from those who arrived already speaking Guinea Coast Creole English that they had acquired in holding forts on the West African coast. In the seventeenth and early eighteenth centuries, many slaves came to what is now the United States not directly from Africa, but after having lived and worked in Jamaica, Barbados, and other colonies, where pidgin and creole-like speech had already begun to form. After South Carolina was founded in 1670, the first blacks it imported came from the Caribbean. In New York, between 1701 and 1726, twice as many slaves were brought from the Caribbean as from Africa.

We have virtually no samples of slave speech from the seventeenth century. One exception is the 1692 testimony of Tituba at the Salem witch trials, recorded by Magistrate John Hathorne and published 174 years later by Samuel Drake. Tituba was actually an Amerindian slave, reared by an African family in Barbados before being transported to Massachusetts in 1680 as a teenager. Her testimony included the sentence:

He tell me he Ø God. (He told me he is / was God.)

Two features common to creoles are found here—absence of the copula, which can be deleted in Caribbean Creole English whether it is present (*is*) or past (*was*), and use of an unmarked "action" verb (*tell*) for past tense, without an *ed* suffix or other verb change (as in *told*).

The eighteenth century. Throughout the eighteenth century, the proportions of blacks in the American colonies increased steadily, as did the numbers who were brought directly from Africa. Disparities between the three colonial regions became even more marked. By 1750, blacks represented only 3 percent of the population in New England, 7 percent of the population in the Middle colonies, but nearly 40 percent of the population in the plantation-rich South. Since 87 percent of all blacks in the American colonies at the time were in the South, it is this region that we must concentrate on when we consider the development of the African American vernacular.

By 1708, blacks outnumbered whites in South Carolina, representing 65 percent of the colony's population in 1720, and 69 percent in 1730. In 1776, on the eve of the War of Independence, there were more than twice as many blacks—the main labor force in the cultivation of rice and indigo—as whites in this colony: ninety thousand blacks to forty thousand whites. In neighboring Georgia, which was founded as a colony only in 1735, and which began importing slaves only in 1750, the black proportion was not as large, but it grew rapidly. Between 1760 and 1773 the black population almost doubled, increasing to fifteen thousand, as against eighteen thousand whites. In the swampy rice-cultivating coastal and Sea Island areas of South Carolina and Georgia, blacks represented even higher proportions— 70 percent and more in some parishes, 90 percent and more on some islands and plantations. The clearest example of Creole English in America—Gullah, or Sea Island Creole—developed in these regions and is still found there.

In eighteenth-century Virginia, Maryland, and North Carolina, the overall proportions of blacks were not as high as in South Carolina and Georgia, but they were still substantial, and black slaves significantly outnumbered white servants. By 1750, for instance, blacks constituted 27 percent of the population in North Carolina, 31 percent in Maryland, and 44 percent in Virginia. But as historian Philip S. Foner has noted, blacks outnumbered whites in three southern counties of Maryland as early as 1712, and "by the mid–eighteenth century, the Negro population had outstripped many times the white laboring class—46,356 Negroes to 6,781 white servants."

Two side effects of the black population explosion of the eighteenth century may themselves have had significant linguistic consequences. The first is that blacks increasingly learned their English not from whites, but from other blacks, who may have been speaking highly vernacular dialects themselves; this reflects the process of language acquisition and the influence of African languages. Historian Peter Wood made this observation in 1974, referring to South Carolina:

> After the first generation, contrary to accepted dogma, most new Negroes learned the local language not from Englishmen but from other slaves, a fact which reinforced the distinctiveness of the dialect.

The second is that whites, feeling threatened and wanting to ensure their economic and social dominance, passed increasingly harsh laws restricting the rights of blacks, stipulating their status as property for life, and prescribing draconian punishments for them. This process had begun since the middle seventeenth century in Maryland and Virginia, but the legislation spread to all the colonies and became harsher in the early eighteenth century. In Virginia, blacks were distinguished from whites as early as 1639 by an act allowing the latter but not the former to receive arms and ammunition. The following year, lifetime service was instituted for blacks but not whites. A series of laws throughout the seventeenth century chipped away at other rights of slaves, such as the right to assemble. But the slave code of 1705 consolidated all the former laws and, in the words of Philip Foner, "fastened the chains of bondage on Negroes more tightly." As he notes, the measure

> increased punishments for slaves by providing that for petty offenses, slaves were to be whipped, maimed or branded; for robbing a house or a store a slave was to be given sixty lashes by the sheriff, placed in the pillory with his ears nailed to the posts for a half-hour, his ears then to be severed from his head. . . . For the first time too, the law prescribed the castration of recaptured fugitive slaves.

Laws like these might have erected or reinforced sociopsychological barriers between blacks and whites, fomenting black resentment and leading to the crystallization of a black identity expressed, in part, through a distinctive vernacular. No slave who had had his ears nailed to a post and severed from his head would have wanted to speak exactly like his persecutors, no matter how many hours he had worked alongside them in the fields.

We begin to find in the eighteenth century not only several literary attestations of slave speech, but also explicit comments about the language of the Africans and about the ways in which black language and culture differed from white. Historians Marvin Kay and Lorin Cary cite the following from contemporary observers:

> Philip Reading, Anglican minister in Delaware, wrote in 1748 that slaves there "have a language peculiar to themselves, a wild confused medley of Negro and corrupt English . . ."

> J. F. D. Smyth, "an English visitor to the colonies at the beginning of the American revolution," described the language used by the Virginia and North Carolina slaves in the 1770s as "a mixed dialect between the Guinea and the English."

> The Reverend James Marye Jr. wrote from Orange County, Virginia, in 1754 that "there are great Quantities of those Negroes imported here yearly from Africa, who have languages peculiar to themselves, who are here many years before they understand English; and great Numbers there are that never do understand it."

Historian Allan Kulikoff explicitly suggests that

> a new creole language may have emerged in the Chesapeake [Virginia and Maryland] region combining the vocabulary of several African languages common among the immigrants, African linguistic structures, and the few English words needed for communication with the master.

And the language that Daniel Defoe put in the mouth of a Virginia slave in his novel *Colonel Jacque* seems to prove Kulikoff right, for it includes such creole features as *me* as subject pronoun (instead of "I" or "Ah") and *no* as negator:

> "Yes, yes . . . me know, but me want speak, me tell something. O! me no let him make de great master angry."

Moreover, as linguist J. L. Dillard has noted in relation to these very sentences:

> The Virginia and Maryland Negroes in *The Life of Colonel Jacque* speak the same Pidgin English which Defoe attributes to his other Africans. The white indentured servants who work beside them speak an entirely different variety of English.

Allan Kulikoff, considering the testimony of late-eighteenth-century observers, noted that black/white differences at the time extended to other aspects of culture besides language:

> White observers agreed that the music, dance, and religiosity of black slaves [in Virginia and Maryland] differed remarkably from those of

whites. . . . The practice of a distinctive culture within their own quarters gave them some small power over their own lives and destinies.

This notion is reinforced by the eighteenth-century observation of the Reverend Alexander Garden that blacks in South Carolina were "a Nation within a Nation. . . . They labour together and converse almost wholly among themselves."

During the War for Independence, fought between 1776 and 1783, thousands of slaves, attracted by promises of freedom, fled to (and sometimes fought for) the British side. John Leacock depicted one of them, Cudjo, in his 1776 play, *The Fall of British Tyranny*. In the passage quoted in chapter 2, Cudjo's speech shows possible influences from creole and/or West African languages, such as copula absence and the use of *me* as both subject and possessive ("*me* come from Nawfok," "*Me* massa Ø name Cunney Tomsee"), and the addition of an extra vowel (a process called epenthesis by linguists) in *disse* (this), and other words to make them conform to the common West African consonant-vowel syllable pattern. Many slaves and ex-slaves like Cudjo settled in Nova Scotia after the war, some eleven hundred of them moving on from there to Sierra Leone, where they founded Freetown in 1792. The descendants of these diasporic African Americans in Nova Scotia and Sierra Leone and Liberia would be recorded by linguists in the latter half of the twentieth century, and their speech used to reconstruct the nature of the African American vernacular of the late eighteenth century.

Evidence on slave speech in the eighteenth century can also be gleaned from newspaper ads about runaway slaves. Assessments of the English of slaves in these ranged from very low ("can't speak English"; "speaks broken English"; "speaks fast and bad English") to very high ("speaks very good English"; "speaks exceedingly good English"; "speaks very proper"), depending on how long the slaves had been in America and other factors. These assessments confirm what might be suspected anyway—that there was variation in slave speech resulting from the varying social circumstances and history of individuals and subgroups. Even J. L. Dillard, a linguist who firmly believes that both West African English and Plantation Creole were in use in eighteenth-century America, also insists that some blacks at the time spoke Standard English, and perhaps other varieties. Insofar as wide linguistic variations existed, eighteenth-century African America was much like the African America of today, although the sociohistorical circumstances shaping the variations were quite different.

The nineteenth century. The 1793 invention of the cotton gin—a machine that facilitated the separation of the cotton fiber from the seed—significantly expanded the production of cotton. Cotton replaced tobacco and other staples as the plantation crop in most parts of the Old South, and fueled the development of new states in the Midwest and Southwest, including Alabama, Arkansas, Louisiana, Mississippi, Missouri, Ohio, and Texas. Not surprisingly, U.S. slave populations underwent massive increases as a result—from seven hundred thousand in 1790 to nearly four million in 1860.

Some of this increase stemmed from the legal importation of slaves from Africa and (to a much lesser extent in this period) the Caribbean, which continued until January 1808, when the importation of slaves was outlawed. But there was also a thriving market in the illegal importation of African slaves that continued well into the nineteenth century, particularly in coastal regions of the South where ships could slip in and unload their cargo quickly and easily. (In 1858—fifty years after the slave trade had been outlawed—more than four hundred African slaves were brought to Jekyll Island, Georgia, on the slave ship *Wanderer*.) A third factor behind the black population spike was "natural" increase, spurred on by prolific slave breeding and the incentives that encouraged it: among them, reduced workloads, gifts of food and livestock to mothers of newborn children, and promises of freedom to women who bore ten or fifteen children.

The main source of new slaves in the newly settled states, however, and in parts of the Deep South where cotton became king, was the domestic or internal slave trade. Under this trade, slaves were moved en masse, by boat or train or, most often, on foot (via forced marches in slave coffles), from Virginia, Maryland, Kentucky, Tennessee, and other states to key cotton-producing states in the lower South—Arkansas, Louisiana, and Texas. Historians Daniel Johnson and Rex Campbell estimate that

> three quarters of a million slaves were removed from the old slave states of Delaware, Maryland, Virginia, [and] North Carolina and the District of Columbia to states in the Deep South and Southwest. . . . In the last decade for domestic slave trading, 1850–1860, migration accelerated, with 193,000 slaves transported over state lines.

One effect of this domestic slave trade was the spread of the black vernacular westward, in a pattern that would be repeated and accelerated in black migrations from the South in the twentieth century.

Much of the apparent uniformity of Spoken Soul may be due to this population diffusion from the South. Another effect was to break up the black family, as mothers, fathers, and children were often separated from each other in the profit-making fervor that drove the nineteenth-century domestic slave trade. Josiah Henson's remembrances of his own forceful separation from his mother at an auction block in Maryland in the early nineteenth century, when he was five or six, make painful reading:

> I seem to see and hear my poor weeping mother now. This was one of my earliest observations of [white] men; an experience which I only shared with thousands of my race, the bitterness of which to any individual who suffers it cannot be diminished by the frequency of its occurrence, while it is dark enough to overshadow the whole after-life with something blacker than a funeral pall.

Such traumatic separations were probably similar to the ear-nailings of the eighteenth century that we cited earlier, in the sense that they would have created or increased the psychic distance between blacks and whites. Blacks experiencing, witnessing, or even hearing about such cruelty would probably not have wanted to talk like their oppressors, and they would probably have become more determined to develop or maintain their own communicative and expressive styles. The fact that Spoken Soul often marks the oppositional identity of blacks vis-à-vis whites and "mainstream culture" is undoubtedly part of the reason for its vibrant existence to this day.

Another key historical development of the nineteenth century was the War of 1812 with Britain, which led to further emigration of blacks to Canada and to a lesser extent the West Indies. In the 1820s and 1830s, colonization movements resulted in the emigration of thousands of blacks to Samaná and other parts of the Dominican Republic and, in even greater numbers, to Liberia. Analyses of modern-day Samaná English and Liberian English have become, in the last decade and a half, important indicators of what the black vernacular may have been like in earlier times.

Of course, the major historical events of the nineteenth century for African Americans were the Civil War between the North and the South, which began in 1861, and their achievement of freedom in the ensuing years. Abraham Lincoln's Emancipation Proclamation of September 1862 offered freedom to all slaves in rebellious Confederate states in January 1863, and the Thirteenth Amendment of 1865 constitutionally abolished slavery everywhere in the United States.

In many parts of the South, slaves achieved their "day of jubilee" even earlier, once Union forces defeated the Confederate forces. Wallace Quarterman, born a slave in Georgia in 1844, gave Zora Neale Hurston and others in 1935 this gripping first-person account of how freedom came to his plantation after the "big gun shot." The event probably took place at or close to the time that fifty Union vessels steamed into Port Royal and the surrounding South Carolina Sea Islands in 1861, and defeated the weak Confederate forces there:

> The overseer ask me what is that, if that is thunder? I tell um I don't know. I know was the Yankee come. . . . An' he call me an' tol' me to run down in the fiel', and tell Peter to turn the people loose, that the Yankee come. An' so I run down in the fiel', an', an' whoop and holler. . . . An that, the people them throw 'way they hoe them. They throw away they hoe, an' then they call we all up, you know, an', an' give we all freedom 'cause we are jus' as much as free as them.

Despite the achievement of legal freedom, the post–Civil War period was one of severe economic hardship for most blacks in the South, ravaged as the region had been by the war and the breakup of the plantation economy. One response was black migration within and out of the region—to bigger cities within the South, to southwestern frontiers such as Kansas and Oklahoma, and to the industrial states of the North. Between 1860 and 1880, the black population in Kansas increased from 627 to 43,100. During the 1880s more than 30,000 Southern blacks migrated to Pennsylvania, New York, and New Jersey. And between 1890 and 1900 more than 105,000 southern blacks migrated to the North. Linguist Don Winford has suggested that "the concentration and intense contact of African Americans of various regional backgrounds in northern and southern cities set the stage for further leveling or convergence among AAVE [African American Vernacular English] varieties, and the emergence of the relatively focussed and uniform urban vernacular."

While the attainment of freedom was replete with hardships, it did allow many blacks to earn a living, especially in the industrial North, and it resulted in increased opportunities for education, in both the North and the South, for election to public office, and for involvement in leadership positions in the church. Those who were fortunate enough to move up economically, educationally, and otherwise would undoubtedly have had more access to standard or mainstream speech.

Although its accuracy is sometimes open to question, the contemporary evidence on black speech in the nineteenth century is voluminous. One finds it in novels, short stories, travelers' accounts, descriptions of minstrel shows, slave and ex-slave narratives, semitechnical studies, dialect sermons, music, and poetry. For a discussion of some of this literary material, see chapter 2.

The twentieth century.   Despite the migratory movements blacks had participated in throughout the nineteenth century, nothing matched in scale and significance the "Great Migration" to the North and West (and specifically to urban centers there) that began around 1916. The initial pull factor was World War I, which increased the need for labor in northern industries at the same time that it caused a precipitous drop in European immigration—from one million in 1914 to a fourth of that in 1916 and a tenth in 1918. Recruiters from the North went south and found many willing migrators among blacks, who were attracted by the promising economic prospects of the North and repelled by the economic stagnation, overt discrimination, inferior education, exclusion from the electoral process, and racial violence (including lynching) that they experienced in the South.

According to one estimate, some 1.8 million black southerners migrated to states in the North or West between 1914 and 1930, about *four* times as many as had done so in the preceding forty years. This process continued in later decades, so that whereas 90 percent of the black population lived in the South in 1900, only 68 percent of the black population lived there in 1950; 15 percent were in north or central states, 13 percent in the Northeast, and 4 percent in the West. By the time of the 1960 census, 1.5 million, or 47 percent, of blacks living in the north central region had been born elsewhere, but only 1.4 percent of the South's black populations had. Illinois showed a net increase of 189,000 black immigrants between 1950 and 1960, and California an increase of 176,000 over the same period. By contrast, Mississippi showed a net decrease of 323,000 blacks from 1950 to 1960, and South Carolina and Georgia a net decrease of more than 200,000 blacks each during this period. It was not until the 1970s that the South, newly industrialized and with good housing and job opportunities, began to show increases in net in-migration, mainly people who had lived or grown up in the South before moving to the North or West, and who were returning rather disillusioned.

Black migration in the twentieth century was not only from South to North and West, but also from rural to urban areas. This was true even for blacks who remained in the South, driven from farms to cities by the collapse of the tenant farming system, by mechanization, and by crop disease. In 1920, 25 percent of southern blacks were urban, but by 1940, that figure had increased to 36 percent, and by 1950 to 48 percent. Urban living was even more characteristic of the North and West. In 1920, 87 percent of north/central blacks were urban, and by 1940, 89 percent were, versus 57 percent of whites. By 1950, fully 94 percent of blacks in the north/central area were urban. By 1970, 74 percent of blacks in the United States as a whole lived in metropolitan areas, and the proportions increased as white flight to the suburbs continued.

Throughout the twentieth century, and especially before the civil rights struggles and legislation of the 1960s, what blacks encountered both in the South and in the "promised land"—the North and the West—was discrimination in jobs and unions, segregation in housing, and distinct inequalities in education. In the 1920s, most blacks in the urban north were working-class, mostly in unskilled occupations (porters, elevator operators, janitors, domestics, and so on). Access to most higher-paying, skilled jobs and their labor unions was blocked by a process of "affirmative action" for whites and "rejective action" for blacks; of the ten thousand apprenticeships in skilled trade unions in New York City in 1920, only fifty-six were held by blacks. In the 1940s, blacks were excluded from most defense industry jobs until the Committee on Fair Employment Practices was established in 1941; between 1942 and 1944, the percentage of blacks in shipbuilding and other war industries increased from 3 to 8 percent, and cities with such industries experienced huge gains in black immigration as a result. Between 1940 and 1944, for instance, the number of blacks in Portland, Oregon, swelled from 2,000 to 15,000, and in the San Francisco Bay Area from 20,000 to 65,000.

Segregation in housing—usually in the form of restriction to overcrowded inner-city ghettoes—was high. In Baltimore in 1941, to name one city, approximately ninety thousand black residents were crammed into an area of one square mile. And in at least 109 cities in the North, South, and West, segregation actually increased between 1940 and 1950. The average index of black segregation for 207 cities surveyed in 1960 (defined by Daniel Johnson and Rex Campbell as "the percentage of blacks [who] would have to move from one block to another to effect an even, unsegregated residential distribution") was 86.2 percent. As upper- and middle-income whites moved to the suburbs, and jobs and industries followed them, the tax base for many cities dropped sharply, and the amount of spending for inner-city schools and other facilities for blacks also plummeted. Linguists William Labov and Wendell Harris, among others, have argued that this intense mid-century segregation in housing and schools led to changes in the grammar of Spoken Soul and increased divergence between black and white vernaculars—an idea we'll take up later.

The civil rights struggles of the 1950s and 1960s—culminating in the 1963 March on Washington, led by the Reverend Martin Luther King Jr.—represented a major attempt to overcome these disparities. The Civil Rights Act of 1964, which legislated an end to segregation in public accommodations and forbade discrimination in hotels and restaurants and in federal spending, was its most spectacular achievement. Voting rights for blacks increased, as did opportunities for education, employment, and access to social services. Affirmative action, providing for preferences in employment for minorities (and women) who had been the earlier victims of discrimination and what we regard as "repressive action," also began in the 1960s. As historian Kennell Jackson has noted: "After the Watts riots in 1965, [President] Johnson signed Executive Order 11246, which required employers using federal funds to set goals for hiring minorities."

Economist Martin Carnoy has argued that such federal interventions as New Deal legislation, the Civil Rights Act, and affirmative action helped produce real gains in black employment and income:

> Between 1939 and the early 1970s, a black male worker pushed his average earnings from 42 to 67 percent of a white male worker's earnings. . . . Black women did even better, almost reaching parity with white women by the end of the 1970s. . . . Black men moved from agricultural to higher-paying, higher-skilled factory jobs, and eventually, office jobs. Black women shifted from domestic service and low-paying factory jobs into retail sales and office work. The fact that black men *and* women were getting more pay helped change the position of the black family. Two-parent black families earned 60 percent of what white, two-parent families were making in 1960, a figure that leaped to 80 percent by 1979—a period of only two decades.

Between the 1970s and the 1990s, however, a series of Supreme Court decisions effectively restricted and outlawed federal affirmative action based on race and gender, and black gains in employment, income, and access to higher education are being eroded. While some blacks have been upwardly mobile (those earning $100,000 or more represented 0.3 percent of all blacks from the 1960s to 1984, but increased to 1 percent in 1987–1989), black-white disparities in employment and income remain very sharp, particularly at the lower levels. In the United States, more than twice as many blacks as whites were unemployed in 1993, and among blacks aged sixteen to twenty-four, nearly 32 percent were unemployed, nearly *three* times as many as whites aged sixteen to twenty-four. Economist Martin Carnoy has argued persuasively that economic and social progress made by blacks between 1940 and the mid-1970s stopped and in some respects reversed since then, and he blames this squarely on reduced government activity and involvement in minority matters. In 1994 he noted some of the grim effects:

> One of two black children now grows up in poverty, a much higher fraction than twenty years ago. One of two young black males has a criminal record, and half of the total prison population is black. One of two black children is born out of wedlock. Again, that number is up over the past two decades. . . . As blacks have moved out of cities into the suburbs, segregated housing has moved with them. Almost all black children grow up in such informally segregated neighborhoods, North and South, most with low-quality services and low-quality schools.

Furthermore, although blacks now occupy some of the highest positions in the land, as congressional representatives, mayors, and police chiefs, among others, they are still disproportionately the victims of criminal injustice and police violence. The 1992 not-guilty decision of an all-white jury for the four Los Angeles police officers who were recorded on videotape savagely beating Rodney King touched off the "largest peacetime civil disturbance of this century," in which fifty-two people died. Even as we write, investigations are proceeding into various incidents of premature and excessive police violence against blacks in New York, New Jersey, and other states across the country.

Some may argue that in summarizing the history of African Americans in the twentieth century we have highlighted the negatives rather than the positives. That may well be so. But the negatives are real, and they explain the existence of the seething "oppositional identity" that anthropologist John Ogbu finds alive and well in the

African American community. That attitude in turn fuels the continued existence and development of the African American vernacular—Spoken Soul.

Sources for studying the nature and development of Spoken Soul in the twentieth century are superabundant, but they have only recently begun to be tapped. In addition to literary sources even richer than those of the nineteenth century (including the works of black writers from the 1920s Harlem Renaissance and their successors), we have the ex-slave narratives and recordings of the 1930s; hoodoo (voodoo) material recorded between 1935 and 1961; recordings made between the 1970s and 1990s of the descendants of African Americans who emigrated to Liberia, the Dominican Republic, and Nova Scotia in earlier centuries; and a wide range of systematic linguistic studies of black speech made in selected cities across the nation from the 1960s to the present. Spoken Soul has come into media prominence during the same period, and the evidence of that coverage is discussed in chapter 10.

Having laid the historical groundwork, we now return to the major linguistic questions about the development of Spoken Soul—the extent of African, English (especially British), and Creole influences on Spoken Soul, and the question of whether it is currently diverging from white vernacular.

African, English, and Creole Influences on the Vocabulary of Spoken Soul

The vocabulary of Spoken Soul is overwhelmingly English in origin, and about that there has never been any dispute. Even the most ardent Africanists and Afrocentrists concede this, contending that African influence is strong in grammar, not vocabulary. Molefi Asante, the leading Afrocentrist scholar in America, notes that "although African lexical items may be found in limited supply among African Americans, they do not make the argument for a more general retention of African linguistic behavior applicable to most black Americans."

At the same time, research over the past half-century has helped dispel the contentions of earlier scholars that "the African brought over or retained only a few words of his jungle-tongue." That indelicately phrased assessment was made in 1922, by Ambrose Gonzales, the same "scholar" who displayed his racism and his ignorance of the fact that physiological factors have little or nothing to do with lan-

guage features, by hypothesizing that South Carolina and Georgia
Gullah originated as follows:

> Slovenly and careless of speech, these Gullahs seized upon the peasant
> English used by some of the early settlers and by the white servants of
> the wealthier colonists, wrapped their clumsy tongues about it as well
> as they could, and, enriched with certain expressive African words, it
> issued through their flat noses and thick lips as so workable a form of
> speech that it was gradually adopted by the other slaves and became in
> time the accepted Negro speech of the lower districts of South Carolina
> and Georgia.

Gonzales's successors avoided putting their feet in their mouths
quite so firmly, but even in relation to Gullah—widely regarded as the
most African and creole-like variety of Spoken Soul—Samuel Stoney
and Gertrude Shelby in 1930 estimated that it had only about twenty
African words, "of which six or seven are in common use." And Mason Crum, writing in 1940, essentially agreed: "perhaps a score of
African words remaining." By contrast, Lorenzo Dow Turner, after
nearly two decades of research, revealed in 1949 that Gullah had approximately four thousand words with plausible African sources. Most
of them were personal names (e.g., *Shiyama*, from a Kongo word
meaning "strength," "security"), but more than two hundred fifty were
words used in conversation (e.g., *goober*, or *guba*, from *ngguba*, a Kim-
bundu word meaning "peanut").

Scholars David Dalby, Joseph Holloway, and Winifred Vass, among
others, have extended Turner's work in regard to African American
English and American English more generally, arguing that even
common expressions such as *jazz*, *tote* (carry), *okay*, and *do one's thing*
have plausible African sources. Africanisms in vocabulary include not
only direct retentions or borrowings from African languages (*goober/
guba*), but also loan translations into English of African compounds
or concepts (*cut-eye*, *bad-mouth*). Because loan translations "pass" as
English words, they tend to survive longer than direct loans.

Arguments that African American English shows creole influences
are, like arguments that it shows African influences, made almost entirely in relation to its pronunciation and grammar rather than its
vocabulary. There are some striking vocabulary parallels between
Caribbean Creole English and African American English, but these
generally involve shared Africanisms such as *tote* and *cut-eye*. Shared
grammatical markers such as *steady* and *come* that do not appear to be
Africanisms are also noteworthy, however.

It should be noted that in addition to the vocabulary obtained from African, English, and Creole sources, Spoken Soul created and innovated many words on its own, as shown by the extensive slang and other expressions that can be found in the dictionaries *Juba to Jive* and *Black Talk*, cited in the notes. Chapter 6 offers several examples.

African, English, and Creole Influences on the Pronunciation of Spoken Soul

Africanists, those who argue for extensive African influences, and Anglicists, those who argue for extensive English—especially British nonstandard—influences, both yield little or no quarter when it comes to the pronunciation of Spoken Soul. For the Africanists, the reason many African Americans pronounce English *th* as *t, f, d,* or *v* (as in *tin* for "thin," *Rufe* for "Ruth," *dem* for "them," and *bave* for "bathe") is simple: The West African languages spoken by the ancestors of today's African Americans did not include the *th* sound, and when acquiring English in the seventeenth through the nineteenth centuries, Africans substituted the consonants most similar to *th* in their own language. Linguist Geneva Smitherman puts it quite plainly. In a column headed "Sound Rule in West African Languages" she gives the feature "no /th/ sound," and in the corresponding column headed "Black English," she gives the result: "Black English speaker substitutes /d/ or /f/ for /th/: thus *souf* (for 'south') and *dis* (for 'this')."

Anglicists are just as adamant that this and other pronunciation features of Spoken Soul are carry-overs from the nonstandard language spoken by settlers from Britain. Most of these settlers, they remind us, were peasant and low-class social types (indentured servants) who were likely to have been speaking vernacular rather than Standard English. As linguist John McWhorter has observed:

> Rural nonstandard dialects in Great Britain are chock full of the very structures that define Black English. In fact if Black English were spoken there, the African Language System notion wouldn't have even made it out of the starting gate because the actual models for most of its constructions would have been closer to hand.
>
> The substitution of *f* for final *th* (*mouf*), the substitution of *d* for *th* at the beginnings of words (*dem, dese* and *dose*), and the simplification of consonant clusters at the end of words are all common in nonstandard British dialects.

Cleanth Brooks, well-known author and literary critic, and a self-styled "amateur" in linguistic matters, is equally obdurate in his claim that such pronunciations as *de, dis,* and *dat* in southern Black English came from southern British dialects, such as that of Sussex, rather than from African languages. He cites evidence from an 1860 pamphlet that such pronunciations were being used in Sussex in the mid-nineteenth century and that they were in use there even earlier, since the sixteenth century. The rural folk in Sussex, he argues, could not have gotten their *des, disses,* and *dats* from blacks, because they had never encountered any, but the black folk in America could and did learn their English from white folk like those who came from Sussex. The blacks kept these and other pronunciations longer and used them more frequently than whites, he claims, because

> the blacks, who were denied education and later on only got a rather poor and limited "book learning," held on to what their ancestors had learned by ear and [what] had been passed on to them through oral tradition. In short, they rather faithfully preserved what they had heard, were little influenced by spelling, and in general actually served as a conservative force.

Is it possible that some of the British settlers might have come to America using the *th* pronunciations? Not really, Brooks avers, for "at this time the standard language had hardly settled down to a generally acknowledged form," and upper-crust Britishers "were few enough in the new American colonies." And is it possible that Africans modified English *th* pronunciations for the same reasons the French do (*zee boy* for "the boy") because this consonant sound is "completely unfamiliar" in their language? Brooks says maybe so for Gullah on the South Carolina and Georgia Sea Islands, where the speakers were "relatively isolated and had little contact with the whites," but outside of this area, no.

We cite Brooks at some length to indicate the uncompromising character of debate on the "origins" issue—concessions are rarely granted to the other side(s)—and to show that arguments are rarely as watertight as they are made to appear. For one thing, while it is certainly possible that Africans learned from whites to pronounce *th* as *d, t,* and so on, it is not necessary to assume this, for influence or "interference" from West African languages, which generally lack *th*, would almost certainly have produced the same result, as Smitherman and others have suggested. This much is clear from the English spoken by

Nigerians, Jamaicans, Gullahs (the one concession Brooks makes), and others in areas where contact between African languages and English took place without the presence of large numbers of British indentured servants and dialect speakers. Moreover, the claim that virtually every British immigrant to America was using nonstandard dialect pronunciations of *th* throughout the more than two hundred years that Africans were being brought to America can hardly be valid, especially since *th* pronunciations are more common among their white descendants today, even those with limited book learning. One problem with the argument of some Anglicists, in fact, is their failure to tell us anything about the frequency with which putative nonstandard features of British dialects occurred in America in the past and occur in Britain today; it is almost as if the attestation of a feature from one British speaker, once, could be the source of the high-frequency use of a similar feature among many if not most African Americans. Since Spoken Soul is often distinguished from surrounding white dialects today by how often particular pronunciations or structures are used, frequency considerations are important in reconstructing its history.

In any case, it is very likely that some Africans coming to America encountered *th* pronunciations among the English speakers they encountered, and produced pronunciations with *t, d, f,* and *v* instead because of the influence of their African languages. It is even more likely that this is one of several features that show mutual or convergent influence from British dialects *and* African languages. Linguist Norma Niles, one of the first to argue British dialect origin for Barbadian Creole English, made precisely this point twenty years ago:

> There may be a significant number of features, grammatical and lexical, with dual African and dialect origins. More significant though is that the similarity of features of the contact languages strengthens the chance of retention and persistence of these features in the developing languages.

In this regard she concedes strikingly more than those who argue for Anglicist origins of Spoken Soul.

Before leaving the subject of *th* pronunciations, we should mention that pronunciations like *t* and *d* could be attributed also to "simplification" from pidgin/creole influence, since *th* consonants are rare, or "marked," among the world's languages, and they are almost universally converted to non-*th* pronunciations in pidgin and Creole

English worldwide, even in the Pacific (Solomon Islands and China Coast Pidgin English, Australian Creole), where African influence is unlikely. This is a feature that could have come from African, English, or creole sources, either individually or jointly.

Another black pronunciation that is claimed by both Anglicists and Africanists is the simplification of consonant clusters by deletion of the final consonant, as in *tes'* for "test" and *han'* for "hand." McWhorter's comment quoted above includes the claim that this, too, is "common in non-standard British dialects," while Smitherman attributes it equally to a sound rule in West African languages disallowing consonant clusters. Ernie Smith elaborates on the Africanist position:

> In the deep phonology of African American speech there is a distinctively West and Niger-Congo African CV (consonant vowel) vocalic pattern that has been retained. As a result of having retained this CV rule, in the deep phonology of African American speech, in consonance with the rules of the West and Niger-Congo African languages, certain consonant clusters or consonant blends do not occur.

Smith's claim receives support from the observation by William Welmers, a leading expert on African languages, that "in Nilo-Saharan as well as in Niger-Congo, consonant clusters are generally rare." And given the evidence of Gullah, Nigerian English, and Caribbean Creoles that Africans with only minimal contact with English speakers simplified their consonant clusters, it is again clear that it is not necessary to appeal to English dialects to explain the presence of this feature in African American speech. Niger-Congo speakers learning English three hundred years ago would have been likely to simplify English consonant clusters because of their African language patterns, just as Africans learning English today do.

Smith makes a further claim that the restriction of consonant cluster simplification in African American speech to homogeneous, or "same voice," clusters (e.g., *nd* in *hand* but not *nt* in *pant*) is also "in consonance with the phonological rules of Niger-Congo African grammars." But no specific Niger-Congo languages are cited in support of this claim, and we could find no evidence in Welmers and other sources for it. On the contrary, the existence of heterogeneous, or "mixed voice," sequences in KiKongo (e.g., *nti,* meaning "tree") weakens the validity of the claim. Although these sequences are not quite the same as the simplified clusters of Spoken Soul (they occur at the beginning or in the middle of words rather than at the end),

Welmers argues for treating them as clusters, and they do involve mixed voicing (*n* is voiced, *t* voiceless).

What of *r* deletion after vowels, for example *afta* for "after," and *yo* for "your"? As in the case of the other Spoken Soul pronunciations discussed in this section, Geneva Smitherman attributes this to a West African language sound rule. Don Winford, while attributing *dem, ting,* and *tes'* pronunciations primarily to West African or creole influence, feels that *r* deletion after vowels, like the use of final *in* for *ing*, comes primarily from British English dialects spoken by indentured servants and other British settlers. However, the normally Anglicist John McWhorter concedes the possibility of West African influence here:

> It is reasonable to trace the absence of *l* and *r* after vowels (*stow* for 'store,' *co'* for 'cold') to West African languages. British dialects did not start dropping *r* in this position until the mid-1700s, after the basics of slave speech here were almost certainly long established, and only a few British dialects are known for dropping *l* after vowels at all.

Although pidgin and/or creole influence is a possibility in the preceding cases, one black pronunciation that seems to make the case for creole influence more strongly than for anything else is the rule deleting *b, d,* or *g* in the preverbal tense-aspect markers, as in "He ain't do it" (He didn't do it) and "Ahma do it" (I'm gonna do it). Parallels to this in Caribbean and other pidgin/creole languages are common (*'on* for *gon, 'a* for *da, 'en* for *ben*) and the feature is unknown in British English dialects. Whether African sources lie behind these creole similarities is not yet clear.

Another feature with strong creole rather than British dialect parallels and possible West African sources is the monophthongal pronunciation of vowels, as in *pay* and *go,* discussed in chapter 6. As linguists Erik Thomas and Guy Bailey recently observed:

> Older AAVE [African American Vernacular English] shows a much higher incidence of monophthongal /e/ and /o/ and of non-front /au/ than Southern White English, and it shares these features with Caribbean creoles. These features may ultimately be derived from African languages.

The authors note that the West African languages seem to favor monophthongal pronunciations, too: "none of the West African systems that have been described by linguists seem to have upgliding diphthongs for /e/ and /o/."

African, English, and Creole Influences on the Grammar of Spoken Soul

Arguments about the sources of the grammar of Spoken Soul are sometimes as trenchant and diametrically opposed as those about its grammar, sometimes even more so. John McWhorter has claimed that "there is not a single sentence structure in Black English that is traceable to West African languages" (see the opening of this chapter) and that virtually all its nonstandard grammatical features come from British dialects of English. At the other extreme, Ernie Smith contends that "Black English" is itself an oxymoron, since "African American speech does not in any way follow the grammar rules of English" but is "the linguistic continuation of Africa in Black America."

The claim that African American speech does not in any way follow the grammar of English is easily refuted. As several linguists have noted (recall the quotation from Stefan Martin and Walt Wolfram cited in chapter 7), Spoken Soul is essentially if not overwhelmingly English in its word order and sentence structure. Moreover, some of the vernacular grammatical features that make it seem distinctive today do indeed have striking parallels if not sources in British dialects. The list includes existential *it* instead of "there" ("*it*'s a lot of girls") and inverted word-order in indirect questions ("I asked him *could he come* with me"). As far as we know, neither of these has parallels in West African or creole languages. Some features of Spoken Soul do have counterparts in Caribbean Creoles, but they may derive from British dialects, in form if not in precise meaning and use. This category includes double negatives ("I *don't* want *nothing*"), double modals ("He *might could* do it"), the use of *ain't* as an all-purpose negator ("I *ain't* lyin"; "He *ain't* gone"), and the use of *done* as a completive ("I *done* had enough"). As Don Winford has recently suggested, however, the meaning of *done* in Spoken Soul and southern white English vernacular, "particularly the sense of 'already,'" differs from that of the British *have / be done [verb](ed)* (e.g., "He *has done* petuously *devour* the noble Chaucer" from Scottish poet William Dunbar, 1460–1513) construction that was its "putative source" and "suggests some degree of creole semantic transfer."

The case can be made for African influence in several aspects of grammar of Spoken Soul, however. For instance, the use of *say* to introduce a subordinate clause, as in this sentence from a Philadelphia man, "They told me *say* they couldn't get it in time," might at first appear to involve nothing more than a nonstandard form (*say* instead of "said"). However, the similar use of *say* with verbs like *think, know,* and *believe* in Gullah and Jamaican Creole—where no "saying" is involved—suggests that more is going on:

> You wouldn't *believe say* i's a colored woman own dat house.
> (Gullah woman)
>
> Me been *know say* him wouldn come. (Jamaican Creole)

Here *say* is functioning much more like English *that,* serving to introduce the complement of a verb. And Lorenzo Dow Turner, who commented on the use of *say* after verbs of saying, thinking, and wishing in Gullah, pointed out that a parallel "use of *sɛ* or a synonym of it [Ewe *be₃*, where the ₃ marks a high tone; Mende *yɛ*] is common in many West African languages." He gives an example from Twi: *ɛnna o susuwi sɛ ɛyɛ ɔkramaŋ foforo bi,* meaning "Then he thought *that* it was some other dog." It is conceivable that in "They told me *say*" we have a West African structure masquerading in English guise, or at least a convergence between West African and English forms.

Molefi Asante has argued that there are some African American parallels to the common West African phenomenon of "serial verbs," in which two or more verbs occur next to or close to one another in a sentence with only one surface subject and special semantic meanings, as in the Vagala sentence that translates literally as "He took knife cut meat," meaning "He cut the meat with a knife." Spoken Soul does not appear to have the wide range of serial verb constructions (inceptive, instrumental, benefactive) one finds in the Caribbean Creoles, but there are suggestive parallels in such structures as "I hear tell you went home," "Go home go see about those children," "He picked up and went to town," and "I'll take a switch and beat you good." This last sentence is instrumental, reminiscent of the Vagala example above ("He took knife cut meat").

Another feature of Spoken Soul that Asante and others attribute to African influence is the primacy of aspect (the manner in which an event occurs) over tense (when it occurs). There is no evidence that tense is unimportant in Spoken Soul, as it is in some West African languages. On the contrary, past-tense marking is very common in black American speech, especially with strong verbs such as *went* and *came,* where there is no possibility for consonant cluster simplification or other pronunciation rules to eat away a final *ed* (as may happen with, for example, *walked*). And Spoken Soul makes distinctions among degrees of future and past (*fitna* is immediate future; BEEN is remote past), which certainly involve tense, the marking of event time.

But the very presence of certain aspect categories in Spoken Soul—particularly the completive (marked by *done*) and the present durative, or habitual (marked by *be*)—may be attributed to their prevalence in West African languages, which is well documented in work by William Welmers and others. Even the existence of a category of remote past (marked by BEEN) may go back to distinctions in languages like LuGanda and KiKongo. Moreover, the tendency of Spoken Soul to encode its most important tense-aspect distinctions through a series of preverbal markers (*be, bin, done*, BIN, *fitna, had,* and so on) rather than through verbal affixes strikingly parallels the pattern in Caribbean Creoles.

In recent years, arguments about African, creole, or British/English sources for Black English features have become more complex, involving frequency considerations, evidence from the African American diaspora, and subtle questions about linguistic constraints. To give an idea of items often discussed and debated, we close this section with two features: copula absence and negation.

Copula absence (as in "He Ø happy" for "He is happy") provides one of the strongest arguments for possible creole and African influences on the grammar of Spoken Soul. In the first place, British dialects of English do not appear to delete their copulas now, nor do they appear to have done so in the past, so the predecessors of today's African Americans cannot be said to have picked up this feature from indentured servants and other English-speaking settlers. Most American white vernacular doesn't delete copulas, either, except for varieties in the South, which, arguably, "learned" to do so from black vernacular. In fact, recent studies of coastal North Carolina communities in which blacks and whites have resided for decades show that the two groups are similar in a number of distinctive pronunciation patterns but differ sharply on some key grammatical features, including copula absence: the blacks deleted *is* 15 to 20 percent of the time, the whites only 1 percent of the time; the blacks deleted *are* 30 to 58 percent of the time, the whites only 4 percent of the time. A study of an old white man and an old black woman who had spent all or most of their eighty-plus years on a South Carolina Sea Island showed similarly dramatic differences with respect to plural marking and other grammatical features, and it was suggested that these linguistic differences reflect differences in both informal socialization networks and expected community norms. Copula absence is one of a number of grammatical variables distinguishing blacks from whites in the present and in the past. While some features of British dialects were adopted, others were not, and differences were either maintained or intensified as part of the social construction of how blacks should talk and how whites should talk. That is something even the most ardent Anglicist has to recognize and explain.

Second, many West African languages and the deep, or basilectal, varieties of Creole English in the Caribbean regularly have no copula before adjectives (Ewe: $a_1 ti_3 la_3 k\jmath_3$ = Tree the tall, "The tree Ø tall"; Guyanese Creole: *De tree Ø tall*), so this could be one model for copula absence in Spoken Soul. Beyond adjectives, both the Caribbean and creole varieties do have copulas, but these differ in form depending on the following grammatical environment. Before nouns, many Caribbean Creoles have *da* or *a* (*He a de teacha*), and Gullah has *duh;* and before locatives, which tell where a person or thing is, many of them use *deh* (*He deh home*). This use of different copulas before different kinds of predicates cannot have come from English, for English uses the same copula form regardless of whether it precedes a noun ("He *is* the teacher"), an adjective ("He *is* sick") or a locative ("He *is* at home"). A much more reasonable source is African languages, which regularly use different copulas according to the following grammatical environment. Yoruba, for instance, uses *ṣe* and *jẹ́* for following nouns, *wà* and *sI* for following locatives, Ø and *ri* for following adjectives, and *ń* for following verbs. The West African system is not perfectly preserved in the basilectal creole equivalents, for different kinds of nouns, locatives, and adjectives are not distinguished by different copula forms. But an African-like distinction among nouns, locatives, adjectives, and verbs is maintained by the different copulas used in the creoles.

When we consider variation in these creoles, especially in mesolectal, or intermediate, varieties somewhat closer to Spoken Soul, things are even more interesting. For the various creole copulas are sometimes deleted and sometimes replaced by English copula forms (*is, are*), and the relative frequency with which you get zero in the different grammatical environments mirrors the relative frequency with which you get zero in Spoken Soul. This is true also for the African American diaspora varieties spoken by the descendants of eighteenth-

and nineteenth-century African Americans who emigrated to Samaná, Liberia, and Nova Scotia, as shown in the table below, which should be compared with its equivalent in chapter 7. It could be argued that the percentages of copula absence that regularly differentiate these following grammatical environments in Spoken Soul and its diasporic and creole cousins essentially maintain the deep creole and African differences among following nouns, adjectives, and verbs that were originally marked with different copulas.

Creole variety or African American diaspora group studied	Copula deletion before noun ("He Ø a man")	Copula deletion before adjective ("He Ø happy")	Copula deletion before gon(na) ("He Ø gon go")
Jamaican Creole	4%	59%	93%
Trinidadian Creole	1%	79%	97%
Barbadian Creole	.08	.42	.77
Liberian Settler (Albert)	32%	65%	100%
Samaná, Dominican Republic	.12	.44	.93
African Nova Scotian English	.31	.46	.73

What about negation? For this we will draw primarily on a recent discussion by linguist Darrin Howe. He begins by noting three respects in which the negation system of modern black speech—as exemplified in studies done in Ohio and New York—differs from white vernacular English and seems closer to Caribbean Creole. They are the use of *ain't* for "didn't" (as in "I *ain't* do it"), the use of *ain't* for "don't" (as in "He *ain't* got none"), and the fact that double or multiple negation is obligatory when there's an indefinite in the same clause ("Nobody *don't* know about *no club*"), just as it is in Guyanese Creole.

But a quantitative analysis of negation in three data sets that provide evidence on nineteenth-century and/or early-twentieth-century speech—African Nova Scotia English, Samaná English, and ex-slave recordings—reveals *less* Creole influence rather than *more*. For instance, *ain't* was used for "don't" only eleven times in the ex-slave recordings and Samaná English corpus combined, and never in the African Nova Scotian English sample. Similarly, *ain't* was used for "didn't" only 6 percent of the time in the Samaná English sample, 3 percent in the ex-slave recordings, and 2 percent in the African Nova

Scotian English data, compared with 40 percent of the time in a modern Spoken Soul sample from Columbus, Ohio. Finally, double negation with an indefinite (*anything, nothing*) in the same clause occurred only 66 percent of the time in Samaná English, 80 percent of the time in the ex-slave recordings, and 89 percent in African Nova Scotian English. These rates are closer to the rate of 75 to 81 percent reported for white nonstandard dialects in the North and South of the United States, but lower than the 98 percent reported for modern African American Vernacular English. It is these data, together with other aspects of negation in the three earlier Black English samples that make them appear more similar to white vernacular varieties, that lead Howe to conclude that the negation system of these early varieties "can be said to have derived exactly from English."

Of course one could temper Howe's conclusion by suggesting that his early Black English texts do not go back far enough, and that they may not have been as vernacular and informal, in terms of the circumstances of recording, as more recent data sets. But his conclusions converge with those of others who have explored the sources of negation in African American speech, and they serve to remind us that African, Creole, *and* British English sources must be acknowledged as having contributed to the development of Spoken Soul.

Divergence

Most of our discussion until now has been about historical influences on Spoken Soul between the seventeenth and eighteenth centuries. The divergence hypothesis, however, brings us into the twentieth century, for it suggests that the Great Migration of blacks to inner cities in the North and West in 1915 and after has led to increasing divergence between black and white vernaculars in the twentieth century, particularly since World War I.

This hypothesis was first presented in the mid-1980s by two Philadelphia-based researchers, William Labov and Wendell Harris, who began by noting that the black population in that city had become increasingly segregated between 1850 and 1970. The proportion of blacks in each census tract had, for instance, increased from 11 percent in 1850 to 35 percent in 1930, 56 percent in 1950, and 74 percent in 1970, and the number of census tracts with 75 percent or more blacks was growing in 1980. For those who believed that segregation had been decreasing since the 1960s because civil rights legislation had dismantled the legal barriers to integration, data like these were a shock; but they reflect white flight to the suburbs and the increasing presence within inner cities of blacks and other people of color. Labov and Harris argued that the increasing segregation of blacks and whites was accompanied by increasing divergence of black and white vernaculars, and they produced two kinds of evidence to support it.

The first kind was the development of new pronunciations among whites that were not spreading to blacks. For instance, whites had begun to produce the diphthong in words like *out* and *doubt* with the tongue farther front, beginning with the vowel of *day* rather than *bat*, and ending with the vowel of *ought*. However, blacks had not adopted this change, beginning their *out* diphthongs with the vowel of *father* and ending them with the vowel of *too*, as in most northern dialects. Independently, Guy Bailey and his students have produced similar evidence in Texas. Of seven ongoing sound changes in Texas, blacks and whites use about the same proportions of the innovative pronunciation for three of them, but the whites are clearly in the lead for the remaining four changes. The difference between the two groups of changes, however, is that those in which blacks and whites appear to be equally involved (such as the pronunciation of *Tuesday* as "*toos*-day" rather than "*tyews*-day") are older changes, which began early in the twentieth century. By contrast, the changes in which blacks are less involved (the pronunciation of the vowel in *night* as long [aa] rather than [ai]) are newer changes, which began to spread rapidly only after World War II. This, together with evidence from other grammatical features, suggests that World War II was a watershed for black-white linguistic divergence.

The second kind of evidence that Labov and Harris pointed to was grammatical usage within the black community. Blacks who had the least contact with whites and were most involved with other blacks in the culture and values of the street used third-person singular present-tense *s* ("he *walks*") and possessive *'s* ("*John's* hat") least frequently, less than 25 percent of the time, and sometimes not at all. Blacks who had the most contact with whites (for instance, musicians) and/or were relatively isolated from street culture, had much higher frequencies of these Standard English features, using them between 60 and 100 percent of the time. Moreover, the black inner-city core group seemed to be using verbal *s* not to mark the third-singular present tense, but to mark the narrative past, and they would frequently put an *s* on the end of the first verb joined by *and* but not the second

("This white guy *runs* behind me an' *bend* down"). However, these findings about the use of *s* as a marker of narrative past were not replicated in the Texas studies (and have not been elsewhere as yet). And although the correlations between contact patterns and vernacular usage that Labov and Harris found seem valid enough, it isn't clear that they represent change from any previous situation, as "divergence" would require.

Bailey and his associates have, however, pointed to other changes in grammatical usage within the black community that have been confirmed from other communities and that qualify better as (mid-) twentieth-century developments. One is a sharp increase in the frequency of invariant durative or habitual *be* over the past fifty years, especially in urban areas, and especially before [verb]*ing* (as in "He *be* dancing"), making it almost the exclusive marker of extended duration or habituality in this linguistic environment. (But contrary to a widespread misconception that *be* was invented from scratch by the youngest generation, note that the adults in this study used *be*, too, and almost always with habitual or extended durative meaning. Urban youth eleven to fifteen years old used invariant *be* 135 times, or 10 percent of the time in the present tense, *am, is, are,* and zero representing the other options. For adults twenty-five to forty-five years old and fifty to one hundred years old, the proportional use of invariant *be* was lower—6 and 2 percent, respectively, of all present-tense copula forms—but this still amounted to a sizable number of *be* tokens, 64 and 72 in each case, respectively.) Another feature that shows twentieth-century change is the use of *had [verb]ed* to mark a simple past rather than a pluperfect, or past-before-the-past (*He had walked* for "He walked"). In Texas, this usage appears to have begun with speakers in the twenty-five-year-old group and to have accelerated among teenagers.

Although these features and others—including *fitna* or *finna* increasingly used as an immediate future—show that Spoken Soul is innovating, like all living speech varieties, its changes are not all away from Standard English and white vernaculars. For instance, the frequency with which black speakers delete the initial unstressed syllables of words like "afraid" (*'fraid*) and "electric" (*'lectric*) in Georgetown County, South Carolina, steadily drops by age group—from 85 percent among sixty- to ninety-two-year-olds, to 70 percent among forty- to fifty-nine-year-olds, to 52 percent among eight- to twenty-year-olds. And in East Palo Alto, California, lax pronunciations of the final vowel in *fifty* and the absence of past-tense marking ("He *go* there yesterday") are both less common among younger age groups; this represents convergence with white norms. In short, while the twentieth century has witnessed the divergence of Spoken Soul from white vernaculars and Standard English in some respects, it has witnessed its convergence with these varieties in other respects.

Author Claude Brown, who coined the term "Spoken Soul" for black talk, praised its "pronounced lyrical quality." (*AP/Wide World Photos*)

Writer James Baldwin described Black English as "this passion, this skill, this incredible music" in a 1979 article. (*Photograph © by Jill Krementz. Courtesy of the photographer.*)

Author Toni Morrison: "The worst of all possible things would be to lose that language [Black English]. I know the standard English. I want to use it to help restore the other language, the lingua franca." (*Photograph © by Jill Krementz. Courtesy of the photographer.*)

The Rev. Jesse Jackson at first called the Ebonics resolution "an unacceptable surrender, borderlining on disgrace." A week later he reversed his position, urging Oakland school board officials to revise the resolution because "your message is not getting through." (*Chuck Painter, Stanford News Service*)

Poet Maya Angelou was "incensed" by the Oakland school board's resolution, but has used Black English in her poems—e.g., "The Thirteens (Black)" and "The Pusher." (*Photograph © by Jill Krementz. Courtesy of the photographer.*)

Paul Laurence Dunbar, renowned for his black dialect poetry, was frustrated that his poems in mainstream English were ignored. (*Schomburg Center for Research in Black Culture*)

James Weldon Johnson, who wrote the Black National Anthem, alternately praised and critiqued the use of black dialect in literature. (*Schomburg Center for Research in Black Culture*)

Zora Neale Hurston used Black English copiously in her novels and critiqued its inaccurate representation in minstrel performances. (*Schomburg Center for Research in Black Culture*)

Alice Walker's *The Color Purple* is the best-known black novel written entirely in Black English. (*Photograph © by Jill Krementz. Courtesy of the photographer.*)

Playwright August Wilson's dialog draws extensively on black talk. As he notes, "Art is within the language of the people." (*Linda Cicero, Stanford News Service*)

Comedian Redd Foxx included a chapter on "Black Language" in *The Redd Foxx Encyclopedia of Black Humor.* In his words, "the black comedian of today uses the language of the streets." (*Schomburg Center for Research in Black Culture*)

Like many black preachers, the Rev. Jeremiah A. Wright Jr. incorporates Black English for dramatic effect, especially in the sermonic climax. (*Erv Cupil, Trinity United Church of Christ, Chicago*)

Oakland school board member Toni Cook, at the center of the 1996 Ebonics firestorm, now manages the African American Literacy and Culture Project. (*John R. Rickford*)

Linguist William Labov, who has been studying Black English since the 1960s, testified before the U.S. Senate's Ebonics panel in 1997. (*John R. Rickford*)

Psychologist Gary Simpkins, coauthor of the *Bridge* readers, which produced big reading gains but were withdrawn because they incorporated Black English. (*John R. Rickford*)

Educator Kelli Harris-Wright, whose bidialectal program for nonstandard dialect speakers in Georgia has produced "improved verbal test scores at every school." (*John R. Rickford*)

A teacher and students in the Academic English Mastery Program for Speakers of Nonstandard Language Forms in Los Angeles. The program is directed by Noma LeMoine, author of *English for Your Success: A Handbook of Successful Strategies for Educators.* (*John R. Rickford*)

Chattanooga Times, cartoon by Bill Plante, December 20, 1996.

San Jose Mercury News, cartoon by Scott Willis, December 22, 1996.

A Beavis and Butt-head Ebonics cartoon by Mike Luckovich that appeared in the *Atlanta Constitution* and other papers early in 1997.

Jeff Danziger's Ebonics *Hamlet* cartoon, which appeared in the *Christian Science Monitor* on January 2, 1997.

Part Four

The Ebonics Firestorm

9

Education

Your message is not getting through. The language and the message must get synchronized.

—The Reverend Jesse Jackson (1996)

Without familiarity with student's traditions, how will teachers see them clearly? How will they recognize their strengths and envision their potential?

—Terry Meier (1998)

On December 18, 1996, the Oakland Unified School District approved its Ebonics resolution and ignited a firestorm. But the measure was only one response to a series of recommendations that the Task Force on the Education of African American Students, established earlier in the year at the request of school board member Toni Cook, had developed in response to evidence that African American students were doing poorly in Oakland schools—worse, in fact, than any other ethnic group. In a school district where more than half the student body and the board of education was black, the concern was well warranted.

It is important to remember—since this fact was obscured in subsequent debates about whether Ebonics (Spoken Soul) was a dialect or a language and whether it was or was not genetically based—that the concerns that led Oakland to establish a special task force and to pass its resolution were not linguistic, but educational. African American students, particularly the majority, who come from working-class and underclass backgrounds, have been failing in schools nationwide. Or rather, schools nationwide have been failing African American students.

Despite media suggestions to the contrary, Oakland schools were not alone in this respect. In 1992–1993, for instance, data from fifty large urban school districts across the country indicated that the reading achievement scores of black students were considerably below grade level. Only 31.3 percent of black elementary students scored above the national median, and only 26.6 percent of black high school students did so. (If these students were representative of American children nationwide, then 50 percent of them should have scored above the national median.) By contrast, 60.7 percent of white elementary students scored above the median, and 65.4 percent of white high school students did so. Data from the 1994 National Assessment of Educational Progress show the same depressing trend: on a 500-point scale, African American students at the age of nine are an average of 29 points behind the scores of their white counterparts; by age thirteen, they are 31 points behind; and by age seventeen, they are 37 points behind.

National findings like these are alarming, and Oakland was in no better shape. The district, concentrating on its own maladies, found more than enough to warrant concern and action. While African Americans constituted 53 percent of the nearly fifty-two thousand students in Oakland, they accounted for a disproportionate number of the youngsters who were facing crisis in the district. Fully 80 percent of suspended students and 67 percent of students classified as truant were black. African Americans constituted 71 percent of students enrolled in Special Education, but only 37 percent of those enrolled in Gifted and Talented Education classes. Nearly one-fifth (19 percent) of twelfth-grade African American students failed to graduate, and the mean grade point average of black students (1.80, or C−) was the lowest of all ethnic groups in the district.

The Task Force's initial recommendations.   In 1996, in an effort to remedy these and other problems, the Task Force came up with nine recommendations, including new criteria to identify, assess, and admit youngsters to Special Education and Gifted and Talented Education classes; improved parental and community involvement; increased funding; and stepped-up efforts to hire African American teachers and staff members. The primary recommendation, however, dealt with language:

> African American students shall develop English language proficiency as the foundation for their achievements in all core competency areas.

This alone would not have provoked objection from anybody. In fact, given the fuss people made about the importance of English in the wake of the Oakland resolution, it was clearly a standard upon which the whole country agreed. But the kindling for controversy lay in the preamble to the Task Force's report. In addressing the challenge of helping students make the transition "from their home language, Ebonics, to achieve greater proficiency in standard English," the Board was challenged "to take bold measures" to:

1. Recognize African American Language/Ebonics as the primary language of many African American students. Add African American Language/Ebonics to all district documents offering optional placement of students in classes or programs serving limited English proficient students.
2. Provide access to all services, current or planned, for limited English proficient students to Limited English African American Language/Ebonics students.

Word of these proposals began to leak to the press nearly three weeks before the school board had approved the resolution. On December 1, 1996, the *Sunday Times* of London ran the following report, hinting, in the editorializing frame within which the information was presented, and in the appended comment by Joan Rattary, at the maelstrom that was to follow:

Despite the move to return to traditional methods, "progressives" have still not given up the fight. In California last week, the Oakland School Board of Education argued that blacks who speak "black English" should qualify for federal bilingual education funds because they speak an authentic language other than English.

The African English is known as Ebonics and the speakers say, for example, "I been done walk" instead of "I have walked."

"I don't call it Ebonics, I call it incorrect English," said Joan Rattary, president of the Institute for Independent Education, a Washington think tank.

Then the December 18 vote was cast. Within days, the resolution had become *the* media story nationally, and while a few people praised the decision, many more were laughing, howling, complaining, and venting about Ebonics. In response to the confusion and criticism greeting the proposal, the school board hired a publicist to serve as go-between with the media, and issued a revised resolution on January 15, 1997. The amended document came on the heels of a series of back-and-forth communications between the Reverend Jesse Jackson, who had become the resolution's most quoted critic, and Oakland administrators, who were determined to set things straight with this powerful potential ally. The culmination of these communications was a couple of tense, closed-door meetings of school board and Task Force members with Jackson, local politicians and educators, and community activists at Oakland School District headquarters on December 30, 1996. While some insiders calmly explained the rationale for the Oakland resolution, one or two participants, stung by Jackson's earlier criticisms, demanded that he issue an apology. But the diplomatic minister deftly sidestepped these demands by listening quietly, talking passionately about the larger problems of education and criminal justice affecting black people, and saying, "Shall we bow our heads in prayer?" Jackson emerged from the huddles with a clearer picture of the Oakland plan, a conviction that the school district had the best interests of black students at heart, and a hope that a national showdown on Ebonics would bring attention to the crisis of black youth. In an auditorium brimming with reporters and cameramen, Jackson reversed his stance on Ebonics publicly, but not before he had delivered an unequivocal message to the Oakland educators: "Your message is not getting through. The language and the message must get synchronized."

In a final effort to clarify its objectives and shake the media loose, the board approved a revised set of Task Force recommendations in May 1997 that made no reference to "Ebonics." But the focus on the "development of a comprehensive English language development program for African American students" remained.

The Oakland school board's resolution.   We provide below the full text of the original resolution, including the January 1997 modifications, and follow this with a discussion of each of its key clauses.

> RESOLUTION (No. 9697-0063) OF THE BOARD OF EDUCATION ADOPTING THE REPORT AND RECOMMENDATIONS OF THE AFRICAN-AMERICAN TASK FORCE; A POLICY STATEMENT, AND DIRECTING THE SUPERINTENDENT OF SCHOOLS TO DEVISE A PROGRAM TO IMPROVE THE ENGLISH LANGUAGE ACQUISITION AND APPLICATION SKILLS OF AFRICAN-AMERICAN STUDENTS

> [Clause numbers have been added here; italicized words were present in the original resolution of December 18, 1996, but deleted in the amended

version of January 17, 1997; wording that was added at that time to re-place or supplement the original wording appears in bold, in brackets; otherwise, in the words of the secretary of the Board of Education, this "is a full, true and correct copy of a resolution passed at a Regular Meeting of the Board of Education of the Oakland Unified School District held December 18, 1996."]

1. WHEREAS, numerous validated scholarly studies demonstrate that African-American students as a part of their culture and history as African people possess and utilize a language described in various scholarly approaches as "Ebonics" (literally "black sounds") or "Pan-African Communication Behaviors" or "African Language Systems"; and

2. WHEREAS, these studies have also demonstrated that African Language Systems *are genetically based* [have origins in West and Niger-Congo languages] and *not a dialect of English* [are not merely dialects of English]; and

3. WHEREAS, these studies demonstrate that such West and Niger-Congo African languages have been officially recognized and addressed in the mainstream public educational community as worthy of study, understanding *or* [and] application of their principles, laws and structures for the benefit of African-American students both in terms of positive appreciation of the language and these students' acquisition and mastery of English language skills; and

4. WHEREAS, such recognition by scholars has given rise over the past fifteen years to legislation passed by the State of California recognizing the unique language stature of descendants of slaves, with such legislation being prejudicially and unconstitutionally vetoed repeatedly by various California state governors; and

5. WHEREAS, judicial cases in states other than California have recognized the unique language stature of African-American pupils, and such recognition by courts has resulted in court-mandated educational programs which have substantially benefited African-American children in the interest of vindicating their equal protection of the law rights under the Fourteenth Amendment to the United States Constitution; and

6. WHEREAS, the Federal Bilingual Education Act (20 U.S.C. 1402 *et seq.*) mandates that local educational agencies "build their capacities to establish, implement and sustain programs of instruction for children and youth of limited English proficiency"; and

7. WHEREAS, the interests of the Oakland Unified School District in providing equal opportunities for all of its students dictate limited English proficient educational programs recognizing the English language ac-

quisition and improvement skills of African-American students are as fundamental as is application of bilingual education **[or second language learner]** principles for others whose primary languages are other than English **[Primary languages are the language patterns children bring to school]; and**

8. WHEREAS, the standardized tests and grade scores of African-American students in reading and language arts skills measuring their application of English skills are substantially below state and national norms and that such deficiencies will be remedied by application of a program featuring African Language Systems principles *in instructing African-American children both in their primary language and in English* **[to move students from the language patterns they bring to school to English proficiency]; and**

9. WHEREAS, standardized tests and grade scores will be remedied by application of a program that teachers and *aides* **[instructional assistants],** who are certified in the methodology of featuring African Language Systems principles *in instructing African-American children both in their primary language and in English* **[used to transition students from the language patterns they bring to school to English].** The certified teachers of these students will be provided incentives including, but not limited to salary differentials;

10. NOW, THEREFORE, BE IT RESOLVED that the Board of Education officially recognizes the existence and the cultural and historic bases of West and Niger-Congo African Language Systems, and each language as the predominantly primary language of **[many]** African-American students; and

11. BE IT FURTHER RESOLVED that the Board of Education hereby adopts the report, recommendations and attached Policy Statement of the District's African-American Task Force on language stature of African-American speech; and

12. BE IT FURTHER RESOLVED that the Superintendent in conjunction with her staff shall immediately devise and implement the best possible academic program *for imparting instruction to African-American students in their primary language* for the combined purposes of *maintaining the legitimacy and richness of such language* **[facilitating the acquisition and mastery of English language skills, while respecting and embracing the legitimacy and richness of the language patterns]** whether *it is* **[they are]** known as "Ebonics," "African Language Systems," "Pan African Communication Behaviors" or other description, *and to facilitate their acquisition and mastery of English language skills;* and

13. BE IT FURTHER RESOLVED that the Board of Education hereby commits to earmark District general and special funding as is reasonably neces-

sary and appropriate to enable the Superintendent and her staff to accomplish the foregoing; and

14. BE IT FURTHER RESOLVED that the Superintendent and her staff shall utilize the input of the entire Oakland educational community as well as state and federal scholarly and educational input in devising such a program; and

15. BE IT FURTHER RESOLVED that periodic reports on the progress of the creation and implementation of such an education program shall be made to the Board of Education at least once per month commencing at the Board meeting of December 18, 1996.

The first notable aspect of the resolution is its uppercase title, which, even in the original version, proclaimed as its mission "to improve the English language acquisition and application skills of African-American students." Nowhere does the board state that its wish is to replace English with Ebonics, or to give up on English, as feared by commentators, many of whom apparently did not read the resolution itself. The resolution's wording clearly indicates (as does the primary Task Force recommendation—see page 164) that the board was concerned about enhancing students' English. The dispute lay in *how* this goal was to be achieved, although many people misunderstood that it was the merits of Standard English at issue.

Clause 1 is less noteworthy for what it includes than for what it excludes. The list of alternative terms for the African American vernacular omits "Black English (Vernacular)" and its successor "African American Vernacular English," the labels that have been most common in scholarly studies by linguists over the past quarter-century. "Black English (Vernacular)," and its predecessor, "Negro Non-Standard," were coined by white linguists including J. L. Dillard, Ralph Fasold, William Labov, William Stewart, and Walt Wolfram, who pioneered the serious study of the African American vernacular in the 1960s. ("Black English" and "African American Vernacular English" continue to be used by the vast majority of linguists, white and black, who entered the field between the 1970s and 1990s.) But these terms were considered derogatory and insufficiently suggestive of African origins by Afrocentric scholars such as psychologist Robert L. Williams and social studies professor Robert Twiggs, who created alternatives in the 1970s.

Twiggs came up with "Pan African Language in the Western Hemisphere" in 1973. This never really caught on, yet it resurfaced in the

Oakland resolution as "Pan African Communication Behaviors." Williams and other African American scholars attending a conference on cognitive and language development of the black child in 1973 coined "Ebonics" (from *ebony* and *phonics*—"black sounds") to avoid the "white bias" and inaccuracy they saw in older terms like "nonstandard English" and "broken English," and "to define black language from a black perspective." But the term "Ebonics" never gained much momentum, either. In fact, Oakland's 1996 resolution gave it more recognition and mileage in twenty-four hours than it had enjoyed in the preceding twenty-three years.

Ernie Smith, professor of medicine, ethnology, and gerontology at Charles R. Drew University of Medicine and Science in Los Angeles, was the scholar who most influenced the wording and philosophy of the Oakland resolution. Smith, who was present at the 1973 meeting where *ebony* and *phonics* were fused, had in the intervening years become the staunchest advocate of the idea that Ebonics was a separate, Niger-Congo–based language rather than a dialect of English. Nabeehah Shakir, a key player in the framing of the Oakland resolution, and a supporter of Smith's ideas, distributed at the height of the controversy a copy of Smith's 1995 paper "Bilingualism and the African American Child." In it Smith insists that

> Afro-American and Euro-American speech emanate from a separate linguistic base. . . . African Americans have, in fact, retained a West and Niger-Congo African thought process. It is this thought process that is dominant in the substratum phonology and morphosyntax of African American speech but stigmatized as being Black English. According to the Africanists the native language of African Americans is Ebonics— the linguistic continuation of Africa in black America. . . . The Africanists posit that Ebonics is not genetically related to English. Therefore the term Ebonics is not a mere synonym for the more commonly used Black English. . . . In fact, they argue that the term Black English is an oxymoron.

Not only does this passage explain the exclusion of "Black English" from the resolution's first clause, but it also clarifies the source and meaning of the resolution's second clause. The initial wording of clause 2, however, ran into a buzz saw of criticism from people who thought that genetics in the biological sense, with all its racist historical baggage, was intended. What Smith meant—and this is quite clear from his 1995 article—was that Ebonics was genetically related to West African languages in the sense that linguists use the word to denote descent from a common origin. But the original phrasing that the resolution's framers chose ("are genetically based") was unusual even in linguistics, and was wide open to misinterpretation. Not surprisingly, this clause was one of the first to be deleted from the January 1997 amendment, although the amended version ("have origins in West and Niger-Congo languages and are not merely dialects of English") betrayed the influence of Smith's article even more overtly. For instance, the "West and Niger-Congo" collocation—a unique mixture of geographical ("West") and language classification ("Niger-Congo") labels—occurs in both. As Caribbean linguist and Afrocentrist Hubert Devonish has noted, highlighting the novel nature of the collocation, "We must presume that what is intended by the phrase 'West and Niger-Congo languages' is the Niger-Congo languages of West Africa."

Clauses 3 and 4 refer, in part, to the Standard English Proficiency program for African American Students (SEP), first approved for use in California in 1981. And the "judicial cases" referred to in clause 5 undoubtedly include the 1979 ruling by Justice Charles Joiner that the Ann Arbor, Michigan, school district had failed to take the "Black English" of students at Martin Luther King Jr. Elementary School into account. (See chapter 10.) Neither the SEP program nor the Joiner decision had hinged on the strongly Afrocentric view that Smith and the Oakland resolution writers were promoting, however. In fact, several linguists, black and white, many of whom were either neutral or negative on the African origins issue, had played key roles in developing the SEP program and winning the Ann Arbor case. In both instances, they had argued that African American speech was distinctive and systematic enough to merit special consideration in schools.

Clauses 6 and 7 make the first link between the language of African American children and federal bilingual education and limited-English-proficiency programs, for which African Americans are not normally eligible. But this connection had already been drawn in Smith's 1995 paper, where he argued that African American children should be treated like "Asian American, White, Hispanic American, Native American, Middle Eastern, and East European children whose limited and non-English proficiencies are acknowledged as being a function of interference from their primary languages." There he urged also that the "discriminatory denial of English as a Second Language (ESL) and Bilingual Education programs for African American children" should be brought to an end. Although they insisted that this was never their intent, Oakland School District officials earned plenty of criticism for the apparent attempt to go after bilingual-education dollars for speakers of what most people considered at best a dialect of English. In February 1997, California assemblywoman Diane Martinez successfully introduced Assembly Bill 1206 to block efforts of this kind. California voters rendered the issue moot by approving Proposition 227 in June 1998, outlawing bilingual education for everyone except as a temporary measure when parents individually requested it.

The original versions of clauses 8, 9, and 12 wound up in the eye of the Ebonics storm because in them lay the suggestion that African American children would be instructed not only in English, but also "in their primary language," namely Ebonics. Many observers took this to mean that teachers would now be expected to teach *in* Ebonics, and to teach Ebonics itself, helping students therefore to master "I be goin', you be goin', he/she/it be goin'," and so on. To clarify matters, the school district issued a supplementary statement in December 1996 emphasizing that:

1. The Oakland Unified School District is not replacing the teaching of Standard American English with any other language.
2. The District is not teaching Ebonics.
3. The District emphasizes teaching Standard American English and has set a high standard of excellence for all its students.

In its January 1997 amendment, the school district tried to erase all doubt on this score by excising the phrases about instruction in the primary language and stressing movement or transition from Ebonics to English proficiency. While we do not believe that the school district intended to teach its students Ebonics, or teach them *in* Ebonics, it should be noted that in helping students switch from the language of Jump Street to the language of Wall Street, teachers must be familiar with the former in order to help children compare and contrast it with the latter—a point we elaborate in the final section of this chapter. In this sense, students would indeed be taught *about* their primary language. But that is a far cry from being taught the vernacular itself. Since many of the students who would benefit from the compare-and-contrast method, known as contrastive analysis, are already fluent vernacular speakers, tutoring them on Ebonics would be like giving a veteran angler a lesson on baiting hooks.

The minor amendment that clause 10 underwent is noteworthy. The word "many" was inserted before "African American students" to counter the insinuation of the original wording that all black students speak Ebonics or African Language Systems as their mother tongue.

Two more comments might be made about the resolution before we briefly consider the May 1997 recommendations. The first is that in the midst of the linguistic and political discussions sparked about whether Ebonics was an English dialect or a separate language, whether it had African roots, whether Oakland was just pursuing bilingual-education funds, and whether it planned to teach in Ebonics, the central educational problems that led to the creation of the Task Force and to the framing of the resolution in the first place (rehashed in clause 8) were lost. And with them was lost a rare opportunity to discuss the devastating malaise of many African American students.

What's more, the resolution's framers did not include or cite any experimental data showing that taking the vernacular into account when teaching Standard English had worked elsewhere. There are several studies from Europe and the United States that support the soundness of Oakland's general approach (we summarize these at the end of this chapter). Failure to cite these experiments—perhaps because the resolution's framers did not know they existed—led California state schools superintendent Delaine Eastin to complain immediately after the resolution was approved that "we are not aware of any research which indicates that this kind of program will help address the language and achievement problems of African American students." Her sentiments were echoed by other educators and policy-makers, and potential solutions to the educational predicament faced by African American children everywhere were largely ignored in the media's six-month frenzy.

The Task Force's revised recommendations of May 1997. The Ebonics furor fizzled, then died, in the spring of 1997, when the school district released to the media the revised recommendations of its Task Force on the Education of African American Students. In her accompanying statement, Superintendent Carolyn Getridge explained that after the media attention elicited by the December 1996 resolution,

> it became increasingly clear that if the nation, and particularly the Oakland community, was to completely understand the driving factors for the resolution and the recommendations, the Task Force needed to pave the way toward a more accurate and meaningful dialogue.

To this end, the Task Force had assembled for four weeks in February and March 1997, intent on revising recommendations and drafting a detailed plan for setting them into action. Getridge herself had then spent a month poring over and modifying the committee's wording before submitting the amended proposal to the school board and putting it in the hands of the press.

In the revised recommendations, the word "Ebonics" had vanished, apparently stripped from the report by Getridge. The omission seemed to surprise Task Force chairman Sylvester Hodges, who told the *Oakland Tribune:* "I felt sure we had that [word there]." But he conceded that "we did not want to focus on the word," which would have likely meant more searing media scrutiny.

Also missing from the seventeen-page recommendation was any suggestion that bilingual education funds be funneled into the district to help African American students improve their English. Instead, the board itself proposed to spend nearly $2 million over the next five years to implement the Task Force's eight main recommendations (which, again, encompassed a broad set of strategies, including reinforcing career training programs for youngsters).

Yet the spirit of the original Ebonics proposal was unbroken. The first recommendation of the finalized report remained the "development of a comprehensive language development program for African American students" with an emphasis on "the need for . . . children to learn Standard English in the schools." The touched-up proposal stressed a "phonics" approach to reading and urged the use of Afrocentric and culturally relevant literature, but it also continued to emphasize respect for home languages, and to suggest that comparisons be made between a student's mother tongue and mainstream English. In fact, the Standard English Proficiency program, previously offered in only a few Oakland schools, was now to be incorporated in all pre-kindergarten to third-grade classrooms where African Americans constituted 53 percent or more of the student body. The SEP strategies were also to be expanded to sixth- through ninth-grade students as the first phase of a broader approach.

After praising these May 1997 recommendations, the media finally left the Oakland School District alone and allowed the African American vernacular to retreat from the spotlight, at least for the time being.

In a subsequent development completely unnoticed by the press, Congress in late 1997 approved a $1 million grant allowing Oakland to continue exploring techniques for tapping the linguistic and cultural resources of black students in order to enhance their school performance. Toni Cook, a former school board member and an administrator centrally involved in the Ebonics controversy, is project manager. Educator Etta Hollins, author and editor of several well-known texts on race, ethnic identity, and culturally responsive teaching, is research director of the cultural component of the research program, based in Oakland. University of Pennsylvania linguist William Labov is the research director of the grant's linguistic component. Labov had testified before U.S. Senate subcommittee hearings on Ebonics chaired by Senator Arlen Specter (Republican, Pennsylvania) in January 1997; Specter's subcommittee (Labor, Health and Human Services, and Education) sponsored the line item in the budget, and Labov worked in Specter's home state. Labov works mostly with children in Philadelphia, but he collaborates with the Oakland School District and with California linguists in analysis of the decoding errors made by black students in reading (e.g., reading *bite* as *bit*), and in development of new texts and exercises to help them improve.

At various times during the Ebonics controversy, a line was drawn by some between linguists in the Afrocentric camp (who attribute Ebonics' origins almost entirely to Africa) and those who were either skeptical or neutral on this matter. This is an intellectual issue on which research and debate should continue, with, one hopes, more substance and less acrimony than we have seen in the past. But the Ebonics controversy confirmed that linguists—whether or not they describe themselves as "Afrocentric"—are generally united in their respect for the legitimacy and complexity of the language spoken by many African American children. This perspective clashed with the more widely held public opinion that Ebonics was simply slang and gutter talk, or the product of laziness and carelessness.

Most linguists supported the educational philosophy behind Oakland and Los Angeles school district attempts to teach children mainstream English by constrasting it with their home language. The roughly six-thousand-member Linguistic Society of America in January 1997 issued an endorsement of Oakland's strategy as "linguistically and pedagogically sound." Other language organizations, among them the American Association for Applied Linguistics and Teachers of English to Speakers of Other Languages, subsequently adopted similar resolutions. And although differences and tensions remained between advocates of Afrocentric and cultural approaches and advocates of English oriented and linguistic approaches, enough of a consensus was struck on the overarching educational dilemma of teaching

English to black inner-city students that the two intellectual camps
could cooperate to seek a cure. And they began to do so—away from
the public eye.

The ultimate value of the approach Oakland announced to the
world in December 1996 remains to be seen. We are hopeful. Far too
many black children in that California school district, and in compa-
rable urban districts nationwide, are not making the grade when it
comes to reading, writing, and the language arts—areas that are critical for success in school and the workplace.

**Research on taking the vernacular into account in teaching Standard
English and reading.**   As we have seen above, the Oakland school
board never intended to replace the teaching of Standard, or mainstream, English with the teaching of Ebonics, or Spoken Soul. But it
did intend to take the vernacular into account in helping students
achieve mastery of Standard English (reading and writing in this variety in particular). And while the board perhaps erred in not citing
studies to support its position, such evidence does exist.

One of the earliest studies was done in the Oakland School District itself, in the early 1970s. The researcher, Ann McCormick
Piestrup, studied two hundred Oakland first-graders, most of them
black, and the ways in which different styles seemed to correlate with
their success in school. Of the several styles she investigated, two were
especially significant. Students who were taught with the "Interrupting Approach"—by teachers who constantly interrupted and cor-
rected them when they read or spoke in Spoken Soul—withdrew
from participation, became hostile to the classroom enterprise, and
posted some of the lowest reading scores. By contrast, students taught
with the "Black Artful Approach"—by teachers who used rhythmic
play and exposed children to Standard English distinctions, but who
did not constantly interrupt or correct their Spoken Soul—participated enthusiastically in the classroom, and recorded higher scores
on reading tests. This study confirms what we know from other studies: that negative and uninformed attitudes toward children's vernacular can be counterproductive, and even harm performance.

Programs such as California's Standard English Proficiency (SEP),
started in the early 1980s and now in use in more than three hundred schools statewide, attempt to do more than improve teachers'
unfavorable attitudes toward Spoken Soul and discourage them from

constantly interrupting and correcting dialect speakers. The basic strategy is contrastive analysis, which involves specifically drawing students' attention to differences between their vernacular and the mainstream or standard language, and helping them develop competence in the latter through a variety of drills and other exercises. In a recent book, Henry Parker and Marilyn Crist extol the virtues of contrastive analysis, noting that they have used the approach successfully to teach "corporate language" to vernacular speakers in Tennessee and Chicago at the preschool, elementary, high school, and college levels.

California's SEP program has a fat handbook of several hundred pages designed to help teachers help their students switch between Spoken Soul and Standard English. The Los Angeles and Oakland school districts don't use the handbook directly, but they do follow the principles of contrastive analysis, asking children to switch between "African Language," or "Nonstandard Language," and "Standard English," or "Academic English," in their classroom exercises.

Unfortunately, the SEP's success has never been closely monitored, via control and experimental groups, so we have no hard evidence of its success. We have, however, seen and read about teachers, ostensibly doing SEP, who ask students to "correct" sentences like "Us wented to the store," which are artificially and exaggeratedly nonstandard, including features (*us* as subject; *wented* as verb) that virtually never occur in real speech. The value of such exercises is questionable, although in fairness to the program, the handbook's exercises are much better.

Much better documented is the ten-year-old program in DeKalb County, Georgia, in which fifth- and sixth-grade students in eight schools are taught to switch from "home speech" to "school speech," using contrastive analysis. As newspaper columnist Doug Cummings noted:

> The program has won a "center of excellence" designation from the National Council for Teachers of English. Last year, students who had taken the course had improved verbal test scores at every school.

The program director, Kelli Harris-Wright, has recently presented results showing that between 1994 and 1997, students in the bidialectal contrastive analysis program showed bigger improvements in their reading scores (as measured by the Iowa Test of Basic Skills) than students in the control group, who were taught by conventional methods. In fact, in the 1994–1995 and 1996–1997 school years, students in the control group scored worse at the end of the school year than they had at the beginning (in a pattern sadly reminiscent of many black students' school performance elsewhere), while the scores of students in the experimental contrastive analysis group steadily improved.

More concrete evidence of the success of contrastive analysis with speakers of Ebonics comes from research on writing done by Hanni Taylor in the late 1980s. She reported that a group of inner-city Aurora University students from Chicago who were taught with contrastive analysis techniques showed a 59 percent reduction in the use of Ebonics features in their Standard English writing, while students taught by traditional methods showed an 8.5 percent increase in the use of such features. In short, the goal of developing proficiency in Standard English, an important one for most of the people who criticized Oakland's resolutions, was better achieved by explicitly contrasting it with Ebonics than by ignoring or degrading the latter, as critics seem to favor doing.

Although it is not what Oakland proposed, we should mention that another approach that takes the vernacular into account—teaching students to read first in their native dialect and then switching to the standard language—has some notable successes to its credit. One of the earliest dialect-reader studies was done by Tore Österberg in Sweden in the early 1960s. One group of dialect speakers was first taught to read in the vernacular, and then taught in standard Swedish, while another group was taught entirely in standard Swedish. After thirty-five weeks, the vernacular-to-standard method showed itself superior in both reading speed and comprehension.

A similar study, reported by Tove Bull, was conducted in Norway in 1990. Ten classes of Norwegian first-graders were taught to read and write either in their Norwegian vernaculars and then in standard Norwegian, or entirely in standard Norwegian. Bull's findings were similar to Österberg's: "The vernacular children read significantly faster and better . . . particularly the less bright children."

The most similar experiment in the United States involved the Bridge readers, coauthored by Gary Simpkins, Grace Holt, and Charlesetta Simpkins in 1977. These provided reading materials in black vernacular, a transitional variety, and Standard English. The 417 students across the United States taught with Bridge showed an average reading gain of 6.2 months over four months of instruction, while the 123 taught by regular methods gained only 1.6 months—showing the same below-par "progress" that leads many Spoken Soul and other dialect speakers to fall further and further behind. Despite their dramatic success, the Bridge readers were discontinued because of hostile, uninformed reactions to the recognition of the vernacular in the classroom. William Stewart and Joan Baratz's promising attempts to introduce dialect readers in a school in Washington, D.C., in 1969 were similarly squelched.

John McWhorter, a critic of contrastive analysis, has recently highlighted a number of studies done in the 1970s that suggest that children tested with Standard English materials performed essentially the same as those tested with Black English materials. However, those studies involve one-time tests and do not systematically help children bridge the gap between the vernacular and the standard over a period of time, as the successful experiments by Harris-Wright, Taylor, and Simpkins, Holt, and Simpkins all do. Moreover, while we agree with McWhorter that more positive attitudes toward the vernacular and Afrocentric curricula could help reverse black students' devastating school failure (they should be a feature of *all* programs), we are skeptical about his suggestion that "immersion" in Standard English—by itself—could significantly improve their ability to read and write fluently in this variety. "Immersion" is what black students already receive in the thousands of schools nationwide that teach entirely in Standard English and ignore Spoken Soul. Yet they show steadily declining scores on language arts tests. With only a few exceptions, Standard English is what black students are exposed to in the media. The evidence is that this passive exposure makes very little difference to their productive control of Standard English. Many have difficulty distinguishing their native vernacular (Spoken Soul) from Standard English when attempting to use the latter. We need more explicit measures to help them bridge that gap.

We are aware that the schools in which speakers of Spoken Soul are concentrated often suffer from larger systemic problems—including limited funding, poor facilities, and undertrained teachers—and that these contribute significantly to the devastating failure rates of black children nationwide. In the face of these looming problems, the relevance of Spoken Soul might seem minimal. But success in reading and writing, especially in Standard English, is central to school success, and the evidence is compelling that black students can be led to success by methods that build on their already developed competence in the vernacular. Although contrastive analysis and dialect readers are not the only viable approaches to teaching the standard, these innovative methods do work. School districts like Oakland that experiment with them to reverse the devastating failures of their dialect speakers should not be hamstrung by carping and criticism from the uninformed.

10

The Media

Language prejudice remains a "legitimate" prejudice; that is, one can generally say the most appalling things about people's speech without fear of correction or contradiction. . . . Let a Fuzzy Zoeller deal with Tiger Woods in an overtly racist manner and he must immediately apologize, drop out of a major golf tournament, and lose his Kmart endorsements. This is not the case for anyone reviling African Americans in general for their language.

—Wayne O'Neil (1997)

In trying to understand the reactions to the Oakland resolution, what was not said—the conversations that did not occur, the topics left unexplored, the voices not heard—is as important as what was said.

—Theresa Perry (1998)

The Oakland Ebonics controversy broke a week before Christmas 1996, amid the slow news season journalists generally spend playing solitaire and praying for a bank heist or a collapsed bridge on their beats. So when Ebonics arrived like an exotic holiday traveler, the media went berserk. Radio talk shows chattered, news wires buzzed, television sets hummed, and magazines and newspapers from coast to coast churned out article after article chronicling, analyzing, and in many cases misinterpreting or maligning the Oakland initiative. The morning after the December 18 resolution was adopted, The *San Francisco Chronicle* announced:

> The Oakland school board approved a landmark policy last night that recognizes Ebonics, or Black English, as a primary language of its African American students, making it the first school district in the United States with such a systemwide approach.

181

Weeks earlier, the UPI news service had reported that Oakland was considering the measure. On December 20, the *New York Times* and the *Washington Post* published their first articles, etching the story into public record. Over the next two weeks, the *Times* ran six more stories on Ebonics, along with a column, an editorial, a few op-ed pieces, and three letters to the editor. Four days after the school board vote, the Reuters wire service had printed more than fourteen hundred words on the topic. If Ebonics was a pop-in guest, it showed no signs of wearing out its welcome.

In fact, by the first week of 1997, Oakland's "landmark policy" had spawned more than twenty-five hundred articles, editorials, columns, and letters in daily U.S. newspapers from Seattle to New Orleans to Boston, to say nothing of the avalanche of coverage on television and in journals, magazines, and newsletters. The fever would run through much of the winter, with Ebonics stories splashed on page one and delivered at the top of the evening news.

The nation had never witnessed such intense and widespread scrutiny of the vernacular. But Black English as a novel (if not white-hot) story was far from new. The media had for years "known the four-one-one" on inner-city dialect—had been aware, that is, that attitudes toward the tongue could be a complicating matter (educationally, socially, and otherwise) for those who relied on it for communication. In 1987, for instance, no less an agenda-setter than Oprah Winfrey hosted a discussion of Standard and Black English on her daytime television show. (Though mostly unfavorable toward the vernacular, the aired comments of Oprah, her guests, and her audience included some strong positives and were more balanced than those prompted by the Ebonics conflagration a decade later.) In 1994, the *New York Times* published a long feature, "Lingering Conflict in the Schools: Black Dialect vs. Standard Speech," which attributed the persistence of Black English to:

> the growing resistance of some black young people to assimilate and their efforts to use language [for] cultural distinction. It also stems from the increasing isolation of black inner-city residents from both whites and middle-class blacks, and . . . from a deep cynicism about the payoffs of conforming.

And the following year, producers of the respected program *60 Minutes* dedicated a segment of one of the television newsmagazine's shows to African American vernacular, with Morley Safer beaming as black adolescents taught him the latest slang and discussed the question of learning Standard English.

Americans who weren't hip to the complexities of Black English, or who had known the variety only as "jive," were probably as intrigued as they were puzzled by these mainstream reports, and by dozens of less notable dispatches on Spoken Soul. But to judge from the many incredulous reactions to the Oakland affair, what some members of the public must have forgotten by 1996 (and others may never even have realized) is that *every decade in the latter half of this century has contained at least one Ebonics flare-up*. One author even theorized that the mass media's relationship with Black English over the past two centuries has followed major twenty-five-to-forty-year cycles and lesser ten-to-twenty-year "intercycles," during which lapses in interest have been broken at fairly regular intervals by periods of intense attention. We won't go back two hundred years, but consider the last thirty:

- In 1985, University of Pennsylvania linguist William Labov prompted some hand-wringing when he warned that Black English and Standard English were diverging—drifting steadily apart as they evolved.

- In 1979, ruling on a lawsuit filed on behalf of eleven black children, a federal judge drew the most intense media coverage of Black English up to that point when he ordered the Ann Arbor, Michigan, school district to educate teachers about Black English in order to allay their negative attitudes toward the dialect.

- In 1977, a trial program involving Bridge readers, a series of short stories written with diminishing doses of dialect and designed to help inner-city children "decode" Standard English more efficiently, vexed community leaders, even as researchers reported striking successes with the readers.

- In 1969, in Philadelphia, the book *Teaching Black Children to Read* sparked a number of misunderstandings, and much defamation of the dialect.

In each case, educators, researchers, and the public jumped into a dispute prompted by a new suggestion that acknowledging and understanding black vernacular might empower inner-city schools to help children take that first stumble, then stride down the path to boardroom English. And in each case, the dispute sent reporters and critics running for their keyboards.

In the May 5, 1985, *Philadelphia Inquirer Magazine,* Neal Peirce, a founder of the *National Journal,* took on Labov's divergence theory:

> But blacks, Labov says, don't share in the evolving local white dialects. Instead, the black vernacular—black English—lives in its own world. The language gap, he warns, is just another reflection of "increasing residential segregation, fewer jobs, fewer contacts between the races." Many young blacks, he says, begin school without ever having conversed before with a white person.

Peirce acknowledged that Black English was the "legitimate and chosen language form of millions of Americans." But he insisted that poverty (rather than race) was to blame for linguistic isolation:

> No one disagrees that young people deprived of learning standard English face bleak, often jobless futures. If you can't speak the language, it's impossibly hard to get ahead except, perhaps, in underclass peer groups. Yet for all the public schools' failings, they do teach standard English. With television blaring away in people's houses "24-seven," who's to say that black America—and for that matter Hispanic or Asian America—doesn't get plenty of exposure to standard English?

Eight years earlier, the remedial reading strategy of dialect readers (see chapter 9) had been at the crux of contention, with the Bridge readers—believed by some researchers to help students swivel more smoothly between Black English and Standard English—were crushed beneath a riptide of condemnation despite their positive results. The *Philadelphia Daily News* had fueled a similar climate of outrage in 1969, when it learned of an internal memo written by a Philadelphia School District administrator and distributed among district personnel; "Order to OK 'Black English' in Schools Comes under Fire," the paper announced. Actually, the memo had only suggested that staff members glance at *Teaching Black Children to Read,* an edited book of papers by linguists who insisted, among other things, that Black English was systematic and legitimate, and that ignoring it or sneering at it could lead to disaster. But the recommendation was misinterpreted as an edict to allow or teach Black English in the classroom.

Of course, the mother of all Black English controversies before the 1990s was the 1979 Ann Arbor decision, sometimes referred to as the "King case." In July 1977, a lawsuit was filed on behalf of fifteen African American students, all of whom attended Ann Arbor's Martin Luther King Jr. Elementary School, alleging that the school, the district, and the state had "failed to properly educate the children, who were thus in danger of becoming functionally illiterate." Judge Charles W. Joiner narrowed the case to whether the school had taken adequate measures to recognize and overcome the barriers to equal educational opportunity posed by the children's home language, Black English. Two years later, the judge ruled in favor of the students in federal court, stating that "the unconscious but evident attitude of teachers toward the home language causes a psychological barrier to learning by students.

The decision did not set a legal precedent. It did, however, set off sirens. Syndicated black columnist Carl Rowan, writing one day before Judge Joiner's decision was released in July 1979, was among the many who bemoaned the impending "tragedy":

> For a court to say that "black English" is a "foreign tongue" and require schools in Ann Arbor, Mich., or any place else *to teach ghetto children in "black English"* would be a tragedy. For that would consign millions of black children to a *linguistic separation* that would guarantee that they will never "make it" in the larger U.S. society.
>
> What black children need is an end to this malarkey that tells them they can *fail to learn grammar, fail to develop vocabularies, ignore syntax and embrace the mumbo-jumbo of ignorance*—and dismiss it in the name of "black pride." [Emphasis added.]

Of course, no one had proposed teaching children in "black English," or telling them that they could ignore syntax and vocabulary. The anxieties surfaced nevertheless. By contrast, Vernon E. Jordan Jr., then president of the Urban League got the story straight:

> Black English became a barrier to learning not because of the children's use of it, but because teachers automatically assumed its use signified inferior intellectual intelligence, inability to learn or other negative connotations. . . . By focusing on the teachers, the judge made the right decision. Sensitizing teachers to Black English will equip them to communicate better with pupils who use the language in their daily lives. And it should help them to make better assessments of their students' ability to read and speak public English.

But even Jordan went on to stress, lest anyone get ideas, that it would be "a big leap from that to advocate teaching Black English in the schools. That would be a big mistake."

Not surprisingly, the King case would roil Michigan and rattle the presses for some time. Between July 1977 and February 1981, nearly five hundred news stories on the case were published. The prim community of Ann Arbor was not to become ground zero for Ebonics on the scale of Oakland (the city where Black Panther radicalism started, after all), but shock waves from the judgment would indeed be felt throughout the country, with dozens of newspaper commentators piling on to snuff out any sympathy for Black English. With the next big tumult over Ebonics, nearly two decades later, the angry sentiment was an echo through the years.

What made Ebonics such a scintillating story in 1996 and 1997? The same characteristics that made it compelling in the sixties, seventies, and eighties, and that all but guarantee another flare-up in the future: that is, its explicit mingling of questions of race and educational justice, and its implicit blending of questions of class, power, identity, and money. Indeed, language is often bound up with volatile political, social, and cultural issues (witness black opposition to Afrikaans in South Africa and jingoistic reactions to what some consider the encroachment of Spanish on the English domain in the United States). Any newsman or newswoman aware of these issues might have predicted that the discussion would grow noisy. But few journalists could have anticipated the intensity of the eruption on December 19, 1996. And after it finally subsided, fewer still would admit they had helped manufacture it.

Although many journalists were confused about how to handle Ebonics, some were fair and thorough. Some did their best to dissect Ebonics and make the story plain for a largely baffled public, even in the face of growing hysteria. Some struggled to understand the Oakland school board's intent, and to translate the convoluted wording of its manifesto. Others tried to trace Ebonics' history, and to unearth the deeper motivations behind the resolution. A precocious few even used the opportunity to scrutinize urban schools that had been overlooked for years, posing such fundamental questions as: Why are so many inner-city African American children having such a tough time mastering Standard English, and what should be done about it?

Overall, though, the coverage had some serious flaws. When Ebonics first hit the scene, journalists hastily identified the handful of public figures who were creating the loudest hullabaloo. The problem was that many of the follow-up articles to appear on or after December 20 and 21 seemed dedicated more to chronicling the ways in which these mouthpieces were spurning the proposal than to examining the curriculum changes Oakland administrators were considering. As is their wont, the media called upon the same handful of pundits to weigh in again and again; Kweisi Mfume, Maya Angelou, and Jesse Jackson appeared to fume anew in every article, but each had in fact issued only one initial statement, which newspapers, radio, and television kept recycling. The debate raged for weeks before advancing beyond pithy sound bites and rhetoric. The country was well into the mess before linguists—among the most informed commentators—were sought out in force. When reporters finally began to call him, University of Pennsylvania professor and Black English expert William Labov told them that Ebonics had been "too emotional a subject to get accurate reporting up to now."

By allowing the same stable of intellectuals to bash the dialect, while ignoring or failing to seek out those of equal caliber who might have praised it (such as novelist Toni Morrison, poet Ishmael Reed, or playwright August Wilson, who in an interview for this book remarked that "art is within the language of the people"), the media overstated the case and almost created a national consensus of scorn. (Indeed, when Reed wrote an op-ed piece to the *New York Times* decrying America's chorus of contempt for Black English, not only did the newspaper decline to publish it, but he was reportedly urged to rethink his position.) And even after Oakland schools superintendent Carolyn Getridge insisted publicly that the school district wasn't making a lunge for government money, newspapers continued to suggest that the Ebonics affair was merely a ploy for federal bilingual education funds. At the same time, Ebonics itself was portrayed, quite deceptively, as a made-up language, a creature engineered overnight in an Oakland basement.

It was the opinion writing that made some people cringe. Several newspapers (among them the *Atlanta Journal-Constitution*) ran almost seven times as much commentary on Ebonics as straight news. Respected periodicals such as *Vanity Fair, Liberty,* the *New Yorker,* the *New Republic,* and *Newsweek* published one-sided essays on the subject. While there were opportunities for clear-headed, well-researched debate, many columnists, editorial writers, and op-ed contributors instead relied on spurious arguments, distortion, condescension, parody, ridicule, and pseudohistory to malign liberal educators, black children, their parents, their communities, and their talk. The diatribes of many of the more reactionary columnists contained little or no discussion of the poor academic performance that had prompted the resolution. Few of these critics seemed to care, or cared to mention, that the average GPA of African American students in Oakland was 1.8, and that traditional strategies for teaching the language arts were failing miserably in a school district filled with speakers of Spoken Soul. As one African American parent complained, "No one worried about what our kids were being taught until this Ebonics thing."

News

The first Ebonics mistake many journalists made was to suggest that Oakland teachers had discarded Standard English and were preparing to give lessons in and on the vernacular. One of the most visible examples of this was seen on NBC's *Meet the Press,* when host Tim Russert asked Jesse Jackson what he thought of the proposal that "Black English, Ebonics, should be taught as an official language." Jackson responded with his oft-quoted statement that the very suggestion was "an unacceptable surrender borderlining on disgrace." As other mainstream television news programs (among them, *Crossfire* and *Talk Back Live*) and talk shows (*Geraldo*) featured discussions on Ebonics, the false assumption underlying Russert's question—that Oakland intended to teach Ebonics—became epidemic.

The January 17, 1997, taping of *Rolanda,* a daytime talk show hosted by Rolanda Watts, an African American woman, offered an almost comical example of how this runaway misconception clouded the national conversation. A cluster of black teenagers on a New York sidewalk were commissioned by the show's producers to provide samples of Ebonics from their everyday speech. Gesticulating dramatically in oversize jackets, the youngsters ran down a brief glossary of hip-hop lingo: *He flooded* or *He iced down* meant "He's got a lot of nice jewelry on," they explained. *I'ma jump in my whip* meant "I'm going to get in my car." *Homeboy flossin'* meant he was "lookin' good" and enjoying a lavish life-style, but *Homeboy flossin' too much* or *frontin'* meant he was looking for trouble. Rolanda's racially mixed studio audience chuckled at the colloquialisms. But believing that this sort of talk was to be encouraged in Oakland classrooms, despite the protests of scholarly guests, they grew serious, and rallied behind a teenager who declared, "You can't progress in society with slang. Slang is for you to get around the hood and all dat." (Linguist and Black English expert

Geneva Smitherman, who was originally featured as a guest, was so incensed that she withdrew and had the producers edit her segments out.) Similar discussions based on misleading information took place on radio programs, fueled by newspapers such as the *Times-Picayune* of New Orleans, which trumpeted, "Oakland to Teach 'Black' English," and the *Sacramento Bee,* which proclaimed, "Oakland Schools OK Teaching of Black Dialect."

Those last two pronouncements represent among the poorest elements of Ebonics coverage: the headlines. A good example of their consistent ambiguity came in March 1997, when the *Toronto Star* titled a story "Ebonics' Garbled Message." The headline implied not only that Oakland administrators had been vague about their intentions (true enough), but that the dialect they wished to redeem was itself garbled, unintelligible, mere gibberish (totally false). There was no such suggestion, however, in the article itself, which mainly probed the motivations of the resolution's framers and punctured the myth that the "home language" they were referring to was, linguistically, a new kid on the block. "While it's as old as slavery in the South," the article stated, "the new debate is about the legitimacy of ebonics, whether it's in the 'hood or in the classroom."

Sometimes the biases were subtle, almost unavoidable, because they came tangled with the attitudes and prejudices that bind our nation's consciousness. Consider the *New York Times,* which on December 30, 1996, announced: "Voice of Inner City Streets Is Defended and Criticized." Now, some speakers of the vernacular may be accurately associated with "the streets." But the streets are certainly not the vernacular's only, or even primary, domain. Indeed, African American vernacular can be heard in black homes and schoolyards, and even in churches (see chapter 3), across the country. Many middle-class readers of all colors got the impression, though, that the dialect was restricted to the streets, and to the "mean streets" at that. For them, "Ebonics" and "hoodlum" had become a natural equation, a duo nicely wed in the shadows of the imagination.

In the same *Times* article, Black English was described as a collection of "idiosyncratic speech patterns." The phrase sounds innocuous enough, but it helped trivialize the dialect, suggesting a linguistic quirk or an absence of the orderliness that is in fact the hallmark of all language varieties, and adding to the sense of weirdness surrounding the already rather alien term "Ebonics." There was much skepticism as far as the legitimacy of Black English (whether spoken inside or outside the classroom) was concerned, and the media often took great pains to avoid presenting it as a credible or even real way of speaking (which it undeniably is).

One reason the press fussed over Ebonics for so long was the emotional outcry the topic continued to evoke. On December 20, 1996, the *San Francisco Chronicle* published an article in which an African American senior at San Francisco High School dismissed Black English as "slave language." On January 5, 1997, the *San Francisco Examiner* ran a feature in which a Bay Area seventeen-year-old commented on Ebonics: "It's rooted in me. I'm very proud of my culture." Elsewhere and at other times, when asked about Ebonics, Spike Lee blistered, rapper Chuck D scoffed, San Francisco 49ers wide receiver Jerry Rice shook his head, and University of California regent Ward Connerly sputtered that it was "just ass-backwards." And yet most of the residents at an Oakland town hall meeting covered by the *San Jose Mercury News* in January supported Ebonics. Said one resident, "If we be cookin', we be cookin'!" Another felt that it was just common sense that a respect for language was elementary to learning: "I saw my peers frustrated and made to feel inferior by teachers and instructors who did not have a background in Black English."

Two weeks before the forum, a white accountant interviewed in an upscale San Francisco shopping center had spoken out against Black English: "They're encouraging kids to use improper language." In an African American section of the same city, an unemployed black welder had staunchly defended it: "They [the school board] said it's all right to talk the way you talk—that you're not stupid, just different." These perspectives reveal as much about our country as they do about the media's approach to covering Ebonics. Despite the distance between the views of the accountant and those of the welder, Ebonics had, in a superficial sense, bridged America's racial gap. People of all complexions were giggling or fuming. But the debate also unveiled the deep socioeconomic fissures within the African American community. The welder's comments, for instance, remind us that while the black middle class was overwhelmingly denouncing Ebonics, many members of the black working class, whose views rarely found their way over the airwaves or onto newsprint, were championing it, or at least grumbling about its getting slammed. In any case, that the *San Francisco Chronicle* would publish the statements of the white accountant and those of the out-of-work black welder one right after the other smelled funny. The implication seemed to be that you could find scarcely anyone with a job who had anything polite to say about Black English.

Reporters committed their most grievous mistake, though, not by using loaded words or sensationalizing headlines or indulging in bits of editorializing, but by excluding from their articles national evidence showing that black students were lagging perilously behind whites when it came to academic achievement. This disparity, after all, was the number-one motivation behind the Ebonics plan in the first place. In the final days of 1996, just as the Ebonics controversy was peaking, the Education Trust released a report indicating that African American students had begun losing ground in reading and writing after years of gaining academically. Minorities had made moderate or significant academic progress in the 1970s and 1980s. But according to a study conducted by the national research group, blacks in the mid-1990s were backsliding in all disciplines, including reading and writing, when compared to whites.

Yet those numbers seldom appeared in articles about Ebonics. This is not to suggest that the press ignored *all* the statistics; many newspapers recounted the discouraging performance of African American students in Oakland schools, and a few even made the crucial point that the district was looking to its Ebonics policy as just one possible solution. But few publications explored the notion of Black English as a universal classroom hurdle as thoroughly as the *Washington Post,* which on January 6, 1997, held that

> in the nation's urban public schools, the scenario is familiar. The academic record of many poor black students is dismal and getting worse. Frustrated educators search for dramatic new ways to get at one root of the problem: language skills.

The *San Jose Mercury News* was also on target, placing Oakland's "disheartening" academic circumstances in the context of a U.S. Department of Education report that revealed that seventeen-year-old blacks were reading at the level of thirteen-year-old whites, and that SAT verbal scores for blacks were on the average almost 100 points lower than those for whites. Clearly, Oakland had no monopoly on failure. Urban schools across the country were reeling. So why did the media often fail to consider these symptoms in the Ebonics diagnosis? We're not entirely sure. That many journalists refused to believe that language could be a central factor in the poor academic performance of many African American students played a part. And certainly, the reality that the educational system, through traditional but often inept teaching methods, was preparing hundreds of thousands of black children for nothing more than poverty was less sexy a story than the prospect of "I be goin' to da sto" replacing "Reading, writing, and arithmetic" as the classroom mantra. As one Stanford University graduate student observed in the aftermath of the Ebonics inquisition, there is often a good distance between what is worthy and what is deemed newsworthy.

To be fair, however, we should recognize what many journalists came up against while trying to tough their way through the wilds of the Ebonics story. It was undoubtedly a story caught in the crosshairs of race and class, and trapped in an elaborate historical web of slavery, segregation, and economic and educational inequity. Folks, white and black, grew touchy or indignant or just plain silly when asked to talk about Black English. Modern scientists themselves had been seriously researching Ebonics only for a matter of decades, and already it had spurred more than its fair share of scholarly quibbling. Even Oakland administrators were conspicuously tight-lipped at first when it came to discussing how the Ebonics plan might be implemented, and at what cost, and who was to pick up the tab—probably because many of these details had yet to be worked out.

The media's later and longer efforts to rescue Black English and the Oakland policy from the muck of public ignorance were, nonetheless, far more auspicious. Just before the new year, for example, the *Oakland Tribune* was one of the few newspapers in the country to publish the full text of the resolution, giving readers a chance to scrutinize the gnarled wording of the document firsthand, "unfiltered by the news media, school officials or their spin doctors." The same day, the *New York Times* reminded readers that Black and White American Englishes, in their slang at least, were "not so separate," pointing out that *uptight, outta sight, groovin', dissin', wannabe, You go, girl,* and *my man* all originated in the 'hood. And to demonstrate that journalists willing to sleuth out the more enduring questions beneath the debate would continue to find plenty of cultural fodder, the *Washington Post* in early January 1997 stated:

> So crucial is a common language to people's sense of security, experts say, that the smallest difference—whether it's a foreign accent or a nonstandard grammar, as occurs in Ebonics—can quickly bring to the surface deep-seated ethnic fears.

In mid-February, the *San Jose Mercury News,* one of the few newspapers to examine some of the instructional strategies used in Oakland's Standard English Proficiency program, offered readers a sample of contrastive analysis, the controversial but promising core of science at the center of the resolution. This was a crucial piece of reporting, as many newspapers failed to provide even one sample of how Black English was being used to teach the standard. The *Mercury News* wrote:

> Haynes cited as an example a lesson in which students are asked to translate into standard English sentences such as "Michael Jackson be dancing. Michael Jackson be the best dancer I know." Supporters of the SEP program have stressed that teachers never instruct in black English. They do, however, ask students to identify the differences between black English and standard English and have students translate black English phrases into standard English.

When Peter Applebome of the *New York Times* went in search of substance, he was able to capture the desperation, the ideology, and the personalities behind the Oakland plan, and after what must have been hours of research, to pen the best Ebonics article of the bunch. But Ebonics as a national topic was a phenomenon of the winter frost, and Applebome's piece didn't appear until March 1997, well into the thaw. Truth came too late, and too little.

Opinion

As 1996 made way for 1997 and Ebonics mania wore on, everyone seemed to be vying for a piece of Oakland. Pundits of all stripes set out to indict Ebonics, to apologize for Ebonics, to try to fix Ebonics, to look for the spin on Ebonics that would suit their own agenda. In the end, the resolution was used to prop up virtually every political platform imaginable. A socialist newsletter, the *International Workers Bulletin,* for instance, claimed that Ebonics had been conjured up by the American aristocracy in order to divert attention from the injustices of class disparity. Another such organ, *Socialist Action,* defended the Oakland school board against the "racist assault" of fascist politicians. Mouthpieces for the mainstream media dug trenches of their own, seeking to resolve some central questions: What is Ebonics, and where did it come from? Who and what is behind the Ebonics movement? And what should be done about it?

Black conservative Thomas Sowell, for one, took the position that Black English "is just as white as any other English." In a newspaper column, Sowell stated that Ebonics apostles were endorsing fairy tales by suggesting that the continent of Africa had anything to do with the way black people talk today. Black English, he maintained, represents nothing more than the last murmurs of an obsolete British dialect (see chapter 8 for our remarks on this):

> From what African language did "ain't" come? And why were whites saying it in England before they ever crossed the Atlantic or ever saw anybody of African ancestry?

Black columnist Walter Williams also insisted that "'I be' talk has no ties to any African heritage." He was among the dozens of critics who wrote a portion or all of their columns in dialect (or some approximation thereof), presumably to illustrate its backwardness most colorfully. In Williams's words: "Y'awl might axin me why Ah be writin dis way." Williams guessed that many of his readers, "intellectual multiculturists" included, would misinterpret the preceding passage as Black English. In fact, he maintained, it was an amalgamation of "regional dialects spoken throughout the south and west of England during the Seventeenth Century" and transplanted to America in later years. Poor whites and blacks in the American South had simply retained such "ill-bred" speech patterns. Williams concluded that "the language we often hear spoken among blacks has little or nothing to do with Africa. It's as English as you want to get."

Williams and Sowell hadn't come up with anything new. Again and again, black intellectuals have tried to drop Black English into the laps of whites and run. As early as 1971, for example, civil rights leader Bayard Rustin, then executive director of the A. Philip Randolph Institute, wrote in a column published as a paid advertisement in the *New York Times:* "'Black English,' after all, has nothing to do with blackness but derives from the conditions of lower-class life in the South (poor Southern whites also speak 'black English')." Shunting off the vernacular, ascribing it to an entirely separate neighborhood, seems to be a much easier policy than confronting it head-on. Some blacks grab whatever convenient scraps of linguistic data they can, and sketch a genealogical chart for Ebonics that they hope will exonerate their great-grandfathers. (But we're all implicated, for as we have shown in chapter 8, the real origins of the dialect are quite diverse and complex.)

White critics tended to fall in with Williams and Sowell, at least in asserting that Ebonics is not what it pretends. Columnist George Will, on an edition of the television program *This Week with David Brinkley,* declared uninformedly that Ebonics

> is clearly not a language. Is there an Ebonics dictionary? No. Is there a canon of Ebonics literature? No. It's not a language. . . . It contributes to the ghettoization of young African Americans.

Other journalists joined Knight-Ridder national correspondent Rachel Jones, an African American, in recognizing that Black English was a "valid part of our cultural history." But many more joined editorial writer Bill Johnson in assailing it as a "linguistic nightmare that refuses to die a natural death." Other less than flattering descriptions of and appellations for the tongue included "mumbo jumbo," "mutant English," "broken English," "fractured English," "slanguage," and "ghettoese." A *New York Times* op-ed went so far as to condemn the "Ebonic Plague." And even Jones's *Newsweek* piece, which began by complimenting the vernacular, ended up as more of a call for "proper speech" than anything else, with Standard English touted as the panacea for much of what was ailing black folk:

> My skill with standard English propelled me from a life of poverty and dead ends to a future I could have scarcely imagined. It has opened doors for me that might never have budged an inch for a poor black girl . . .

Jones testified that she herself didn't "talk white," just "right." Though she was willing to confer on Black English all the validity of an anthropological relic, she apparently still considered it categorically wrong. Standard English, she seemed to suggest, had cornered the market on clarity, eloquence, and when you got down to it, any sort of inherent value. Whether or not they came right out and said it, this was the fundamental conviction of many of the black journalists who sounded off on Ebonics. Whether liberal or conservative, Black English in their minds represented a dark side, a streak of backwardness that had to be shunned, purged, stripped away, or lopped off like an unsightly carbuncle in order for the race to advance. Researchers could have lectured these intellectuals all day long, arguing that the goal of Oakland's Ebonics policy was actually Standard English and that a youngster who has mastered a home language can be taught to use the same cognitive abilities to master a school language. But as soon as the word "Ebonics" left their lips, the debate, as far as many African American pundits were concerned, was over. Something deep in the psyche of many blacks refused to accept that anything good could come of this "I be" jive.

A handful of writers, however, considered Black English a commodity. Writing in the *Boston Globe,* Derrick Jackson suggested that Ebonics was just good marketing:

> Oakland said it wants to recognize Ebonics as a way of helping youths bridge the gap to mainstream English. This is a source of outrage? White people have no problem bridging the gap to black English when they make money off it, like sneaker and insurance companies that borrow "You go, girl," like white editors of rap magazines, like John Belushi and Dan Aykroyd parading as "Blues Brothers," or like white college basketball and football recruiters who talk more jive than Cab Calloway to get black men to come to their school to play ball.

Author Ishmael Reed insisted in *Newsday* that the dialect was a currency no American lacks:

> Like other forms of African-American culture, Ebonics is something that whites sleep with at night and don't recognize during the day. When they do recognize it they give it a stepfather. Many young whites believe that Bill Haley invented rock 'n' roll.

But Reed took exception with the Oakland school board and others who casually lumped Ebonics together with African languages:

> I have studied Yoruba, which is still spoken and written in Cuba and Brazil, and have found only superficial resemblances between it and black English. I wonder how many of the op-ed writers who've claimed that there are strong connections between "African language systems" and black English have actually studied one of these West African languages.

What made Reed bristle, this "everybody's an expert" attitude, also makes linguists crazy. They often complain about the popular perception that anybody and everybody who *uses* language is qualified to speak with authority *about* language. To scholars who spend much of their lives contemplating the nuances of human communication, that's like saying that anybody with a belly button is qualified to perform brain surgery. But that didn't stop many an individual with access to a keyboard from pontificating about the source and system of Black English during the Ebonics controversy.

As to the question of who and what was behind Ebonics, most commentators, again, were less than complimentary. On one edition of *Forum*, a KQED public education radio program, *Oakland Tribune* urban affairs reporter Chauncey Bailey ripped into the Oakland school board and its defenders, calling them all "poverty pimps in Kente cloth." No doubt Oakland educators eventually got used to that kind of talk; again and again they were accused of being radical Afrocentrists, wild-eyed separatists, and racist crackpots. More often than not, though, anti-Ebonics crusaders left the authors of the resolution alone after one or two jabs. Unfortunately, it was the black community at large that sometimes took the roundhouse punch.

This was the case with "Ebonics: Bridge to Illiteracy," a long, searing five-page essay penned by Nicholas Stix and published in a libertarian political magazine. Like many other columnists, Stix believed Ebonics to be a dangerously subversive scheme. And like several other columnists, he wound up revealing some of his own deep-seated stereotypes and animosities while slamming the proposal. Arguing that a federal government with a jones for "counter-institutions" was coaxing Afrocentrists out of the cracks, Stix declared that

> the movement for Ebonics is just one division of the movement for bilingual education in which we see the partnership of the welfare state and racism in making the world safe for illiteracy.

Stix certainly had a right to protest the possibility that national funds would be spent on an Ebonics program he considered backward and sure to fail. But not only is the notion that illiteracy is a necessary consequence of Ebonics ignorant and insulting, it requires us to look at peculiarities of culture as if they were determinants of ability, an exercise that leads irrevocably to racism. And yet this antagonism toward Ebonics, bilingual education, and other perceived tabernacles of "liberalism" was merely symptomatic of the fever for "pure" English and for a homogeneous America that we were suffering from during the time of the Ebonics affair—and that we will likely continue to suffer from well into the twenty-first century. In such a climate of intolerance, it's only natural to blame the victim.

Stix was not alone in crying racism while propping up distinctly racist attitudes. Jack White fell into the same trap when he wrote "Ebonics According to Buckwheat" for *Time* magazine. Common sense dictates that teachers in the inner city recognize that some black youngsters speak differently from how other students do. White was willing to allow that much. And faced with such an alarming rate of high school dropouts, Oakland had to try something new, he conceded. But White sneered at the hypocrisy of the "Afrocentric jargon and education-speak" of the resolution. Yet in trying to satirize the Ebonics policy by resurrecting Hollywood's old racial caricatures, White succeeded in doing little more than just that—resurrecting racial caricatures:

> I put in a call to the Home for Retired Racial Stereotypes in a black
> section of Hollywood. The Kingfish answered. "Holy mack'rul dere,
> Andy, somebody wants to talk 'bout dis 'ere Ebonics. Could you or
> Tonto tell Buckwheat come to da phone? He de resident expert."

Protests to the editor followed, mostly because the article contained some of the same minstrel-style speech ("paragiraffe" for *paragraph*) that blacks had long worked to erase from literature and the American stage (see chapter 2). But many people agreed with the point White was trying to make, that tolerance for Ebonics was a shuck-and-jive that would ultimately only validate stereotypes and send the race backsliding. And it was this same unmitigated intolerance for Ebonics that drove some white writers, perhaps unwittingly, to make the most condescending and paternalistic statements about blacks. In an article entitled "Hooked on Ebonics," for instance, *Vanity Fair* contributor Christopher Hitchens stated:

> There is tragedy and history and emotion involved in the survival of
> a black speech in America, and giggling at its expense is not good
> manners. But the worst irony of all would be to congratulate, hypo-
> critically, the "richness" of something that threatens to imprison
> its speakers . . .

And in the *New Yorker,* an essayist submitted that

> multiculturalism, of the strident sort that the Oakland board has
> espoused, is no favor to American subcultures. In the short run, it
> may enliven everyone's appreciation of the variety of American styles,
> but in the long run it can only turn that variety into mainstream
> mush.

Both these excerpts reveal a tendency to belittle the dialect, to encapsulate it, to write it off as just one more spirited attempt at multiculturalism, or as nothing more than the gurgling of a "subculture." Once defined as such, some writers must have figured, the thing could be shelved away and perhaps forgotten. But such dismissive attitudes indicate a profound disrespect for the experience of blacks in America. To attribute a system of communication used consistently by millions to a quaint emotion or to liken it to a plaything to be pulled out for cultural show-and-tell is to subscribe to the same one-dimensional matrix that produced the great mascots of white fantasy—Buckwheat included.

Occasionally, though, someone sounded a note of praise for Black English. Several newspapers joined the *San Diego Union-Tribune* in cautioning that "the backlash against Black English overlooks the beauty of the words." In some cases, recognized columnists such as the *Miami Herald*'s Leonard Pitts and the *Washington Post*'s William Raspberry rethought their initially negative positions and adopted more moderate stances on the vernacular. While Pitts swore in December 1996 that he was "insulted" by black "slanguage," by the next month he was ready to acknowledge that Ebonics could be "a bridge to success" and to make a plea for tolerance:

> We come here, we Americans, from a thousand different bypasses, back yards, bayous and boulevards, from outposts of culture and enclaves of speech, any one of which has potential to seem strange and outlandish to the rest of us.

Other writers cautiously sided with some of the Oakland school board's philosophies. There was the *Essence* magazine contributor, for instance, who reasoned that

> it can't help our children to be told at every utterance that their mode of expression—which is intimately linked to their identity—is wrong, wrong, wrong, when others who plagiarize them are getting paid.

And in an unusual move, the *Oakland Tribune* produced an editorial that gave the Oakland school board the benefit of the doubt:

> We hope good news eventually comes out of this controversy, because Oakland school children need and deserve success. If as the district tells us, the Ebonics program is one way we can raise the achievement level of African-American students, we have to say, "Go for it."

Of course, these were the exceptions. Far too many columnists, editorial writers, and op-ed contributors saw the Ebonics story as an opportunity to poke fun at black policy-makers, ridicule an act of black self-determination, and smear the vernacular spoken by the black masses while still enjoying the applause of the black middle class. And all this at a time when minorities, having finally added a dash of color to what for years were milk-white newsrooms, were increasingly taking their editors to task for slanted or stereotypical representations of their communities.

For those who sought balance and reason rather than a blind backing up or vicious hacking up of Black English—one of the most organic and distinctive speech varieties in the United States—these were confusing, even troubling times. Amid the fray, the question of whether Ebonics was a language or a dialect kept recurring. But the real question was: Who would decide? As long as Ebonics could be kept underfoot and condemned publicly as bastardized speech, who cared whether the variety lived or died in the ghetto, or that it was spreading to the tongues of young white suburbanites? The debate seemed at times to hinge less on why black inner-city children were doing so badly on tests of Standard English proficiency than on which critics would triumph in a battle too often waged with deception on behalf of ethnic fear or embarrassment.

And as for what should be done about Ebonics? Most of the media had an easy answer: Spin it to death. In an op-ed that appeared in the *New York Times* in January 1997, Frank Rich wrote:

> There isn't a public personage of stature in the land . . . who doesn't say that the Oakland, Calif., school board was wrong, if not deranged, to portray black English as a "genetically based" and "primary" language . . . and to imply that it was worthy of public funds set aside for bilingual education.

Rubbish. Actually, at least half a dozen people that we know of, including a well-published and widely acclaimed writer, a documentary film director, an education council director who testified at the congressional hearing on Ebonics, and three leading linguists, all sent op-eds to the *Times* defending the vibrancy and legitimacy of Black English, espousing its potential as a bridge to Standard English, or decrying its widespread condemnation. But the *Times* published none of these. The contribution by University of Chicago Linguistics Chair Salikoko Mufwene, solicited by the *Times,* was rejected in favor of one written by a lawyer opposed to Ebonics. While the paper must of course be selective about op-ed submissions, it is striking that it never printed an opinion piece on this issue that was neutral, much less positive, and that it ignored the contributions of experts in the field.

Ebonics coverage, by and large, was yet another case of the mainstream media's not merely establishing the national agenda, but shaping the national consciousness in the style described by linguist and social critic Noam Chomsky in *Manufacturing Consent.* The beating the vernacular was getting in the press encouraged the bruising it was getting on the street, and created a lasting climate in which the very mention of Ebonics elicited funny looks, giggles, or tirades of intolerance.

On October 9, 1998, the *Times* set off a fresh wave of tremors among linguists and educators by running, free of charge, an arresting quarter-page anti-Ebonics ad. Created by the Ketchum advertising agency (of Pittsburgh) for a group identified as "Atlanta's Black Professionals," the ad had won the prestigious $100,000 Athena award (Award to Honor Excellence in Newspaper Advertising) from the Newspaper Association of America. Depicting a rearview silhouette of the Reverend Martin Luther King Jr. superimposed with "I has a dream" in large, bold letters, the ad included this message:

> Does this bother you? It should. We've spent over 400 years fighting for the right to have a voice. Is this how we'll use it? More importantly, is this how we'll teach our children to use it? If we expect more of them, we must not throw our hands in the air and agree with those who say our children cannot be taught. . . . The fact is, language is power. And we can't take that power away from our children with Ebonics. . . . If you haven't used your voice lately, consider this an invitation. SPEAK OUT AGAINST EBONICS.

Advertising executives at the *Times* ran the ad for free in recognition of the Athena award. But when more than two hundred linguists and educators wrote to the *Times* in protest, urging that it publish the Linguistics Society of America's pro-Ebonics resolution for the sake of balance, the newspaper turned them down, explaining that it had "a policy that mandates against giving away advertising space."

But the "I has a dream" represents just another of the many Ebonics blunders catalogued in this chapter and this book. First, contrary to the widespread misconception that any sentence with "bad" Standard English grammar would be "good" Ebonics (the "anything goes" fallacy), "I has a dream" is *not* acceptable in Ebonics or Spoken Soul. Although speakers of this vernacular commonly use *have* where SE requires *has* (with third-person-singular subjects, as in "He *have* a car"), they never or very rarely use *has* where SE requires *have* (with non-third-person-singular subjects, as in *"I *has* a dream"). In the recorded speech of a sample of forty-four black teenagers in New York City, for instance, *have* for "has" occurred 67 percent of the time, but *has* for "have" (the nonstandard construction maligned in the ad) occurred 0 percent of the time—that is, never.

Second, the ad falsely suggests that those who framed and supported the Ebonics resolutions wanted to teach children Ebonics and deny them access to the English of Martin Luther King Jr. and other leaders. But the intent, as observed in chapter 9, was to use the former to increase proficiency in the latter, and as noted in chapter 3, Dr. King is but one titan in a rhetorical tradition that includes both Standard English *and* Spoken Soul. Finally, although the *Times'* version of the ad appeared to have been sponsored by the National Head Start Association (its name and address were listed at the end of the ad), it was not. Head Start's board had not approved the use of its name and had not taken a position on Ebonics, and after the controversy created by the publication of the ad, Head Start made that known publicly. The *Times,* which normally checks such attributions, did not do so in this case.

In fairness, it was the *Times* that had published James Baldwin's paean to Black English (see chapter 1) three decades earlier, and that provided some of the best reportage on the subject. But in its one-sided selection of opinion pieces on the Ebonics issue, and in its generous publication of the misleading "I Has a Dream" ad, the nation's newspaper of record appeared to be as much under the sway of the dominant ideology on this issue as the rest of the media were.

11

Ebonics "Humor"

It was a funny type of humor, which on its surface appeared to be of the ha-ha! type, but at a deeper level of the more serious uh-hmm type.
——Jerrie C. Scott (1998)

Mock Ebonics on the Internet blurs the distinction between public and private discourse, thereby distancing producers and consumers from responsibility for language that would be highly offensive in other public venues, such as call-in talk shows, neighborhood bars, and letters to the editor.
——Maggie Ronkin and Helen E. Karn (1999)

Long after the media abandoned Ebonics, humorists continued to stoke the coals. In fact, Ebonics seemed to have become a national punch line the very instant the Oakland school board released its resolution. At first, the raillery was part of the media's response, as cartoonists and columnists wove their wit into pages crowded with serious news reports, headlines, letters, and op-ed pieces. But before long, comedians, public speakers, preachers, and people on the street and on the World Wide Web—especially on the Web—jumped in to create and spread new varieties of Ebonics humor.

John Leo suggested in a *U.S. News Online* column that "the nationwide roar of laughter over Ebonics is a very good sign." He took the open laughter as an indication that Americans in the later 1990s had less tolerance for political correctness than they had had before, and that they were more willing to respond to what they considered wrongheadedness with chuckling, satire, and ridicule. While Ebonics

203

humor revealed that political correctness had fallen out of favor, some of it revealed also that crude racial stereotyping and overt expressions of racism were as much in vogue as they ever were. More often than not, the satire proved how little most people understood not only Ebonics itself but also Oakland's proposal to use it to teach Standard English.

Ebonics jokes fall into four main categories: *-onics* jokes; jokes involving the verb *be;* translation humor; and racial caricatures. As is evident below, there is a considerable gap between the first and last categories in terms of how closely they relate to Ebonics and how sinister the humor is.

-onics **jokes.**   The earliest and most innocuous jokes to emerge often poked fun at the term "Ebonics"—which sounded to many like some weird science—and mocked the claim that it referred to a distinctive way of speaking. Fanciful varieties of *-onics* languages sprang up on the Internet, and circulated on fliers that were nearly indecipherable because they had been photocopied so many times:

> *Languages Being Taught in Oakland, California*
> Afro-American Speak—Ebonics ("Ebony" + "Phonics")
> Irish-American Speak—Leprechaunics
> Native-American Speak—Kimosabics
> Italo-American Speak—Spumonics (or Rigatonics)
> Chinese-American Speak—Won-tonics
> Japanese-American Speak—Mama-san-ics
> Jewish-American Speak—Zionics
> Russian-American Speak—Rasputonics
> Spanish-American Speak—Burritonics
> Eskimo-American Speak—Harpoonics
> German-American Speak—Autobahnics (or Teutonics)
> French-American Speak—Cornichonics (or Escargonics)
> Oakland-School-Board Speak—Moronics

Here the humor stems from the play on ethnic stereotypes, in some cases more entrenched than in others. The list is perhaps less offensive than it might have been, because the strings of virtually every ethnic group are yanked. Two points are noteworthy: First, the etymology (or origin) of "Ebonics" is given at the outset. Second, the final item names the school board. So whether one thinks it lame or clever, the joke is firmly based in the substance of the Ebonics issue—educational policy and language.

Other *-onics* gags resembled this list. In the first cartoon following page 160, notice that the linguistic subtypes are not only ethnic but geographic and occupational. The second cartoon, by Scott Willis, even includes a new term, "Waveonics," for the speech of surfers.

These cartoons imply that there are so many different ways of speaking in America that to recognize and cater to them all would be lunacy. The case is made more explicitly in a cartoon by Barbara Brandon that was published in the *Detroit Free Press* on January 12, 1997. It ends with the lines, "What's next? Will we validate poor English spoken by white folks by calling it . . . Ivoronics?" A cartoon by Mike Keefe that appeared in the *San Francisco Examiner* on December 29, 1996, has a teacher introducing to her class "your new Ebonics interpreter . . . and your interpreters for Brooklynese, east Texan, Appalachian, Minnesotan, Down Eastern, Deep Southern, Chicagoan, Valley Speak, Surfer, Cajun, Clevelandic . . ." The point that's lost, however, is that Ebonics is more than the narrow, specialized, and often ephemeral words that characterize such dialects or styles. In fact, Ebonics is a full-fledged language variety with distinctive features of pronunciation, grammar, and vocabulary. And its deep-rooted and widespread use among African Americans affects the teaching of reading and the language arts in ways that most other American dialects do not.

The suggestion in the next cartoon that even the inane "huh-huhs" of MTV characters Beavis and Butt-head would qualify as a "distinct language" in Oakland illustrates how nonchalantly many critics dismissed Ebonics as gobbledygook.

Invariant *be* jokes.   The linguistic feature most often picked on by humorists trying to parody Ebonics (see the first three cartoons) was the particular use of the verb *be.* Linguists call it invariant *be,* because, unlike the Standard English *be,* its present-tense form does not change according to its subject (although it sometimes occurs as *be's* or *bees,* especially among older people). In Ebonics, one says "I *be,*" "you *be,*" "he/she/it *be,*" and so on, while in Standard English one says "I *am,*" "you/we/they *are,*" "he/she/it *is.*"

As early as the 1970s and 1980s, invariant *be* had appeared in jokes involving blacks. Bill Cosby recalled a "racist joke" a friend had told him in the early 1980s:

Q: Do you know what Toys 'Я' Us is called in Harlem?

A: We Be Toys.

The following one-liner, a supposedly black version of the airline advertising jingle "Delta is ready when you are," had appeared even earlier:

> Delta be ready when you is.

The use of invariant *be* was not always derogatory, however, and was often employed playfully by African Americans. Arsenio Hall, for one, used to begin his 1980s late-night talk show by declaiming:

> Arsenio Hall! We be havin a ball!

Linguists have found that between the 1960s and the 1990s, the frequency of invariant *be* in the speech of African Americans skyrocketed, especially among teenagers. In the late 1960s, William Labov and his fellow researchers reported that the eighteen teenage members of the Thunderbirds, a gang they recorded in New York City, used only some five examples each in their interviews. Walt Wolfram, writing around the same time, found that the four dozen African Americans from all age groups whom he and his colleagues interviewed in Detroit used even fewer—about two examples each. By contrast, Foxy Boston, a teenager in East Palo Alto, California, whom Faye McNair-Knox first recorded in 1986, used 385 examples of invariant *be* in her hourlong interview. Guy Bailey and Natalie Maynor reported in the late 1980s that twelve- and thirteen-year-old African Americans in Texas were using invariant *be* three times as often as black Texans over the age of seventy.

It's not surprising, then, that invariant *be* would become *the* icon of African American vernacular during the Ebonics imbroglio. Unlike rarer and more complex grammatical patterns of Ebonics, such as negative inversion ("Didn't nobody leave"), invariant *be* appeared to be a simple word, a straightforward substitute for Standard English *am, is,* or *are.* The story is more complicated, but that didn't stop the proliferation of *be* quips.

Some of the jokes in this category were clever and creative:

> Q. What do you call an Ebonics transvestite?
> A. Susan B. Anthony [Susan be Anthony].

Others showed that their creators were hip to the dialect, as does the cartoon by Jeff Danzinger (see the photo and cartoon insert following page 160), in which he exploits authentic Ebonics lingo—*chillin', main man, dat's whuzzup,* and *nome sane* (a condensed version of "Know what I'm saying?") that has become popular in the black community.

But although the cartoonist correctly uses *don't* (rather than *ain't*) as the appropriate negative form of *be* in Ebonics grammar, the appearance of *be* at the end of a clause without an adjective or verb following it ("I be or I don't be") is virtually nonexistent in recordings of everyday Ebonics conversation.

Most of the satirists who aped Black English had no idea how to re-create the dialect accurately. They didn't know (and perhaps didn't care) that the use of invariant *be* and other features is governed by subtle grammatical and semantic rules that most outsiders, white and black, bungle when they try to imitate Spoken Soul.

Consider the following Ebonics joke:

Q. Why were there only forty-nine contestants for the Miss Ebonics USA Pageant?

A. No contestant wanted to wear a banner that said "Idaho" (I da ho').

Cute. But linguistically incorrect. While Ebonics speakers regularly leave out forms of *is* and *are,* they almost never omit *am.* They often contract *am,* as in "I'm da bomb," but they don't delete it. "I da bomb" would be ungrammatical, just as "I da ho" is.

A more fundamental mistake made by cartoonists and columnists who tried to parody invariant *be* was their failure to use the verb form only for actions that occur frequently or habitually, as in this example recorded from the speech of teenager Foxy Boston:

And every day, every day, "Did you go shopping today? What you go buy? You bought this? You bought that? You like it?" And I *be* going, "Yep, Yep, yep."

Most Ebonics satirists used every opportunity to substitute *be* for Standard English's *am, is,* or *are,* whether or not the situations they were referring to occurred regularly. See, for instance, the Scott Willis cartoon in the insert following page 160, where it is clear that the conversation is about what the big guy is doing right then, at the moment of speech ("What you be doin'?" . . . "I be chillin'"). In genuine Ebonics, the exchange would go more like this: "What you doin'?" . . . "I'm chillin'."

The mistake was made repeatedly in the popular press. In a *Doonesbury* cartoon dated February 16, 1997 (www.doonesbury.com/flashbacks/pages/1997/oz/db970216.html), a college president is shown reading a headline announcing that "the Oakland School Board is still sticking with Ebonics," while he mutters to himself, "This be perverse." Journalist Patricia Smith opened a syndicated column in the *Oakland Tribune* with the statement, "This don't be no new thang," instead of "This ain't no new thing." And Bill Cosby himself, in the *Wall Street Journal,* wrote, "After all, Ebonics be a complex issue."

Equally off the mark was *Washington Post* columnist William Raspberry, who began a piece entitled "Ebonics Debate: Who Will Benefit?" as follows:

> "'Sup?" the cabbie said.
>
> "No thanks," I said. I was trying to cut back on my caloric intake. "Besides," I pointed out, "it looks to me like you've only got half a filet of fish and what's left of a small order of fries."
>
> "What you be talkin' bout, my man?" he said, "I don't be offerin' you my grub; I be saying hello. You know, like, *what's up?*"

In genuine Ebonics, "What you *be* talkin' bout" would be "What you talkin' bout." "I don't *be* offerin' you my grub" would be "I ain't offerin' you my grub." "I *be* saying hello" would be simply "I'm sayin' hello." But Raspberry's most egregious error comes when he claims, later in the whimsical taxi dialogue, that Ebonics is formed willy-nilly—that it is a language variety without discernible rules or restrictions:

> "I noticed a couple of errors when you tried your French and Spanish on me a while back," I said. "Just out of curiosity, who corrects your Ebonics?"
>
> "That's the beautiful part," the cabbie said. "Ebonics gives you a whole range of options. . . . My brother-in-law tells me that you can say pretty much what you please, as long as you're careful to throw in a lot of 'bes' and leave off final consonants."
>
> As a former proofreader, I couldn't believe my ears.
>
> "They'll have teachers learn a language that has *no right or wrong expressions, no consistent spellings or pronunciations and no discernible rules?* How will that help children learn proper English? What is the point?" [Emphasis added.]

Many of the critics who scripted letters to the editor and Internet tirades insisted that the notion of Ebonics as a systematic form of English was ridiculous. But as any undergraduate college student taking Linguistics 101 knows, all languages and dialects are systematic and rule-governed. The evidence lies both in empirical findings—from studies of thousands of language varieties—and in theoretical assumption. If languages and dialects were not structured, how could speakers communicate reliably with one another, and how could children acquire language or dialect?

Translation jokes.   The logical extension of *be* jokes are jokes involving translations of longer stretches of speech or writing. Jokes that translate Ebonics have been around for a number of years. In the 1987 movie *Hollywood Shuffle*, black drama students attending acting school are tutored in crude Ebonics ("You jive turkey mutha-fucka!") so they can more "authentically" play black parts. Even before that, in the 1980 movie *Airplane!*, a white flight attendant finds herself unable to comprehend the speech of a black passenger until a white woman sitting nearby steps in as interpreter:

FLIGHT ATTENDANT *(to black male #1, after he says something indecipherable to her):* I'm sorry, I don't understand.

BLACK MALE #2 *(sitting beside black male #1):* Cutty say he can't hang.

WHITE PASSENGER: Oh, stewardess, I speak Jive!

FLIGHT ATTENDANT: Oh, good!

WHITE PASSENGER: He said that he's in great pain, and he wants to know if you can help him.

FLIGHT ATTENDANT: All right. Would you tell him to just relax, and I'll be back as soon as I can with some medicine?

WHITE PASSENGER: Just hang loose, blood. She gonna catch up on the rebound on the medi-side.

BLACK MALE #1 *(offended):* What it *is*, big momma? My momma didn't raise no dummies! I dug her rap!

WHITE PASSENGER: Cut me some slack, jack!

At least one Internet website (www.AtlantaGA.com), no longer active, included another sample of *Airplane* "Jive" dialogue. This time the conversation was translated from Ebonics into a very formal register:

Person	Ebonics	English Translation
Man 1	Sheeeet. Man, that honky mus' be messin' with my old lady. Got to be runnin' col' upside down his head!	I don't believe this. That white man should stay away from my wife or I will be forced to inflict on him a blunt force trauma to his head with a vengeance, and that is a dish best served cold.
Man 2	Hey Home, I can dig it! You know he ain't gonna lay no mo' big rap upon you, man!	Yes, brother from my home land, I would feel the same way. He is wrong for doing that. He would never have you arrested either, because neither he or anyone else would have you arrested for defending your right.

Another tongue-in-cheek Internet translation from Ebonics to high English was introduced as an entry "turned in by an Oakland High School student who received highest honors at the school district's Ebonics translation competition." The assignment was to render into Standard English the song "One More Chance," by the late rap artist Notorious B.I.G.:

Ebonics	English Translation
So, what's it gonna be? Him or me? We can cruise the world with pearls Gator boots for girls. The envy of all women, crushed linen Cartier wrist-wear with diamonds in 'em. The finest women I love with a passion Ya man's a wimp, I give that ass a good trashin'.	The ultimate decision rests with you. Whom do you choose as your sexual partner? I can take you on cruises around the world. I will dress you in the finest jewelry and footwear. You will be envied by women worldwide in your fine clothes and jewelry. There is a special place in my heart for beautiful women. I will defeat your man in an altercation because he is effeminate.

Sparing neither his rampaging materialism nor his misogynistic ravings, the "translator" lampooned Biggie's lyrics with a keen ear for the nuances of hip-hop's insider lingo. But textbook Ebonics this was not. With a few exceptions, the verbiage of today's rap artist draws more on slang than it does on the grammar of Ebonics.

Most translation jokes involved translations in the other direction, from Standard English into Ebonics. They reveal both what people took Ebonics to be, and what they took its speakers to be like. Several loose versions of Clement Moore's "The Night Before Christmas" (originally entitled "A Visit from St. Nicholas") were striking in this respect. One of the first was circulated via electronic mail in January 1997:

'Twas da Night Befo' Christmas

'Twas da night befo' Christmas and all in the hood
Not a homie was stirring cuz it was all good
The tube socks was hung on the window sill
And we all had smiles up on our grill

Mookie and BeBe was snug in the crib
In the back bedroom cuz that's how we live
And moms in her do-rag and me with my nine
had just gotten busy cuz girlfriend is fine

All of a sudden a lowrider rolled by
Bumpin phat beats cuz the system's fly
I bounced to the window at a quarter pas'
Bout ready to pop a cap in somebody's ——
well anyway

I yelled to my lady, "Yo peep this!"
She said, "Stop frontin', just mind yo' bidness!"
I said, "For real, doe, come check dis out!"
We weren't even buggin, no worries, no doubt

Cuz bumpin an thumpin' from around da way
Was Santa, eight reindeer and a sleigh
Da beats was kickin', da ride was phat
I said, "Yo, red Dawg, you all that!"

He threw up a sign and yelled to his boyz
"Ay yo, give it up, let's make some noise!
To the top of the projects and across the strip mall
We gots ta go, I got a booty call."

He pulled up his ride on the top a da roof
And sippin' on a 40, he busted a move
I yelled up to Santa, "Yo ain't got no stack!"
He said, "Damn homie, dese projects is wack!

"But don't worry, black, cuz I gots da skillz
I learnt back when I hadda pay da billz."
Out from his bag he pulled three small tings
A credit card, a knife, and a bobby pin

He slid down the fire escape smoove as a cat
And busted the window with a b-ball bat
I said, "Whassup, Santa? Why'd ya bust my place?"
He said, "You best get on up out my face!"

His threads was all leatha, his chains was all gold
His sneaks was Puma and they was five years old
He dropped down the duffle, Clippers logo on the side
Santa broke out da loot and my mouf popped open wide.

A wink of his eye and a shine off his gold toof
He cabbage patched his way back onto the roof
He jumped in his hooptie with rims made of chrome
To tap that booty waitin at home

And all I heard as he cruised outta sight
Was a loud and hearty . . .
"WEEESSTSIIIIDE!!!!!!!"

This translation offered an authentic approximation of hip-hop speech, complete with Ebonics pronunciations (*da, befo', smoove, toof*) and slang (*buggin'*, or worrying; *frontin'*, or faking; *40*, for a forty-ounce container of malt liquor; *homie*, or home boy; *hood*, or neighborhood; *hooptie*, or car, usually decrepit, but not in this case; *phat*, or great). But the parody obviously swarms with stereotypes as well.

We have discussed the old-time black-faced minstrel performer and his ludicrous speech. In this recent incarnation, he rides in a "hooptie with rims made of chrome," but he is still grinning. The stereotypes and antics have shifted with the times: handkerchiefs have been swapped for do-rags, worn to protect a hairdo, and straight-razors for nines, nine-millimeter handguns. But the modern stereotypes are as deplorable as ever; the narrator is concerned with superficial externals (gold, leather, designer accessories), obsessed with sex (Santa is hurrying to make a "booty call," and the narrator himself has "just gotten busy"), and poised for violence ("ready to pop a cap in somebody's ———"), while Santa is well practiced in burglary ("I gots da skillz").

Breaking as it did in the Christmas season, the Ebonics controversy spawned many other full-length translations of "The Night Before Christmas," including this less authentic but equally racist one "De Ebonics Crimmus Poem" (from the site www.AtlantaGA.com/crimmus.htm; no longer active):

> I looked out thru de bars;
> What covered my doe;
> 'spectin' de sheriff;
> Wif a warrent fo sho.

> And what did I see;
> I said, "Lawd, look at dat!"
> Ther' wuz a huge watermellon;
> Pulled by giant warf rats!!

Such parodies held a hidden irony. In the 1960s, William Stewart argued that stories written in dialect might help some Ebonics-speaking children learn to read because it is easier, theoretically, to "decode" a text that mirrors the way one speaks than to grapple with a text that is foreign. Once the students mastered the dialect stories, they would turn their attention to narratives rendered in Standard English. Stewart said the idea had come to him when he was penning a black-dialect version of Moore's poem for a greeting card. Stewart's version, which followed the wording of the original more closely than the caricatures cited above, began:

> It's the night before Christmas, and here in our house,
> It ain't nothing moving, not even no mouse.
> There go we-all stockings, hanging high up off the floor,
> So Santa can full them up, if he walk in through our door.

This vernacular "Night Before Christmas" was distant from its 1996 counterparts in conception and purpose. (According to Stewart, a twelve-year-old African American student who was having difficulty reading could recite the Ebonics version fluently and accurately. But when she was given the original version, "all the 'problem reader' behaviors returned.")

The "Ebonics Lectric Library of Classical Literature" was the single largest source of Ebonics translation humor on the Internet (www.novusordo.com/indexn.htm; no longer active). It opened with these words:

> Since the recent decision to make Ebonics (Ebony-Phonics) a second language in our schools it has become obvious that e-bliterations of the classics will be required. We will cover here the greater works of world Literature (Litershure) in the hopes of bridging the gap between English and the new Slanguage. The Illuminatus Foundation has come to the web to meet that need. . . . Educators are encouraged to study the writing style and incorporate it into their daily lesson plans as they will be required to teach it under the new laws. Students are encouraged to read these works in their own language with a clearer comprehension than has ever been possible.

The translated works available on the site included selections from Plato, Milton, Shakespeare, Ovid, and Sophocles. The first few lines of Coleridge's "Rime of the Ancient Mariner" read as follows:

> It be an ancient Marina',
> And he stoppeth one o' three. Sheeeiit.
> "By dy long grey beard and glitterin' eye,
> Now wherefore stoppst dou me?
> The bridegroom's door's be jimmy'd wide,
> And Ah am next o' kin;
> De guests be met, de feast be set, dig dis:
> Mayst hear de merry din."

The translation strategies tended to be simple, and their products were stilted and counterfeit, unlike those of the spoken Ebonics exemplified elsewhere in this book. *Sheeeiit* and *dig dis* were inserted from time to time, "is" and "are" were universally replaced by *be*, in accordance with the misconception about this verb noted previously, and selected words and pronunciations were replaced by their often disparaging "Ebonics" equivalents: "opened" by *jimmy'd*, "I" by *Ah*, "of" by *o'*, and so on. The website, in fact, invited visitors to "e-bliterate" any work of literature they wished, using a filter available on-line. The Ebonics Translator (at www.AtlantaGA.com/ebonics.htm; no longer active) offered a similar service.

These translators and others were similar or identical to Jive, a filter posted on the Internet long before the Ebonics controversy. Jive replaced "man" with *dude*, "woman" with *mama*, "something" with *sump'n*, "buy" with *steal*, "did" with *dun did*, "ask" with *ax'*, "hi" with *'sup, dude*, and so on. As linguists Maggie Ronkin and Helen Karn noted in 1999, these and other translation devices invariably introduced vulgarities and linguistic derogation. The effect was a mock Ebonics that conveyed the "outgroup ideology that the denigration of English and Western culture in general" would result from Oakland's "having gone too far in respecting and embracing the 'legitimacy and richness of Ebonics.'"

Racial caricatures.   The fourth and final category of Ebonics jokes involved racial caricatures or stereotypes. Spoofs along the lines of "Ebonics Homework Assignment" and "Hooked on Ebonics" were by far the most popular of this genre. "Leroy," a fifteen-year-old ninth-grader, was said to have received an "easy homework assignment," requiring him to use fifteen words in as many sentences. In other versions, Leroy was twenty, still in the ninth grade, and an Oakland resident, and the number of words on the assignment had swollen to eighteen or twenty. But these chucklers almost always remained:

> **Catacomb.**   Don King was at the fight the other night . . . Man, somebody get dat *catacomb*.
>
> **Israel.**   Alonso tried to sell me a Rolex. I said, Man, that look fake. He said, No, *Israel*.

This strategy of fusing two or more words to resemble another word or phrase also helped "I. B. White" (wordplay on "I be white") compile his 1997 glossary *The Old, Fat, White Guy's Guide to Ebonics*. There were entries for *delight* ("the light, as in, 'Turn off delight, got dammit'") and *splay* ("an expression meaning 'let's start the game'").

This sort of wordplay was benign. Less harmless was the implication in "Ebonics Homework" that Leroy was too stupid to recognize the puns in his slurred interpretations of "cat a comb" and "it's real" and that his teachers were equally clueless ("Leroy got an A!"). Yet these jabs amounted to little more than a lighthearted lampooning of the Oakland proposal.

The list, however, grew ugly. As the fictional homework assignment unfolded, Leroy became much more than just doltish. He was transformed into the image of the Brute Negro (one of the seven black stereotypes of American fiction identified by the late literary scholar Sterling Brown). He became a criminal, an adulterer, and a rapist:

Hotel.   I gave my girlfriend da crabs and the *hotel* everybody.

Income.   I just got in bed wit dis hoe and *income* my wife.

Fortify.   I axed da hoe how much? She said *fortify.*

Disappointment.   My parole officer tol me if I miss *disappointment* he gonna kill me.

Honor.   At the rape trial, the Judge axed my buddy, "Who be *honor* first?"

When one learns that between 1930 and 1967, 89 percent of the 455 prisoners executed for rape in the United States under civil authority were African American—a proportion far in excess of their representation in the general population—the last joke turns sour in one's mouth. Indeed, many of the same prejudices that fueled that disparity may have contributed during the 1990s to the fact that one in every three black men in the country between the ages of twenty and twenty-nine was either in prison, on parole, or otherwise in the cluthces of the criminal justice system.

Such sobering considerations did not stem the Ebonics satire that rose from the bellies of bigots. There was the "Ebonics Loan Application," for instance:

Approximate Estimate of Income

Thefts $_____, Relief $_____, Unemployment $_____, Welfare $_____
Activities: Gov't Employee _____, Evangelist _____, VD Spreader _____,
Hubcap Salesman _____, Rapist _____

As late as October 1998, nearly two years after the first Ebonics resolution, an undergraduate at a major American university circulated via his dormitory's electronic mailing list a "Gangsta Aptitude

Test," or GAT (hip-hop for "firearm"). Described as "an Ebonics version of the SAT," the test included such multiple choice items as this:

> You just robbed sum jack mo fo with $20 in his wallet. You can buy
> A. A dime and two 40's.
> B. A new pair of Fila's.
> C. Dashiki down the block.
> D. Yo mama.

And in November 1998, another undergraduate at the same university received an e-mail with this new and even more odious caricature, from which we quote only a few excerpts:

> **Ebonics Meets Windows 98**
>
> Compton City Schools has announced that its special Ebonics version of Windows 98, entitled "Dis be a fresh window," has been leaked to several white suburbs, causing confusion for unsuspecting Caucasian users. . . . On the main screen, My Computer is replaced with "Dis My Shit." The Recycle Bin has been replaced with a Goodwill dumpster, and the Internet Explorer reads, "Titty and Booty Sites." . . .
>
> Users have their choice of three animated screen savers: "Marquee," a li'l G spray-painting dirty words that move across the screen; "Mystify," a 15-year-old crack whore giving birth to 12 children on screen, or "Flying Bullets," a '64 Olds loaded with gangstas doing a desktop drive by. . . .

The "Mystify" screen saver, in particular, gave us the shivers. One has the sense of eavesdropping on a twisted mind, from some earlier century when racist depravity of this type could be expressed more overtly.

What is startling and revealing about such caricatures is that some of them, at least, were created by blacks. Black illustrator Keith Lovett, for instance, threw together a slim paperback in 1997 entitled *Hooked on Ebonics*. It included a twenty-five-item version of the "Ebonics Homework Assignment," as well as a number of innocuous jokes revolving around the theme "Clues That You May Be Hooked on Ebonics" ("You call a girl a 'sister' and she's no kin to you"). Some of the cracks, however, involved insidious stereotypes:

> **Clues That You May Be Hooked on Ebonics**
>
> You see your parole officer more than you see your father.
> You use your ski mask as your ATM card.
> Your gold necklace is thicker than any book you've ever read.

In these and similar "jokes," Ebonics no longer stood for the language variety being debated in Oakland. Instead, it was a cruel proxy for African Americans themselves, an opportunity to resurrect or perpetuate the grossest stereotypes about them. Nowhere is this clearer than in "Ebonic Olympic Games" (novusordo.com/elympic.html; no longer active). In this spoof, the satire is invidious and grotesque, and the creator's fear of or loathing for African Americans, and the clearinghouses of liberalism that he/she sees as sympathetic toward them, crackles like a Roman candle:

Ebonic Olympic Games
(Event List)

Opening Ceremonies
The Torching of the Olympic City
Gang Colors Parade

Track and Field
Rob, Shoot & Run
9MM Pistol Toss
Molotov Cocktail Throw
Barbed Wire Roll
Chain Link Fence Climb
Peoplechase
Monkey Bar Race
100 Yard Dog Dash (100 Yard Dash While Being Chased By Police Dog)
200 Yard Trash Can Hurdles
500 Yard Stolen Car Battery Run
1000 Meter Courtoom Relay (Team of four passing murder weapon—
    not getting caught)
1500 Meter Television Set Relay
Bitch Slapping (Bruises inflicted on wife/girlfriend in three one-minute
    rounds)
Ebo-Decathlon
    Rob Liquor Store
    Guzzle One-Fifth of Fortified Wine
    Drink Six-Pack of Old English 800
    Steal One BMW
    Commit One Car Jacking
    Have Sex With Prostitute
    Pimp Girlfriend to Family Member
    Complete One Drug Deal
    Remove Serial Numbers From One Stolen Gun
    One Additional Felony of Choice

Miscellaneous Events
Graffiti Wall Painting
Name Your Father (Canceled, Considered Too Difficult)
Lying to Police (Canceled, Considered Too Easy)
Welfare Fraud (Canceled, Considered a Lifestyle, Not an Event)

Closing Ceremonies
Grand Finale Firearms Display & Gang War Shoot Out

Sponsors: ACLU, Oakland Board of Education, Congress, and the
Supreme Court

For those behind this most virulent strain of Ebonics "humor,"
Ebonics was never a language. Or a dialect. Or an educational policy.
Or a matter of public outrage. For bigots, Ebonics simply served as a
metaphor for their stereotypes of African Americans—as criminals
and crackheads and welfare defrauders and liars and gangbangers
and sex addicts and objects. Originally intended to stir black consciousness, the term was twisted into the symbol of a degenerate culture and class. Because everyone supposedly agreed that Ebonics was
ludicrous and laughable, one could use this consensus as a cover for
much darker kinds of humor about the stereotypical speakers of
Ebonics, and broadcast over the Internet—and elsewhere—what was
previously uttered only behind cupped hands. And one could implic-
itly invite those who encountered the jokes to share the stereotypes.
In short, "Ebonics" became a new slur, a "nigger" upon whom one
could inflict a Rodney King–style beating while wearing the helmet
of "wit."

Part Five

The Double Self

12

The Crucible of Identity

*One ever feels his two-ness—an American, a Negro: Two souls, two
unreconciled strivings; two warring ideals in one dark body . . . The history of the American Negro is the history of this strife—this longing . . . to
merge his double self into a better and truer self. In this merging, he wishes
neither of the older selves to be lost.*

—W. E. B. Du Bois (1903)

*I who am poisoned with the blood of both
Where shall I turn, divided to the vein?
I who have cursed the drunken officer of British rule, how choose
Between this Africa and the English tongue I love?
Betray them both, or give back what they give?*

—Derek Walcott (1969)

Here is a conversation as ordinary in its context as breathing. It took
place recently in the office of a California elementary school, between
three black people: a second-grade student, or eight-year-old; Miss P.,
the school secretary, in her forties; and a parent in his thirties who
happened to be in the office at the time.

STUDENT: Miss P., my teacher sen' me to the office.

MISS P.:   What she sen' you here fuh?

STUDENT: She say I got a rash.

MISS P.:   A rash? Where the rash at?

STUDENT: Right here on my chin . . .

MISS P.:   Come over here an' lemme see. [The child walks over to her, and she examines his chin.] So what you want me to do? [No answer.] I'ma call yo' dad, boy. [She phones his father, learns that he can't come for his son right then, and hangs up.] You know yo' dad got to go to school, boy, he can't come an' get you. . . .

STUDENT: Where Miss G. at? [Miss G. is a staff member the student likes.]

MISS P.:   Miss G. in the room nex' to the library. [The child leaves to look for Miss G.]

PARENT: [To Miss P.] That boy sound jus' like me. He remind me of me. He remind me of me. Don' seem like that long ago. Seem like jus' yesterday . . .

These speakers, youth and adults alike, used Spoken Soul because it is the language in which comfortable informal conversation takes place daily for them—as is true within vast segments of the African American community. They drew on it for reasons similar to those that the novelists, playwrights, poets, preachers, pray-ers, comedians, actors, screenwriters, singers, toasters, rappers, and ordinary folk whose extensive and creative use of the vernacular we've documented in this book drew on it: because it came naturally; because it was authentic; because it resonated for them, touching some timbre within and capturing a vital core of experience that had to be expressed *just so;* because it reached the heart and mind and soul of the addressee or audience in a way no other variety quite did; because to have used Standard English might have marked the relationships between the participants as more formal or distant than the speaker wanted. For these individuals, not to have used Spoken Soul might have meant they were not who or what or where they were and wanted to be.

The question remains about why Spoken Soul persists despite the negative attitudes toward it, and its speakers, that have been expressed for centuries. The primary answer is its role as a symbol of identity. This is the driving force behind the maintenance of low-prestige languages and dialects around the world, including "Schwyzerdeutsch in Switzerland, Canadian French in Canada, Appalachian English . . . in the United States, and Catalan Spanish in Spain," all of which, as psychologist Ellen Bouchard Ryan has noted, have survived despite "strong pressures to succumb" to the standard languages that dominate them. Pidgin and creole languages worldwide provide additional examples. Often derided as illegitimate, even degenerate, they are also exalted and embraced as markers of solidarity; local, national, or ethnic identity; and truth.

For many African Americans, the identity function of Spoken Soul is paramount, and very old. The repressive slave codes enacted in America between the late seventeenth century and the early eighteenth century (including whipping, maiming, branding, ear-nailing and -severing, and castration for various "offenses") may have helped forge an oppositional identity among blacks vis-à-vis whites, expressed in part through a distinctive vernacular. Continued hardships of the nineteenth and twentieth centuries (including lynchings, the denial of equal access to education and employment, segregation, poverty, police persecution, and criminal injustice) not only would have facilitated the development and/or maintenance of distinctive black ways of talking, dressing, dancing, making music, and behaving, but also would have made black Americans reluctant to mimic white ways of talking and behaving.

In the 1980s, anthropologists Signithia Fordham and John Ogbu found black inner-city teenagers in Washington, D.C., hostile to the adoption of a cluster of behaviors defined as "acting white"—at the top of which was "speaking standard English." The opposition is not just to speaking Standard English, which can be done in an identifiably black way, with a black accent and rhetorical style, but also and especially to talking proper or talking white (whether standard or vernacular), with white pronunciation patterns or accents. This attitude remains deeply ingrained today. Working-class teenagers from East Palo Alto and Redwood City, California, recently articulated for us their opposition to talking white and their defiant defense of talking black. For them, Spoken Soul is a litmus test for anyone who claims to be black (although one has to be cautious about the shrinking of Du Bois's consciousness to a one-soul paradigm):

> Then i's these . . . black girls jus' like—ack lak white girls. Ah say, "You wanna be white, go change yo' sk[in] color. Shut up! [Tinky]

> Over at my school . . . first time they catch you talkin white, they'll never let it go. Even if you just quit talkin like that, they'll never let it go! [Reggie]

> It pisses me when the Oreos [black on the outside, white on the inside]—they be trying to correct your language, and I be like, "Get away from me! Did I ask you to—correct me?! No! No! No, I didn't! Nuh-uh!" [Fabiola]

As hip-hop culture and the language, body movements, dress, and music that embody it spread among young Americans of virtually every ethnicity and are adopted by teenagers in countries as distant as Russia and Japan, the status of black language and culture at the popular level is rising, and young African Americans of every class proudly claim it as originally and most authentically theirs.

We shouldn't let this mention of teenagers delude us into thinking, as many do, that Spoken Soul figures in the identities of young people only. Black adults of all ages talk the vernacular, and it functions to express their black identity, too. While it is true that African Americans with less education and earning power use the grammatical features of Spoken Soul more extensively than do those with more education and earning power, the vernacular is often wrongly associated with ignorance. The use, enjoyment, and endorsement of the vernacular by blacks who are well educated and hold good jobs reveal that much more is going on. This category includes not only such writers as June Jordan and such comedians as Steve Harvey, for whom the vernacular is part of their occupational art. It also includes business administrators such as Arch Whitehead (featured on *60 Minutes* and referred to earlier in the book), who eschew Spoken Soul in the world of work and extol it as the language they prefer at home or with friends.

A series of studies conducted since the 1970s reveals that attitudes toward Spoken Soul and Standard English, particularly among blacks, are more complex than what is commonly reported in the press—namely that the former is disdained and the latter extolled. Acknowledging this complexity is one key to understanding the persistence and significance of Spoken Soul.

In the 1970s, education specialist Mary Hoover polled forty-eight parents of elementary students in East Palo Alto and Oakland, California, about their attitudes toward vernacular and standard Black English. (Standard Black English or Black Standard English is a variety in which the speaker uses standard grammar but still sounds black, primarily because of black rhetorical strategies and selected black pronunciations, among them intonation and emphasis.) Hoover also asked about Superstandard, or "talking proper," in which the speaker sheds all traces of black pronunciation and affects a stilted syntax. She found little support for "talking proper," long the butt of humor and deprecation within the black community, but plenty of support for Standard Black English and a distinct preference for it over the vernacular in the classroom and at work, and for reading and writing. However, there was strong support for the vernacular in informal spoken interaction at home and in the community, especially with black family members and friends.

One of the most frequent explanations that the parents gave for wanting to retain the vernacular was its role in the preservation of their distinctive history, worldview, and culture—their soul. The sentiment is not unique to African Americans. As T. S. Eliot observed some fifty years ago: "For the transmission of a culture—a peculiar way of thinking, feeling and behaving—and for its maintenance, there is no safeguard more reliable than a language." Literary critic Cleanth Brooks, noting the maintenance of Welsh in the face of English domination, and other examples, observed that:

> The soul of a people is embodied in the language peculiar to them. . . .
> It is significant that peoples throughout history have often stubbornly
> held on to their native language or dialect because they regarded it
> as a badge of their identity and because they felt that only through it
> could they express their inner beings, their attitudes and emotions,
> and even their own concepts of reality.

Another reason for blacks' accepting and preserving the vernacular is its usefulness in "getting down" with other blacks. A black professor at a midwestern university, interviewed in a study in the early 1990s, explained that she not only used Spoken Soul with her black friends as a release from the stresses of her white-dominated professional life, but also employed it at times to create a positive relationship interaction with black students:

> I think it [black vernacular] can be a unifier in developing a certain
> kind of rapport with them. . . . The personal rapport perhaps gives
> them a greater sense that "I am on your side. . . . There's no barrier
> between us. I can identify with you"—[it's] kind of a signal with the
> language.

We should remember that for many, speaking the vernacular is a source of great pleasure, as well as great utility. As Toni Morrison pointed out, there are some things that soul speakers cannot say, or say as well, "without recourse to my language."

The most recent study of attitudes toward black vernacular and Standard English is an ongoing one being conducted by Jacquelyn Rahman, a linguistics graduate student at Stanford University. In spring 1999, she asked black undergraduates and graduate students there what they thought of the two varieties of English, and found that even among these upwardly bound black academics and pre-professionals, the value of both varieties was endorsed, much as Mary Hoover had found with black parents two decades earlier. On the one hand, Standard English was defended as the variety needed "in a white-dominated world . . . to gain respect and get good jobs," "in formal settings (work, school reports)," and "when I am around the white majority . . . because that is what my audience understands and it's socially more appropriate." On the other hand, Black English was praised for its "spirit, creativity, resilience and soul," for its "character and history," for "being more expressive and vibrant," and because "it keeps me close to my family and friends, as well as serving as a living reminder of my history as a member of a distinctive ethnic group in this country." Virtually all the students said that they were bidialectal, some becoming so after initial school experiences in which they were derided by black classmates for talking white. They draw on one variety or the other as audience and situation demand.

Because we have celebrated Spoken Soul throughout this book, one might be tempted to group us with those who argue that Standard English is unnecessary, and who insist that vernacular speakers need not extend their repertoires. On the contrary, we feel that shunning Standard English too easily lets the power structure and our own would-be spokespeople off the hook, allowing the former more wantonly to disregard the raw voice of protest, and the latter to have one less weapon hopelessly mute in affairs of business and the state.

That mainstream English is essential to our self-preservation is indisputable. Without it, how could we have wrested judgeships and congressional seats and penthouse offices from those who have long enjoyed such privileges almost unchallenged? We have come this far thanks, in part, to a distinguished lineage of race men and women who used elegant Standard English as a template for their struggle against the very oppressor responsible for imposing the language on them. Malcolm X's speeches show his command of Standard English, especially a black Standard English that, like Jesse Jackson's, is non-vernacular in grammar but soulful in its rhetorical style and pronunciation, including intonation and emphasis. (Malcolm himself was quite critical of "ultra-proper-talking Negroes," including "those with their accents so phonied up that if you just heard them and didn't see them you wouldn't even know that they were Negroes.") But in making the transition from the street to the podium, brother Malcolm also had to develop his expertise in speaking and writing Standard English, and his initial discouragement is described in his *Autobiography*:

> I became increasingly frustrated at not being able to express what I
> wanted to convey in letters that I wrote, especially those to Mr. Elijah
> Muhammad. In the street, I had been the most articulate hustler out
> there—I had commanded attention when I said something. But now,
> trying to write simple English, I not only wasn't articulate, I wasn't even
> functional. How would I sound writing in slang, the way I would *say* it,
> something such as "Look, daddy, let me pull your coat about a cat,
> Elijah Muhammad."

Before we even fix our mouths to snub the speech of the marketplace, we must remember Malcolm, and remember also Frederick Douglass's "What to the Slave Is the Fourth of July? An Address delivered in Rochester, New York, on 5 July 1852." Drawing his imposing form upright before the president of the United States and other assembled statesmen, Douglass declared that:

> This Fourth [of] July is yours, not mine. You may rejoice, I must
> mourn. To drag a man in fetters into the grand illuminated temple of
> liberty, and call upon him to join you in joyous anthems, were inhuman
> mockery and sacrilegious irony. Do you mean, citizens, to mock me,
> by asking me to speak to-day? If so, there is a parallel to your conduct.
> And let me warn you that it is dangerous to copy the example of a
> nation whose crimes, towering up to heaven, were thrown down by
> the breath of the Almighty, burying that nation in irrecoverable ruin!
> I can to-day take up the plaintive lament of a peeled and woe-smitten
> people.

By bequeathing to us such eloquence, Douglass commands us not only to master Standard English but also to learn it in its highest form. And we must. For in the academies and courthouses and legislatures and business places where policies are made and implemented, it is as graceful a weapon as can be found against injustice, poverty, and discrimination. Like Douglass and Malcolm X, we must learn to carry Standard English like a lariat, unfurling it with precision. We must learn to use it, too, for enjoyment and mastery of literature, philosophy, science, math, and the wide variety of subjects that are conducted and taught in Standard English, in the United States, and, increasingly, in the world. We must teach our children to do so as well. This, as you know, is no mean feat. It requires time, money and other resources, patience, discipline, and understanding, all of which

tend to be in tragically short supply in schools with large black populations. But treating Spoken Soul like a disease is no way to add Standard English to their repertoire. On the contrary, building on Spoken
Soul, through contrast and comparison with Standard English, is
likely to meet with less resistance from students who are hostile to
"acting white." It is also likely to generate greater interest and motivation, and as experiments have shown (see chapter 9), to yield greater
success, more quickly.

But if we could wave a magic wand and have all of black America
wake up tomorrow talking like television anchorman Bryant Gumbel,
shouldn't we do so? Actually, no. Sampling Standard English should
not lead us to forget the flavor of Spoken Soul, or vice versa. Just ask
yourself: Why would our forefathers and foremothers "sing the Lord's
song in a strange land" (Psalm 137:4), if their voices hadn't created a
note that was decidedly their own? Without that note, how could they
have described to their children their intimate relationships with love
and freedom and death, relationships that were dissimilar to those of
their masters? In the end, all words (and the rules for pronouncing
and combining them) are mighty. As the African concept of *nommo*
asserts, spirits are conjured by the saying of words. Ancestors are in-
voked by the speaking of words. If our enemies can make us forget
these words, and then make us forget that we have forgotten, they will
have robbed us of our ability to honor and summon our ancestors,
whom we so desperately need now more than ever.

True, the vernacular has been abused. (How could we ever forget
the prattle of the blackface minstrels?) But we must reclaim it. We
must stop importing this shame that is manufactured beyond our
communities for something as cellular and spiritual as our language.
We must refuse to allow Spoken Soul to remain a stepchild in the
family of tongues. We must begin to do for language what we have
done historically (in some cases only very recently) for our hair, our
clothes, our art, our education, and our religion: that is, to determine
for ourselves what's good and what's bad, and even what's *baaad*. The
crucial thing is that we hold the yardstick, and finally become sover-
eign guardians and arbitrators and purveyors of our culture. For all
who share this vision, we close with four modest suggestions:

■ Develop a new awareness about the origins, structure, politics,
and larger significance of Spoken Soul. We're not suggesting that you
case the 'hood thinking about etymology or phonology. Rather, try
to keep in mind that all languages and dialects are systematic, rule-

governed, and righteous, and that none has ever fallen out of a black hole or been spontaneously conceived.

■ Be conscious of our love-hate relationship with Spoken Soul. The next time a brother or sister starts speaking in deep vernacular during a city council meeting and you feel yourself stinging with embarrassment, try to remember the social conditioning and the historical circumstances behind that private shame. We don't promise that you'll overcome your shame, only that you may begin to understand it and, one hopes, reverse it. By the same token, the next time you find yourself submerged in and surrounded by Spoken Soul, acknowledge it silently. Adore it. Taste it as if for the first time. Try to imagine the same scene, the same ethos and ambience, without it.

■ Strike such phrases as "broken English," "lazy English," "bad English," and "careless English" from your vocabulary, and teach your friends and family to put little stock in such uninformed and absolutist judgments. You can't speak soul simply by being lazy or careless about speaking Standard English. At the same time, urge youngsters to appreciate and become proficient in Standard English, especially the black Standard English that the Reverend Martin Luther King Jr., Malcolm X, Maxine Waters, Maya Angelou, and other leaders have commanded so well.

■ Don't ever shun or jeer a brother or sister because of the way he or she speaks. It is only when we have claimed both Spoken Soul and Standard English as our own, empowering our youth to appreciate and articulate each in their respective forums, that we will have mastered the art of merging our double selves into a better and truer self. Remember: to become an accomplished pianist (jazz *or* classical), you've got to be able to work both the ebonies and the ivories.

We should remember and do these things, because issues of language, class, culture, education, and power will continue to smolder, and will flare up again. As the African American proverb—cast in Spoken Soul—cautions us, "Every shut eye ain't asleep, every goodbye ain't gone."

Notes

Part One
Introduction

1. *What's Going On?*

The definitions for *soul* are from *The American Heritage Dictionary* (Boston: Houghton Mifflin, 2000). Claude Brown's comments on "Spoken Soul" are from his article "The Language of Soul," *Esquire*, April 1968, pp. 88, 160–161. James Baldwin's remarks are from "If Black English Isn't a Language, Then Tell Me, What Is?" originally published in the *New York Times*, July 29, 1979, and reprinted in Geneva Smitherman, ed., *Black English and the Education of Black Children and Youth* (Detroit: Wayne State University Press, Center for Black Studies, 1981), pp. 390–392, and in Theresa Perry and Lisa Delpit, eds., *The Real Ebonics Debate* (Boston: Beacon Press, 1998), pp. 67–70. Toni Morrison's quotation is from Thomas LeClair, "A Conversation with Toni Morrison: 'The Language Must Not Sweat,'" *New Republic*, March 21, 1981, pp. 25–29. June Jordan is quoted from "Nobody Mean More to Me Than You and the Future Life of Willie Jordan," in her book *On Call: Political Essays* (Boston: South End Press, 1985), pp. 123–139.

Maya Angelou's remarks on the Ebonics resolution were made during a visit to Wichita, Kansas, on December 20, 1996, and were quoted in the Associated Press article "Oakland Decision Spurs Debate over Ebonics," *Wichita Eagle*, December 22, 1996, p. 7A. Kweisi Mfume's denunciation was quoted in John Leland and Nadine Joseph, "Hooked on Ebonics," *Newsweek*, January 13, 1997, p. 78. Jesse Jackson's comment was made on NBC's *Meet the Press* on December 22, 1996, and quoted in Maria Puente, "Calling Black English a Language Prompts Chorus of Criticism," *USA Today*, December 23, 1996, p. 1A. Ward Connerly's critique was quoted in Elliot Diringer and Lori Olszewski, "Critics May Not Understand Oakland's Ebonics Plan," *San Francisco Chronicle*, December 21, 1996, p. A17. Henry Louis Gates Jr.'s comment was quoted by Frank Rich in "The Ebonic Plague," *Wall Street Journal*, January 8, 1997. Bill Cosby's column "Elements of Igno-Ebonics" was published in the *Wall Street Journal*, January 10, 1997. William Bennett's description of the Ebonics resolution and Mario Cuomo's reaction were quoted in Maria Puente, "Calling Black English a Language Prompts Chorus of Criticism," *USA Today*, December 23, 1996, p. 1A. Richard Riley's remarks were quoted in Nanette Asimov, "U.S. Says Ebonics Isn't a Language," *San Francisco Chronicle*, December 25, 1996, p. 1.

Information on legislative efforts to ban Ebonics from use in schools and other official contexts is in Elaine Richardson, "The Anti-Ebonics Movement: 'Standard' English Only," in *Journal of English Linguistics* (Special Issue: Ebonics), vol.

26, no. 2 (June 1998), pp. 156–169. The report of the America Online poll about Ebonics appeared in John Leland and Nadine Joseph, "Hooked on Ebonics," *Newsweek,* January 13, 1997, p. 78. For the America Online quotations cited in this chapter, we are grateful to linguist and school volunteer Lucy Bowen of Menlo Park, California, who printed out hundreds of them and passed them on to us. Full citation information on each America Online comment, including exact time of transmission, is available.

For summaries of Justice Joiner's ruling, see the *New York Times,* July 13, 1979. The ruling itself is reprinted in Geneva Smitherman, ed., *Black English and the Education of Black Children and Youth* (Detroit: Wayne State University Press, Center for Black Studies, 1981). Carl Rowan's comment about the Ann Arbor court case was in a column entitled "Black English," which appeared in the *Philadelphia Bulletin,* July 11, 1979. For information on proposals by Caribbean linguists to consider Creole English in schools, see John R. Rickford, "Using the Vernacular to Teach the Standard," in his book *African American Vernacular English* (Oxford: Basil Blackwell, 1999). One book that exemplifies the 1990s concern with what unites us rather than what separates us as Americans is Arthur M. Schlesinger Jr., *The Disuniting of America: Reflections on a Multicultural Society* (New York: W. W. Norton, 1991, 1998). For more about Propositions 209 and 227 and similar measures in California and other states, see Jewelle Taylor Gibbs's monograph *The California Crucible* (San Francisco: Study Center Press, 1998). The income statistics for African Americans are from Martin Carnoy, *Faded Dreams: The Politics and Economics of Race in America* (Cambridge: Cambridge University Press, 1994). For other income statistics, and for a discussion of the generation gap within the black community, see Faral Chideya, "Money. Power. Respect?" *Emerge,* October 1998, pp. 35–38. For more information on the differences of opinion among African American writers with respect to Ebonics, see chapters 2 and 10, and references there.

Part Two
"This Passion, This Skill, This Incredible Music"

2. *Writers*

We are grateful to Arnold Rampersad, Sonia Sanchez, and Meta Duwa Jones for feedback on an earlier version of this chapter.

The opening epigraph is from Paule Marshall, "From the Poets of the Kitchen," *New York Times Book Review,* January 9, 1983, reprinted in Henry Louis Gates Jr. and Nellie Y. McKay, eds., *The Norton Anthology of African American Literature* (New York: W. W. Norton, 1997), pp. 2072–2079. Marshall attributes the closing quotation to writer Grace Paley. The second is from Henry Louis Gates Jr., *The Signifying Monkey: A Theory of Afro-American Literary Criticism* (New York and Oxford: Oxford University Press, 1988), p. xxii.

John Leacock's play *The Fall of British Tyranny; or, American Liberty Triumphant* was published by Styner and Cist in Philadelphia in 1776. Richard Allsopp's *Dictionary of Caribbean Usage* (Oxford: Oxford University Press, 1997, p. 333) defines *Kojo* or *Cudjoe* as "a name loosely applied to any black man, usually from a rural area, who has a reputation for rough-and-ready force, crude strength, or stubborn resistance," and derives it from "Fante *Kodwo* . . . Ghanaian *Kodzo*," name of a male born on a Monday. The quotations from Stephen E. Henderson are from *Understanding the New Black Poetry: Black Speech and Black Music as Poetic References* (New York: William Morrow, 1973), pp. 31–33. Sterling Brown's "Southern Road" poem, reprinted in part, is from his *Southern Road* (New York: HarperCollins). The quotation about Johnson's reevaluation of dialect use in Brown's poetry comes from *The Norton Anthology of African American Literature*, cited above, p. 121. Arnold Rampersad's comment on "Mother to Son" is from *The Life of Langston Hughes*, vol. 1: 1902–1941. *I, Too, Sing America* (New York and Oxford: Oxford University Press, 1986), p. 43. For the full text of "Queens of the Universe" by Sonia Sanchez, see Woodie King, ed., *BlackSpirits: A Festival of New Black Poets in America* (New York: Random House, 1972), p. 186. Don Lee's poem "Move Un-Noticed to Be Noticed" is in Stephen E. Henderson, *Understanding the New Black Poetry*, cited above, pp. 340–343.

The passage from Claude Brown's *Manchild in the Promised Land* (New York: Macmillan, 1965) is on p. 63. The excerpt from Walter Mosley's *Devil in a Blue Dress* is from chapter 2 (New York: W. W. Norton, 1990). Sherley Anne Williams's "Tell Martha Not to Moan," first published in *Massachusetts Review* in 1967, is anthologized in *The Norton Anthology of African American Literature*, cited above, pp. 2365–2375. The passage from June Jordan's *His Own Where* is from chapter 1 (New York: Thomas Y. Crowell, 1971). Paul Stoller is quoted from his book *Black American English: Its Background and Its Usage in the Schools and in Literature* (New York: Delta, 1975), p. 194. Alice Walker's *The Color Purple* was first published in New York by Harcourt Brace Jovanovich in 1982. The Ntozake Shange excerpt is from *for colored girls who have considered suicide / when the rainbow is enuf* (New York: Simon & Schuster, 1975.)

The Zora Neale Hurston passage is from *Their Eyes Were Watching God* (Philadelphia and London: J. B. Lippincott, 1937). Henry Louis Gates Jr.'s comment about Sterling Brown's and Hurston's reverence for black vernacular is in *The Signifying Monkey*, cited above, p. xii. Daryl Cumber Dance's comment about the ubiquity of dialect in black folklore is in the introduction to *Shuckin' and Jivin': Folklore from Contemporary Black Americans* (Bloomington: Indiana University Press, 1978), p. xx. The quotation from Chapman Milling within the comment is from his foreword to J. Mason Brewer's *Dog Ghosts and Other Texas Negro Folk Tales* (Austin: University of Texas Press, 1958), p. xii. For analyses of black folklore, see Alan Dundes, ed., *Mother Wit from the Laughing Barrel: Readings in the Interpretation of Afro-American Folklore* (Englewood Cliffs, N.J.: Prentice-Hall, 1973). For further analysis of Walter Simmons's watermelon story and other lies, see John R. Rickford, "Riddlin and Lyin: Participation and Performance," in Joshua A. Fishman, ed., *The Fergusonian Impact* (The Hague: Mouton, 1986), vol. 2, pp. 89–106. The "Aunt Dinah Died" jump-rope rhyme is from Linda Goss and Marian Barnes, *Talk That Talk: An Anthology of African-American Storytelling* (New York: Simon & Schuster/ Touchstone, 1989), p. 443. The excerpt from James Baldwin's *Blues for Mister Charlie* is from p. 40 of the 1964 edition (New York: Dial Press).

Christopher Hitchens's comments about Baldwin and Black English are in his essay "Hooked on Ebonics," *Vanity Fair*, March 1997, p. 95. The extract from *A Raisin in the Sun* is from pp. 29–30 of the 1966 edition (New York: New American Library; original copyright Robert Nemiroff 1958, unpublished manuscript). John Rickford's interview with August Wilson was conducted on January 14, 1999, at Ujamaa Lounge, Stanford University, and transcribed with the assistance of Akua Searcy. The extract from *Fences* is from pp. 2–3 of the 1986 edition (New York: New American Library/Plume). The *People* magazine article on August Wilson, "Street Talk: Hearing Voices Makes Playwright August Wilson the Talent He Is," by William Plummer and Tony Kahn, appeared in the May 13, 1996, issue, pp. 64–66.

Sylvia Wallace Holton's account of the minstrel show tradition is in her book *Down Home and Uptown* (London: Associated University Presses, 1984), p. 102. Nathan Huggins's remarks about minstrelsy are from *Harlem Renaissance* (New York: Oxford University Press, 1971), p. 251. Three of the best general books on blackface minstrelsy are Robert C. Toll, *Blacking Up: The Minstrel Show in Nineteenth-Century America* (New York: Oxford University Press, 1974); Eric Lott, *Love and Theft: Blackface Minstrelsy and the American Working Class* (New York: Oxford University Press, 1993); and W. T. Lhamon Jr., *Raising Cain: Blackface Performance from Jim Crow to Hip-Hop* (Cambridge, Mass.: Harvard University Press, 1998). The minstrel show dialogue featuring "End" and "Mid" is from Jack Haverly, *Negro Minstrels* (Chicago: Frederic J. Drake, 1902), and was cited in Elizabeth Riles, Phillip Klemmer, Lauren Neefe, and Haresh Kamath, "Minstrelsy: A History and Analysis," in John R. Rickford and Lisa Green, eds., *The AAVE Happenin'* (Stanford, Calif.: Stanford University Department of Linguistics, 1994), pp. 108–124). Zora Neale Hurston's complaint about the inaccuracy of dialect in minstrel shows is from "Characteristics of Negro Expression," a 1934 article reprinted in *The Norton Anthology of African American Literature*, cited above, pp. 1019–1032. James Weldon Johnson's comments on the same topic are in *Along This Way: The Autobiography of James Weldon Johnson* (New York: Viking Press, 1933), pp. 158–159.

The quotation about Joel Chandler Harris playing minstrelsy in his youth is from Eric Lott's *Love and Theft*, cited above, p. 33. The Uncle Remus story is from Joel Chandler Harris, *Uncle Remus: His Songs and Sayings*, ed. Robert Hemenway (New York: Penguin, 1986; orig. pub. D. Appleton, 1880), p. 55. Robert Hemenway's commentary on Uncle Remus is in his introduction to the Penguin Classics edition of Joel Chandler Harris, *Uncle Remus: His Songs and His Sayings* (Middlesex, England, and New York: Penguin, 1982, p. 22). Sylvia Wallace Holton's comments on Thomas Nelson Page are in her book *Down Home and Uptown*, cited above, p. 86. The "Marse Chan" passage is from Thomas Nelson Page, *In Ole Virginia; or, Marse Chan and Other Stories* (New York: Scribner, 1887). Thomas Dixon's *The Clansman: An Historical Romance of the Ku Klux Klan* was first published in 1905 (New York: Doubleday, Page).

Alain Locke's comment about "jingling and juggling" is in his article "Sterling Brown: The New Negro Folk Poet," originally published in *Negro Anthology*, 1934, pp. 111–115, and reprinted in Jeffrey C. Stewart, ed., *The Critical Temper of Alain Locke: A Selection of His Essays on Art and Culture* (New York and London: Garland, 1983), p. 50. The critique of Langston Hughes's *Fine Clothes to the Jew* is quoted from Langston Hughes, *The Big Sea: An Autobiography* (New York: Thunder's Mouth Press, 1986 [1940]), p. 266. Hughes's response to his critics is also in *The Big Sea*, p. 268. "When Malindy Sings" is quoted from *The Complete Poems of Paul Laurence Dunbar* (New York: Dodd, Mead, 1922 [1913]), p. 82. Dunbar's remark about his ability to write in dialect is quoted in James Weldon Johnson, *Along This Way*, cited above, p. 160. Johnson's assessment of Dunbar is in the same book, p. 161. "The Poet" is quoted from *The Complete Poems of Paul Laurence Dunbar*, cited above, p. 191.

The verse of "Sence You Went Away" is quoted from Johnson's *Fifty Years and Other Poems* (New York: AMS Press, 1975), p. 63. (This is a reprint of a 1917 edition published by Cornhill in Boston; individual poems were published elsewhere, 1871–1938.) James Weldon Johnson's remarks about black poets' use of quaint and musical folk speech are from *The Book of American Negro Poetry* (New York: Harcourt, Brace, 1922), pp. xxxix–xl. His subsequent, more critical remarks are from his preface to the revised edition (New York: Harcourt, Brace, 1931), p. 4. The quotation from the preface to Johnson's "Negro folk sermons" is in *God's Trombones: Seven Negro Sermons in Verse* (New York: Viking Press, 1927), p. 7. The lines from "The Pusher" and "The Thirteens (Black)" are reprinted from *The Complete Collected Poems of Maya Angelou* (New York: Random House, 1994), pp. 39, 94.

3. Preachers and Pray-ers

The first epigraph is from the sermon "Guidelines for a Constructive Church," delivered by the Reverend King at Ebenezer Baptist Church, Atlanta, June 5, 1966, which is reprinted in Clayborne Carson and Peter Holloran, eds., *A Knock at Midnight: Inspiration from the Great Sermons of Reverend Martin Luther King, Jr.* (New York: Warner Books, 1998), pp. 105–115). The second epigraph is from John R. Rickford's recording of a prayer meeting on Daufuskie Island, South Carolina, on May 24, 1970, presided over by Deacon Walter Simmons.

A more recent study of the African American preaching style is Walter Pitts's *Old Ship of Zion: The Afro-Baptist Ritual in the African Diaspora* (New York and Oxford: Oxford University Press, 1993). Pitts is justifiably critical (see pp. 4–5) of some aspects of an older work on black preaching, William H. Pipes's *Say Amen, Brother! Old-Time Negro Preaching: A Study in American Frustration* (New York: William-Frederick Press, 1951). An excellent article-length study of black preaching is Faye Vaughn-Cooke's "The Black Preaching Style: Historical Development and Characteristics," *Language and Linguistics Working Papers,* 5 (Washington, D.C.: Georgetown University Press, 1972).

As noted above, Deacon Walter Simmons's prayer was recorded on Daufuskie Island, South Carolina, May 24, 1970. The prayer recorded in Austin, Texas, is reprinted from Walter Pitts's *Old Ship of Zion*, cited above, p. 19; and Pitts's comment about the similarities between current prayers and prayers of the 1920s and 1930s is on p. 70 of the same work. Patricia Jones-Jackson's analysis is in *When Roots Die: Endangered Traditions on the Sea Islands* (Athens: University of Georgia Press, 1987), pp. 80–81. The remarks on the religious motif of the train are in the introduction to James Weldon Johnson's *God's Trombones* (New York: Viking Press, 1927). The claim that the Reverend King "delighted in euphony" was made by Richard Lischer in *The Preacher King: Martin Luther King, Jr., and the Word That Moved America* (New York and Oxford: Oxford University Press, 1955), p.120; the passage from Dr. King's sermon is from page 121 of the book.

The Reverend Emil Thomas's remarks are from a service at Jerusalem Baptist Church, Palo Alto, January 3, 1992. Geneva Smitherman is quoted from *Talkin and Testifyin: The Language of Black America* (Detroit: Wayne State University Press, 1986), p. 134. The first passage with the "hunh" expression is from Grace Sims Holt, "Stylin' outta the Black Pulpit," in Thomas Kochman, ed., *Rappin and Stylin Out: Communication in Black America* (Urbana: University of Illinois Press, 1972), p. 193. The second "hunh" passage is from a sermon by Ernestine Cleveland Weems, pastor of a Berkeley Church of God in Christ congregation featured in the documentary *The Performed Word* (Red Taurus Films, The Anthropology Film Center Foundation, 1982, produced by Gerald L. Davis).

Grace Sims Holt's 1972 essay "Stylin' outta the Black Pulpit" is cited above. "The Creation," one of seven "Negro folk-sermons" in *God's Trombones*, by James Weldon Johnson, is cited above. The list of black denominations that exemplify physical possession of the Holy Spirit is from Geneva Smitherman, *Black Talk: Words and Phrases from the Hood to the Amen Corner* (Boston and New York: Houghton Mifflin, 1994), p. 31. The sermon "When You Fail in Your Trying" was presented by the Reverend Jeremiah A. Wright Jr. before Trinity United Church of Christ, Chicago, Father's Day 1998; it can be found in the videotape series *Great Preachers* (Odyssey Productions, 1998, distributed by Vision Video, Worcester, Penn.). Rev. Wright discusses African American language very positively in a sermon entitled "Ain't Nobody Right but Us," in his book *What Makes You So Strong: Sermons of Joy and Strength from Jeremiah A. Wright, Jr.* (Valley Forge, Pa.: Judson Press, 1993: 13–26.

Grace Sims Holt's comment on how black preachers begin their sermons is from "Stylin' outta the Black Pulpit," cited above, p. 191. Henry H. Mitchell is quoted from *Black Preaching* (Philadelphia and New York: J. B. Lippincott, 1970), p. 148. Richard L. Wright's findings are in his Ph.D. dissertation, "Language Standards and Communicative Style in the Black Church" (University of Texas at Austin, 1976). Walter Pitts's less dramatic demonstration of the same point is in *Old Ship of Zion*, cited above, pp. 139–141. The sample of the black vernacular version of the Bible is from *Rappin' with Jesus: The Good News According to the Four Brothers* (New York: African American Family Press, 1994), p. 62. A Gullah version of the Gospel According to Luke (*De Good Nyews Bout Jedus Christ Wa Luke Write*) was made available in 1994 through the American Bible Society. Rev. Green shared the anecdote about his parishioners' enthusiastic reaction to the Gullah version with John Rickford and his students in March 1999.

Minister Louis Farrakhan's "black agenda" speech was presented in Atlanta in 1988. The excerpt from the Reverend Jesse Jackson's 1988 speech is from "Jesse Jackson: The Sermons in His Speeches," a paper by Stanford undergraduates Michael Canul, David Hirning, Heidi Durrow, Matt Langley, and Jervey Tucker, in John Rickford, Bonnie McElhinny, and Arnetha Ball, eds., *The B.E. Happenin* (Stanford, Calif.: Stanford University Department of Linguistics, 1989).

4. Comedians and Actors

The Redd Foxx epigraph is from his and Normal Miller's invaluable book for the study of black comedy, *The Redd Foxx Encylopedia of Black Humor* (Pasadena, Calif.: Ward Ritchie Press, 1977), p. 264. The Dance epigraph is from *Shuckin' and Jivin': Folklore from Contemporary Black Americans* (Bloomington: Indiana University Press, 1978), p. xx. Another general study of black comedy is William Schechter, *The History of Negro Humor in America* (New York: Fleet Press, 1979). The most comprehensive and valuable recent book on this topic is Mel Watkins, *On the Real Side: A History of African American Comedy* (Chicago: Lawrence Hill Books, 1999 [1994]).

The lyrics to "Nobody" are by Alex Rogers, and the music by Bert Williams himself; the text appears in *The Redd Foxx Encylopedia of Black Humor*, cited above, p. 47. Sammy Davis Jr. is quoted from the same book, pp. 91 and 92.

Richard Pryor's "Eulogy" is on his audiotape cassette *Is It Something I Said?* (Burbank, Calif.: Warner Bros. Records, 1975, M5 2285). Adele Givens's routine is from an HBO *Comedy Half Hour* that aired on October 8, 1996. Steve Harvey's firing episode is from a live performance broadcast on television on December 23, 1997.

One example of "puttin' on ole massa" is reported in John R. Rickford and Angela E. Rickford, "Cut Eye and Suck Teeth," *Journal of American Folklore,* 89 (1976), pp. 294–309: "The story [was] told to us by Richmond Wiley, a native of the South Carolina Sea Islands, of a slave who used to answer his master's queries and commands with the words 'You ass, sir!' The insult, so obvious to his fellow slaves, was passed off on the master as the slave's slurred pronunciation of 'Yes, sir.'" For three slave narratives that fit into this genre, see Gilbert Osofsky, *Puttin' on Ole Massa* (New York: Harper & Row, 1969). For a description and several examples of "shuckin' and jivin'" to avoid encounters with police and other authority figures, see Thomas Kochman, "Toward an Ethnography of Black American Speech Behavior," *Rappin' and Stylin' Out: Communication in Black America* (Urbana: University of Illinois Press, 1972), pp. 241–264.

Kochman's comment about differences between black and white modes of public debate is from *Black and White Styles in Conflict* (Chicago: University of Chicago Press, 1981), p. 18. Claudia Mitchell-Kernan's description of "marking" is from "Signifying and Marking: Two Afro-American Speech Acts," in John Gumperz and Dell Hymes, eds., *Directions in Sociolinguistics* (New York: Holt, Rinehart & Winston, 1972), pp. 161–179; the marking example involving an Uncle Tom character is from p. 178.

The excerpt from Chris Rock's "My Father" routine is from the cassette recording *Born Suspect* (New York: Atlantic Recording, 1991, 7-82159-4). The excerpt from Bill Cosby's "The Lower Tract" is from the cassette recording *Inside the Mind of Bill Cosby* (Universal City, Calif.: MCA Records, 1972, MCAC-554). Ronald L. Smith's commentary on and quotation from Cosby is from his book *Cosby: The Life of an American Legend* (New York: Prometheus Books, 1997). The segment cited here was part of an excerpt from the first edition of the book (New York: St. Martin's Press, 1986), reprinted in the *Philadelphia Inquirer,* April 15, 1986, p. C03.

Dick Gregory is quoted from *Dick Gregory: From the Back of the Bus,* ed. by Bob Orben (New York: Avon, 1962, p. 16). Moms Mabley is quoted from Jim Lowe, "Jackie 'Moms' Mabley: Star of the Chitlin Circuit," in *Retro,* an on-line magazine (www.retroactive.com/jan98/moms.html), January 1998. Redd Foxx's comments on civil rights marchers are from *The Redd Foxx Encyclopedia of Black Humor,* cited above, p. 239; his observations about black street language and blackface and dialect are from pp. 264 and 234.

House Party, written by Reginald Hudlin, was a Hudlin Brothers film and a New Line Cinema production. The sixth-grade "snaps" from East Palo Alto were recorded by Stanford student Charles Philips in 1989; they appear in an article by F. Charles, R. Haynes, G. Lee, and Philips in John R. Rickford, Arnetha Ball, and Bonnie McElhinny, eds., *The B.E. Happenin: A Mini-Conference on the Expressive Uses of Black English* (Stanford, Calif.: Stanford University Department of Linguistics, 1989). James Percelay, Monteria Ivey, and Stephan Dweck's observations about snaps, and examples, are from *Snaps* (New York: Quill, 1994). See also their *Double Snaps* and *Triple Snaps* (New York: Quill, 1995 and 1996), and James Percelay, *Snaps Four* (New York: Quill, 1998).

Good Times was produced by CBS from 1974 through 1979. *Superfly,* a Sig Shore production, was released in 1972 by Warner Bros. *Hollywood Shuffle,* written by Robert Townsend and Keenen Ivory Wayans, and produced and directed by Robert Townsend, was released in 1989.

Three collections of black humor worth looking at are Philip Sterling, *Laughing on the Outside: The Intelligent White Reader's Guide to Negro Tales and Humor* (New York: Grosset & Dunlap, 1965); Langston Hughes, *The Book of Negro Humor* (New York: Dodd, Mead, 1966); and Dillibe Onyeama, *The Book of Black Man's Humor* (London: Dillibe Onyeama, 1975).

5. *Singers, Toasters, and Rappers*

The first epigraph is from the introduction to Leroi Jones, *Blues People* (New York: Quill, 1963). The second epigraph is from "Street Conscious Rap: Modes of Being," in James Spady, Charles G. Lee, and H. Samy Alim, *Street Conscious Rap* (Philadelphia: Black History Museum Umum/Loh Publishers, 1999), p. xx. Carole Simpson's remarks to the Howard University graduating class were delivered at Commencement, May 1997. James Brown's "Soul Power," originally produced by King Records in 1971, was found on *The CD of JB: Sex Machine and Other Soul Classics* (Polygram Records, 1985).

The lyrics to "You Gotta Move" were attributed to Fred McDowell and the Reverend Gary Davis in the liner notes of the Rolling Stones' 1971 album *Sticky Fingers*. The Georgia Sea Island Singers' version of "I Got to Move," attributed to Mrs. Janie Hunter and the Moving Star Hall congregation, appears in *Ain't You Got a Right to the Tree of Life: The People of Johns Island, South Carolina—Their Faces, Their Words and Their Songs*, recorded by Guy and Candie Carawan (New York: Simon & Schuster, 1966), p. 163.

The lyrics of "Steal Away to Jesus" are from Henry Louis Gates Jr. and Nellie McKay, eds., *The Norton Anthology of African American Literature* (New York: W. W. Norton, 1997), p. 13. "I Will Move On Up a Little Higher" is on *Mahalia Jackson: The World's Greatest Gospel Singer* (Sony Music, 1992). "Mannish Boy" is on *Muddy 'Mississippi' Waters Live* (CBS Records, 1971).

The comments on "signifying" are from Claudia Mitchell-Kernan's "Signifying and Marking: Two Afro-American Speech Acts," in John J. Gumperz and Dell Hymes, eds., *Directions in Sociolinguistics* (New York: Holt, Rinehart & Winston, 1972), pp. 161–179. The definition of toasts by Labov and his colleagues Paul Cohen, Clarence Robins, and John Lewis is from "Toasts," in Alan Dundes, ed., *Mother Wit from the Laughing Barrel* (Englewood Cliffs, N.J.: Prentice-Hall), p. 335. Roger Abrahams's comments on toasts are from *Deep Down in the Jungle . . . Negro Narrative Folklore from the Streets of Philadelphia* (Chicago: Aldine, 1970), p. 97. The "Signifying Monkey" toast is reprinted from p. 153 of that book; the "Great Mac-Daddy" toast, from p. 162; and the *"Titanic"* toast from p. 127. Abrahams's remarks on the kinds of heroes celebrated in toasts are in chapter 3 of his book. The work by Henry Louis Gates Jr. is *The Signifying Monkey: A Theory of Afro-American Literary Criticism* (New York and Oxford: Oxford University Press, 1988). The Dolomite toast is from Bruce Jackson, *Get Your Ass in the Water and Swim Like Me: Narrative Poetry from Black Oral Tradition* (Cambridge, Mass.: Harvard University Press, 1974), pp. 57–59.

LL Cool J's "I'm Bad" is from his *Bigger and Deffer* album (Def Jam Recordings, 1987). Smooth Da Hustler's "Broken Language" is on the *Once Upon a Time in Amerikkka* album (Profile, 1997). Nas's "If I Ruled the World" is from the

Illmatic album (Columbia Records, 1996). For more on freestyling, see the documentary video by Jacquie Jones, *Freestyle* (Department of Communications, Stanford University, 1995). "The Day After" by Goodie Mob is found on the *Soul Food* album (La Face Records, 1995). For information about the ring shout, see Art Rosenbaum, *Shout Because You're Free: The African American Ring Shout Tradition in Coastal Georgia* (Athens: University of Georgia Press, 1998). DMX's "How's It Going Down" is from *It's Dark and Hell Is Hot* (Def Jam Recordings, 1998). "Rapper's Delight," by the Sugarhill Gang, was released as a single in 1979 by Sugar Hill Records, Englewood, N.J., and it was the title rap on the 1996 CD/cassette album *Rapper's Delight: The Best of Sugarhill Gang* (Rhino Records). There are many variant transcripts of the lines we cite from this rap, as a web search for the lyrics of "Rapper's Delight" will confirm. Lauryn Hill's "Lost Ones" appears on the album *The Mis-education of Lauryn Hill* (Columbia Music, 1998). For an older example of *done done* in song, see Ma Rainey's 1924 version of "See, See Rider" ("See, See Rider, see what you done done!") in *The Norton Anthology of African American Literature* (cited above), p. 27. In linguistics circles, the recognized authority on vernacular usage in rap and hip-hop music is Marcyliena Morgan, whose forthcoming books are *Say It Loud: Discourse and Verbal Genres in African American Culture* (Cambridge: Cambridge University Press, 2000) and, with Stephen DeBerry, *Thursday Night at Project Blowed: Underground Hip Hop and Urban Youth Resistance* (Durham, N.C.: Duke University Press, to appear).

Part Three
The Living Language

6. *Vocabulary and Pronunciation*

We are grateful to Thomas Wasow of Stanford University for comments on an earlier version of this chapter.

The epigraphs are from AOL on-line discussions of the Ebonics controversy, December 1996. James Baldwin's article "If Black English Isn't a Language, Then Tell Me, What Is?" was in the *New York Times,* July 29, 1979.

Clarence Major's dictionary is *Juba to Jive: A Dictionary of African-American Slang* (New York: Penguin, 1994). Geneva Smitherman's *Black Talk: Words and Phrases from the Hood to the Amen Corner* was published by Houghton Mifflin, New York, in 1994. A revised and updated version is forthcoming (January 2000). Rudolph Fisher's "Introduction to Contemporary Harlemese" is in *The Walls of Jericho* (New York and London: Alfred A. Knopf, 1928); pp. 295–307. *The New Cab Calloway's Hepster's Dictionary: Language of Jive* was published by Calloway, New York, in 1944. *A 2 Z: The Book of Rap and Hip-Hop Slang,* by Lois Stavsky, I. E. Mozeson, and Dani Reyes Mozeson, was published by Boulevard Books, New York, in 1995. Another recent glossary is Monica Frazier Anderson's *Black English Vernacular: From "Ain't" to "Yo Mama"* (Highland City, Fl.: Rainbow Books, 1994). J. L. Dillard's *Lexicon of Black English* was published by Seabury Press, New York, in 1970. Edith Folb's *runnin' down some lines: the language and culture of black teenagers* was published by Harvard University Press, Cambridge, Massachusetts, in 1980.

Teresa Labov's study, entitled "Social and Language Boundaries Among Adolescents," was published in *American Speech,* 67, 4 (1992), pp. 339–366. Robert

Williams's 1972 Black Intelligence Test of Cultural Homogeneity was copyrighted by him (Black Studies Program, Washington University, St. Louis).

The students who reacted with interest and amazement to the distinctiveness of *ashy* were members of the Society of Black Engineers from various California colleges to whom John Rickford lectured at Stanford in November 1998. The *cut-eye* and *suck-teeth* survey was conducted by John and Angela Rickford in the early 1970s and first reported in their article, "Cut Eye and Suck Teeth: Masked Africanisms in New World Guise," *Journal of American Folklore*, 1976, pp. 294–309; the article has since been reprinted, most recently in John R. Rickford, *African American Vernacular English* (London and New York: Blackwell, 1998). For more on African origins of words in Ebonics, Gullah, and American English, see Joseph E. Holloway and Winifred K. Vass, *The African Heritage of American English* (Bloomington: Indiana University Press, 1993).

The *Dictionary of American Regional English* (Frederic G. Cassidy, chief ed., Joan Houston Hall, associate ed.) is being published by Belknap Press, Cambridge, Massachusetts, in a series of volumes several years apart. The first, A–C, was published in 1985; D–H in 1991; and I–O in 1996. Definitions of *ace-boon-coon*, *bid whist*, *bubba*, *bad-eye*, *bad-mouth*, and *big-eye* given here are from vol. 1. For a list of all the "black" terms in DARE up to vol. 2, see *An Index by Region, Usage and Etymology to the Dictionary of American Regional English vols. I and II* (*Publication of the American Dialect Society*, 77) (Tuscaloosa: University of Alabama Press, for the American Dialect Society, 1993). The Mandingo source for *bad-mouth* is from Geneva Smitherman, *Talkin and Testifyin* (Detroit: Wayne State University Press, 1986), and the Hausa and Mandingo sources are from Holloway and Vass's *The African Heritage of American English*, cited above, p. 137. The various African sources for *suck-teeth* are from John and Angela Rickford's "Cut Eye and Suck Teeth," cited above, and from Richard Allsopp's *Dictionary of Caribbean English Usage* (New York: Oxford University Press, 1996).

The domains of black vocabulary use were derived from information in the following sources cited above: J. L. Dillard (1977), Edith Folb (1980), Clarence Major (1994), and Geneva Smitherman (1994). Folb's comment on class differences is from *runnin' down some lines*, cited above, p. 201. Major's notion about black slang as a living, breathing form of expression is from *Juba to Jive*, cited above, p. xxviii. The innovative character and meaning of *shorty* were first noted in an October 1996 assignment by Sterling K. Brown for John Rickford's course "African American Vernacular English" at Stanford; Brown's observations were corroborated by Anakela C. Rickford, a Spelman College student.

Claude Brown's comment on *uptight* is in "The Language of Soul," *Esquire*, April 1968, p. 160. Clarence Major's comment on the same word is in *Juba to Jive*, cited above, p. xxix. Edith Folb provides additional discussion of the evolution of the word in *runnin' down some lines*, cited above, p. 208. James Baldwin's comment on diffusions of black vocabulary is from "If Black English Isn't a Language," cited above, p. 391. Margaret Lee presented her paper "Out of the Hood and into the News: Borrowed Black Verbal Expressions in a Mainstream Newspaper" at the twenty-seventh annual conference on New Ways of Analyzing Variation, University of Georgia, Athens, October 1998. For an excellent discussion of words that cross over from black to white and mainstream usage, see pp. 16–22 of Smitherman's *Black Talk*, cited above. Clarence Major's comment on the inevitability of diffusion is from *Juba to Jive*, cited above, p. xxix.

Claude Brown's comments are from "The Language of Soul," cited above, pp. 88, 160. *How to Speak Southern* by Steve Mitchell was published by Bantam, New York, in 1976. The classic overview of black vernacular pronunciation and grammar, still useful although dated in some respects, is Ralph W. Fasold and Walt Wolfram, "Some Linguistic Features of Negro Dialect," in Ralph W. Fasold and Roger W. Shuy, eds., *Teaching Standard English in the Inner City* (Washington, D.C.: Center for Applied Linguistics, 1970). For a more recent overview, see John R. Rickford, "Phonological and Grammatical Features of African American Vernacular English" in *African American Vernacular English* (Oxford: Blackwell, 1999). For a more technical and detailed recent account of black vernacular pronunciation, see Guy Bailey and Erik Thomas, "Some Aspects of African-American Vernacular English Phonology," in Salikoko S. Mufwene, John R. Rickford, Guy Bailey, and John Baugh, eds., *African American English* (London: Routledge, 1998), pp. 85–109.

Walter Edwards's statistics on the differential use of monophthongal pronunciations like *mah* and *Ah* by blacks and whites in Detroit come from "Sociolinguistic Behavior in a Detroit Inner-City Black Neighborhood," *Language in Society*, 21, pp. 93–115. Erik R. Thomas and Guy Bailey are quoted from "Parallels Between Vowel Subsystems of African American Vernacular English and Caribbean Anglophone Creoles," *Journal of Pidgin and Creole Languages*, 13, 2 (1998), p. 284; for details of pronunciation differences, see pp. 271–281. For data on black pronunciation in the 1930s, see George Dorrill, "A Comparison of Stressed Vowels of Black and White Speakers in the South," in Michael B. Montgomery and Guy Bailey, eds., *Language Variety in the South* (Tuscaloosa: University of Alabama Press, 1986), pp. 149–157.

On Guyanese East Indians and Creole, see Derek Bickerton, *Dynamics of a Creole System* (Cambridge: Cambridge University Press, 1975). For further discussion of past and present relations between black and white speech in the South, see Crawford Feagin, *Variation and Change in Alabama English: A Sociolinguistic Study of the White Community* (Washington, D.C.: Georgetown University Press, 1979), pp. 245–247.

The transcript of Johnnie Cochran's comments was obtained from the following website: http://v90-137.cchono.com/~walraven/simpson/#lists. John McWhorter's comment is from *The Word on the Street: Fact and Fable about American English* (New York: Plenum, 1998), p. 133.

John Rickford's 1972 study was reported in an unpublished term paper, "Sounding Black or Sounding White: A Preliminary Investigation of a Folk Hypothesis," for the course Linguistics 521 at the University of Pennsylvania. A tracing of the spectrograph showing variation in the black male speaker's voice was reprinted in his article, "The Question of Prior Creolization in Black English," in Albert Valdman, ed., *Pidgin and Creole Linguistics* (Bloomington: Indiana University Press, 1977), pp. 190–221. For further discussion of intonation in black speech, see Elaine E. Tarone, "Aspects of Intonation in Black English," *American Speech* 48 (1973), pp. 29–36. The speaker identification study by G. Richard Tucker and Wallace E. Lambert, "White and Negro Listeners' Reactions to Various American-English Dialects," was published in *Social Forces*, 47 (1969), pp. 463–468. Roger Shuy's speaker identification study, "Subjective Judgments in Sociolinguistic Analysis," was published as *Georgetown University Monograph Series on Language and Linguistics*, 22 (1969). The speaker identification study by William

Labov, Paul Cohen, Clarence Robins, and John Lewis is reported in *A Study of the Non-Standard English of Negro and Puerto Rican Speakers in New York City* (1968), vol. 2, sect. 4.7. For more recent speaker identification studies, see Guy Bailey and Natalie Maynor, "The Divergence Controversy," *American Speech,* 64 (1989), pp. 12–39; and John Baugh, "Perceptions Within a Variable Paradigm: Black and White Racial Detection and Identification Based on Speech," Edgar W. Schneider, ed., *Focus on the USA* (Amsterdam: John Benjamins, 1996), pp. 169–182.

The March 1995 segment of the CBS television program *60 Minutes* on black speech was entitled "The Language Factor." For more on the rule deleting initial voiced stops, see John R. Rickford, "The Insights of the Mesolect," in David DeCamp and Ian F. Hancock, eds., *Pidgins and Creoles: Current Trends and Prospects* (Washington, D.C.: Georgetown University Press), 1974.

Walt Wolfram's Detroit study was published as *A Sociolinguistic Description of Detroit Negro Speech* (Washington, D.C.: Center for Applied Linguistics, 1969). Catherine Chappel's study is *A Generational Study of Oakland AAVE [African American Vernacular English]: Linguistic Variation by Class and Age among Oakland Females* (Ph.D. qualifying paper, Department of Linguistics, Stanford University, 1999). Oprah Winfrey's pronunciation is analyzed by Jennifer Hay, Stephanie Hannedy, and Norma Mendoza-Denton in "Oprah and /ay/: Lexical Frequency, Referee Design, and Style," to appear in *Proceedings of the 14th International Conference of Phonetic Sciences* (San Francisco, 1999). The replication by Walter Edwards is reported in his 1992 *Language in Society* article cited above. For another classic study of pronunciation variation by social class, age, and style, see the New York City study by William Labov and others cited above. Quantitative variation in final consonant clusters is reported there and in William Labov, *Language in the Inner City: Studies in the Black English Vernacular* (Philadelphia: University of Pennsylvania Press, 1972; reissued 1998), p. 45.

7. *Grammar*

We are grateful to Thomas Wasow of Stanford University for feedback on an earlier version of this chapter.

The epigraph from J. L. Dillard is from *Black English: Its History and Usage in the United States* (New York: Random House, 1972). The epigraph from Geneva Smitherman is from *Talkin and Testifyin: The Language of Black America* (Detroit: Wayne State University Press, 1986).

The New York City study, by William Labov, Paul Cohen, Clarence Robins, and John Lewis, was published as *A Study of the Non-Standard English of Negro and Puerto Rican Speakers in New York City* (New York: Columbia University Press, 1968). The Detroit study, by Walt Wolfram, was published as *A Sociolinguistic Description of Detroit Negro Speech* (Washington, D.C.: Center for Applied Linguistics, 1969).

The classic overview of black vernacular pronunciation and grammar is Ralph W. Fasold and Walt Wolfram, "Some Linguistic Features of Negro Dialect," 1970, cited above (p. 242). For a more recent overview, see John R. Rickford, "Phonological and Grammatical Features of African American Vernacular English," 1999, also cited above.

Stefan Martin and Walt Wolfram's comment about similarities in sentence structure between African American Vernacular English and other English dialects is from "The Sentence in African American Vernacular English," in Salikoko S. Mufwene, John R. Rickford, Guy Bailey, and John Baugh, eds., *African American*

English (London: Routledge, 1998), p.11. For more on plural marking and pronoun use in AAVE, see Salikoko S. Mufwene, "The Structure of the Noun Phrase in African American Vernacular English," in the same volume, pp. 69–81.

Data on the frequency with which Foxy Boston and Tinky Gates deleted third-person-singular *s* and possessive *'s* is from John R. Rickford, "Grammatical Variation and Divergence in Vernacular Black English," in *African American Vernacular English,* cited above.

Two of the best sources on invariant *be, done, be done,* and other tense-aspect markers in AAVE are Ph.D. dissertations by Lisa J. Green, "Topics in African American English: The Verb System Analysis" (University of Massachusetts, Amherst, 1993) and Elizabeth Dayton, "Grammatical Categories of the Verb in African American Vernacular English" (University of Pennsylvania, 1996). Both are available from UMI Dissertation Services, Ann Arbor, Michigan (800-521-0600 or 313-761-4700). Green's work is also available in "Aspect and Predicate Phrases in African American Vernacular English," *African American English,* cited above, pp. 37–68. Although our discussion of invariant *be* highlights its most common use as a marker of habituality, several researchers have noted that it is sometimes used to mark events that take place over an extended period at one time, as in the following examples from John Baugh, *Black Street Speech* (Austin: University of Texas Press, 1983), p. 72: ". . . and we be tired from the heat, but he just made everybody keep on working. So they be runnin . . . right . . . really bookin . . . and the police had all the streets blocked off." For further discussion of *steady,* see pp. 85–89 of the same book.

One of the earliest, most comprehensible, and most technical discussions of restrictions on the deletion of the copula in African American English is William Labov, "Contraction, Deletion, and Inherent Variability of the English Copula," in *Language in the Inner City* (Philadelphia: University of Pennsylvania Press, 1972), pp. 65–129. For comparisons of copula absence in African American English with copula absence in Arabic, Hungarian, and other languages, see Charles A. Ferguson, "Absence of the Copula and the Notion of Simplicity," in Dell Hymes, *Pidginization and Creolization of Languages* (Cambridge: Cambridge University Press, 1971), pp. 141–150, and Geoffrey Pullum, "Language That Dare Not Speak Its Name," *Nature,* 386 (March 27, 1997), pp. 321–322. The data on copula deletion frequencies according to grammatical environment is from John R. Rickford, "The Creole Origins of African American Vernacular English: Evidence from Copula Absence," in *African American English,* cited above. The reason some of the copula deletion figures in the chart are given as .25, .12, and so on instead of as 25 percent and 12 percent is that while they are based on observed percentages, they represent deletion probabilities as calculated by a computer program (VARBRUL) that estimates how much various factors contribute to the likelihood that copula deletion will take place. For further information, see John R. Rickford, Arnetha Ball, Renee Blake, Raina Jackson, and Nomi Martin, "Rappin on the Copula Coffin: Theoretical and Methodological Issues in the Analysis of Copula Variation in African American Vernacular English," *Language Variation and Change,* 3 (1991), pp. 103–132.

Irma Cunningham's unstressed *been* sentence from Gullah is quoted from her Ph.D. dissertation, "A Syntactic Analysis of Sea Island Creole" (Ann Arbor: University of Michigan, 1970), p. 65. Beryl Bailey's unstressed *been* sentence is from *Jamaican Creole Syntax* (New York: Cambridge University Press, 1966), p. 46. For more on stressed *BEEN,* see the dissertations by Lisa Green and Elizabeth Dayton, cited above, and John R. Rickford, "Carrying the New Wave into Syntax: The Case of Black English BIN," *African American Vernacular English* (Oxford: Blackwell, 1999). The example of *been like* in Lindsey's play is cited in G. Krapp, *The English Language in America* (New York: Century, 1925), pp. 258–259. The statistics on differences in black/white interpretations of BEEN are in Rickford, "Carrying the New Wave into Syntax," cited above. The "We had BEEN married" example is from Elizabeth Dayton's dissertation, cited above. The "five present tenses" of AAVE were discussed, with the same examples used in this chapter, in John R. Rickford, "Suite for Ebony and Phonics," *Discover,* December 1997, pp. 82–87.

For examples and analysis of *done,* double modals, and other AAVE features in Southern white speech, see Crawford Feagin, *Variation and Change in Alabama English* (Washington, D.C.: Georgetown University Press, 1979). For discussion of the meaning of *fixing to* in Southern white English, see Marvin K. L. Ching, "How Fixed Is *fixin' to*?" *American Speech,* 62, pp. 332–345.

For further discussion of past-tense *had,* see John R. Rickford and Christine Theberge Rafal, "Preterit *had* in the Narratives of African American Preadolescents," *American Speech,* 71, pp. 227–254, reprinted in Rickford, *African American Vernacular English,* cited above; and Patricia Cukor-Avila, "The Evolution of AAVE in a Rural Texas Community: An Ethnolinguistic Study" (Ph.D. dissertation, University of Michigan, 1995). The classic study of indignant *come* is Arthur K. Spears, "The Black English Semi-Auxiliary Come," *Language,* 58 (1982), pp. 850–872.

For a thorough study of *ain't, don't,* and other negative auxiliaries in black speech, see Tracey Weldon, "Variability in Negation in African American Vernacular English," *Language Variation and Change,* 6 (1994), pp. 359–397. The most detailed study of multiple negation is William Labov, "Negative Attraction andNegative Concord," in *Language in the Inner City* (Philadelphia: University of Pennsylvania Press, 1972), pp. 130–196. The negative inversion examples are from William Labov, Paul Cohen, Clarence Robins, and John Lewis, *A Study of the Non-Standard English of Negro and Puerto Rican Speakers in New York City,* cited above, vol. 1. The double-negation example from Chaucer is from *The American Heritage Dictionary of the English Language,* 3rd ed. (Boston: Houghton Mifflin, 1992), p. 555, "double negative." For a more recent discussion of negative inversion, see Peter Sells, John R. Rickford, and Thomas A. Wasow, "Negative Inversion in African American Vernacular English," *Natural Language and Linguistic Theory,* 14, 3 (1996), pp. 591–627.

For discussion of the Harlem repetition experiment with *if,* see William Labov, *Language in the Inner City,* cited above, pp. 61–63. For the Washington, D.C., version of this experiment, see Joan Baratz, "Teaching Reading in an Urban Negro School System," in Joan Baratz and Roger Shuy, eds., *Teaching Black Children to Read* (Washington, D.C.: Center for Applied Linguistics, 1969).

The *Ahma git me a gig* example is from John Gumperz, *Discourse Strategies* (Cambridge: Cambridge University Press, 1982), p. 30. The examples of deleted relative pronouns and double modals from Stefan Martin and Walt Wolfram are "The Sentence in African American Vernacular English," cited above, pp. 31–33. For information on double modals in southern white English and other English varieties, see Crawford Feagin, *Variation and Change in Alabama English,* cited above, pp. 151–174.

For variation by social class, gender, age, and style in the grammar of Spoken Soul, see Walt Wolfram, *A Sociolinguistic Description of Detroit Negro Speech,* cited above. The East Palo Alto data on copula absence and other age-related variations recorded by Faye McNair-Knox are from John R. Rickford, "Grammatical Variation and Divergence in Vernacular Black English," in *African American Vernacular English,* cited above. The study of variation in Foxy Boston's language is John R. Rickford and Faye McNair-Knox, "Addressee and Topic-Influenced Style Shift" (1994), reprinted in John R. Rickford, *African American Vernacular English* (Oxford: Basil Blackwell, 1999).

8. *History*

The epigraph quoting Carter G. Woodson is from *The Mis-Education of the Negro* (Trenton, N.J.: Africa World Press, 1998; originally published 1933), p. 19. The epigraph quoting John McWhorter is from *The Word on the Street: Fact and Fable about American English* (New York: Plenum, 1998), pp. 174–175.

Information on slaves brought to America by the Spanish in the sixteenth century and on the twenty Africans brought to Jameston in 1619 is from Daniel M. Johnson and Rex R. Campbell, *Black Migration in America: A Social Demographic History* (Durham, N.C.: Duke University Press, 1981), pp. 7–8, and Daniel P. Mannix, *Black Cargoes* (New York: Viking Press, 1962), pp. 54–55. John Hope Franklin and Alfred A. Moss Jr. are quoted from *From Slavery to Freedom: A History of Negro Americans,* 6th ed. (New York: Alfred A. Knopf, 1988), p. 53.

Statistics on black population proportions in Virginia and South Carolina come from Philip S. Foner, *History of Black Americans* (Westport, Conn.: Greenwood Press, 1975), vol. 1, p. 188; Allan Kulikoff, *Tobacco and Slaves: The Development of Southern Culture in the Chesapeake, 1680–1800* (Chapel Hill: University of North Carolina Press, 1986); and Peter Wood, "The Changing Population of the Colonial South: An Overview by Race and Region," in Peter H. Wood, Gregory A. Waselkov, and M. Thomas Hatley, eds., *Powhatan's Mantle* (Lincoln: University of Nebraska Press, 1989), pp. 38, 46. Among those who believe that seventeenth- and early-eighteenth-century African English in the United States outside of Gullah territory was not significantly pidginized or creolized are Peter Wood, *Black Majority* (New York: Alfred A. Knopf, 1975), p. 175; Salikoko S. Mufwene, "The Founder Principle in Creole Genesis," *Diachronica,* 13 (1996), pp. 83–134; and Don Winford, "On the Origins of African American Vernacular English— A Creolist Perspective, Part I: The Sociohistorical Background," *Diachronica,* 14 (1997), pp. 305–344.

Data on Suriname, Jamaica, and colonial America in the seventeenth and early eighteenth centuries come from various sources cited in John R. Rickford, "Prior Creolization of African American Vernacular English? Sociohistorical and Textual Evidence from the 17th and 18th Centuries," *Journal of Sociolinguistics,* 1 (1997), pp. 316–336. Among the most important are: Robert B. Le Page and Andrée Tabouret-Keller, *Acts of Identity: Creole-Based Approaches to Language and Identity* (Cambridge, England: Cambridge University Press, 1985); Bettina M. Migge, "Substrate Influence in Creole Language Formation: The Case of Serial Verb Constructions in Sranan" (M.A. thesis, The Ohio State University, Columbus); and John Hope Franklin and Alfred A. Moss Jr., *From Slavery to Freedom,* cited above. For Derek Bickerton's claim that language learners must constitute 80 percent or more in the contact situation for creoles to emerge, see *Roots of Language* (Ann Arbor, Mich.: Karoma, 1981), p. 4. Data on the proportions of Africans in the first twenty-five years of the founding of Haiti and Martinique are from John Singler, "The Demographics of Creole Genesis in the Caribbean: A Comparison of Martinique and Haiti," in Jacques Arends, ed., *The Early Stages of Creolization* (Amsterdam: John Benjamins, 1995), pp. 203–232.

The Sranan and Ewe versions of "Dogs are walking under the house" are from John McWhorter, *The Word on the Street: Fact and Fable about American English*, cited above, p. 159. For more on Guinea Coast Creole English, see Ian Hancock, "The Domestic Hypothesis, Diffusion, and Componentiality," in Pieter Muysken and Norval Smith, eds., *Substrata versus Universals in Creole Genesis* (Philadelphia: John Benjamins, 1986), pp. 71–102. For more about Tituba's origin and speech, see Samuel G. Drake, *The Witchcraft Delusion in New England* (Roxbury, Mass.: W. Elliot Woodward, 1866), and Elaine G. Breslaw, *Tituba, Reluctant Witch of Salem* (New York: New York University Press, 1996).

Statistics on black-white proportions in various American colonies in 1750 come from John Hope Franklin and Alfred A. Moss Jr., *From Slavery to Freedom*, cited above, p. 61. Table 3 in John Rickford's "Prior Creolization" paper, cited above, reprints and reorganizes the Franklin/Moss data in detail. The quotation from Philip S. Foner about blacks outnumbering whites in parts of Maryland is from *History of Black Americans*, cited above, vol. 1, p. 201. Wood's remark is from *Black Majority*, cited above, p. 187. The quotations from Foner about the 1705 Virginia slave code are from pp. 194–195.

The comments about distinctive black language and culture in eighteenth-century America are adapted from John Rickford's "Prior Creolization" paper, cited above. Marvin L. M. Kay and Lorin L. Cary are quoted from *Slavery in North Carolina 1748–1775* (Chapel Hill: University of North Carolina Press, 1995), pp. 149–150. Allan Kulikoff is quoted from *Tobacco and Slaves*, cited above, pp. 327–328 and 351. The Garden comment about blacks interacting with blacks is cited in Michael Mullin, *Africa in America: Slave Acculturation and Resistance in the American South and the British Caribbean, 1736–1831* (Urbana: University of Illinois Press, 1992), p. 187. The citation from Defoe is from *The History and Remarkable Life of the Truly Honourable Col. Jacque Commonly Called Col. Jack* (London, 1722). Dillard's remarks about language differences between blacks and whites in the novel are in *Black English*, cited above, p. 78.

The Fall of British Tyranny was published in 1776 in Philadelphia by Styner and Cist. The quotations from eighteenth-century newspaper ads about runaway slaves are from Walter M. Brasch, *Black English and the Mass Media* (Lanham, Md.: University Press of America, 1981), pp. 6–8. Dillard's statement about variation in black speech in the eighteenth century is in *Black English*, cited above, p. 85.

For information on slaves landed illegally on Jekyll Island, Georgia, in 1858, see Tom Henderson Wells, *The Slave Ship Wanderer* (Athens: University of Georgia Press, 1968 [1967]). Data on the increase in the U.S. slave population between 1790 and 1860 come from Daniel M. Johnson and Rex R. Campbell, *Black Migration in America*, cited above, p. 25; the estimates of the number of slaves moved by the internal slave trade are from the same source. Josiah Henson's remembrances are narrated in *Father Henson's Story of His Own Life*, ed. Walter Fisher (1962), quoted at some length in Donald R. Wright, *African Americans in the Early Republic, 1789–1831* (Arlington Heights, Ill.: Harlan Davidson, 1993), pp. 40–41.

The Wallace Quarterman transcript is from John R. Rickford, "Representativeness and Reliability of the Ex-Slave Narrative Materials, with Special Reference to Wallace Quarterman's Recordings and Transcript," in Guy Bailey, Natalie Maynor, and Patricia Cukor-Avila, eds., *The Emergence of Black English: Text and Commentary* (Amsterdam: John Benjamins, 1991), pp. 206–208.

Data on post–Civil War black migration come from Daniel M. Johnson and Rex R. Campbell, *Black Migration in America,* cited above, pp. 52–63. Don Winford's remarks about African American dialects are from "On the Origins of African American Vernacular English," cited above, p. 318. For information about African American gains and losses after the war, see chapters 12–14 of John Hope Franklin and Alfred A. Moss Jr., *From Slavery to Freedom,* and chapter 27 of Philip S. Foner's *History of Black Americans,* vol. 3, both cited above.

The list of nineteenth-century sources on black speech essentially follows that presented by Walter M. Brasch, *Black English and the Mass Media,* cited above, pp. 23–58 and 59–145. Brasch's book contains excerpts from and analysis of many sources, including Francis Anne Kemble's *Journal of a Residence on a Georgian Plantation,* written in 1838–1839 and published by Harper and Bros., New York, in 1863.

The estimate of 1.8 million black southerners emigrating comes from Dernoral Davis, "Portrait of Twentieth Century African Americans," in Alferdteen Harrison, ed., *Black Exodus: The Great Migration from the American South* (Jackson: University Press of Mississippi, 1991), p. 11. Other demographic data on the twentieth century come primarily from Daniel M. Johnson and Rex R. Campbell, *Black Migration in America,* cited above; their definition of the index of black segregation, and data on this, are from pp. 149–150. William Labov and Wendell A. Harris outlined the divergence hypothesis in "De Facto Segregation of Black and White Vernaculars," in David Sankoff, ed., *Diversity and Diachrony* (Amsterdam and Philadelphia: John Benjamins, 1986), pp. 1–24. Kennell Jackson's comment on affirmative action is from *America Is Me: The Most Asked and Least Understood Questions about Black American History* (New York: Harper Perennial, 1996), p. 418.

Information on 1993 unemployment rates is from the *Statistical Abstract of the United States,* 115th ed. (Washington, D.C.: Bureau of the Census, 1995), tables 628 and 635. Martin Carnoy's book is *Faded Dreams: The Politics and Economics of Race in America* (Cambridge: Cambridge University Press, 1994); the quotation is from p. 3. The comment about the 1992 riots in Los Angeles is from Kennell Jackson, *America Is Me,* cited above, p. 385. For John Ogbu's concept of "oppositional identity," see "Class Stratification, Racial Stratification and Schooling," in L. Weis, ed., *Race, Class and Schooling. Special Studies in Comparative Education,* 17 (State University of New York at Buffalo, Comparative Education Center, 1986), and Signithia Fordham and John Ogbu, "Black Students' School Success: Coping with the 'Burden of Acting White,'" *The Urban Review,* 18,3 (1986), pp. 176–206.

Molefi Asante's remark on the limited significance of Africanisms is from "African Elements in African-American English," in Joseph E. Holloway, ed., *Africanisms in American Culture* (Bloomington: Indiana University Press, 1990), p. 21. Ernie Smith is quoted from *Ebonics: The Historical Development of African-American Language* (San Francisco: ASPIRE Books, 1997), pp. 7, 9, 21. Ambrose Gonzales is quoted from *The Black Border: Gullah Stories of the Carolina Coast* (Columbia, S.C., 1922), pp. 17–18 and 10. Samuel G. Stoney and Gertrude N. Shelby's assessment of the African words in Gullah is in *Black Genesis* (New York, 1930), p. xv. Mason Crum's is in *Gullah: Negro Life in the Carolina Sea Islands* (Durham, N.C., 1940), pp. 111, 121, 123. The preceding three sources are cited in Lorenzo Dow Turner, *Africanisms in the Gullah Dialect* (Chicago: University of Chicago Press, 1949). For other work on Africanisms in American dialects, see David Dalby, "The African Element in Black English," in Thomas Kochman, ed., *Rappin' and Stylin' Out:*

Communication in Urban Black America (Urbana: University of Illinois Press, 1972); Joseph E. Holloway and Winifred K. Vass, *The African Heritage of American English* (Bloomington: Indiana University Press, 1997 [1993]), and their references. The point about loan translations from African languages was made in John and Angela Rickford, "Cut Eye and Suck Teeth: African Words and Gestures in New World Guise," *Journal of American Folklore*, 89 (1976), pp. 294–309.

Geneva Smitherman's listing of the sound rule in West African languages is in *Talkin and Testifyin: The Language of Black America* (Detroit: Wayne State University Press, 1986), p. 7. John McWhorter's remarks about English sources are in *Word on the Street: Fact and Fable about American English*, cited above, p. 162. Cleanth Brooks's discussion is in *The Language of the American South* (Athens: University of Georgia Press, 1985), pp. 8–13. For more on *th* sounds and their replacement in Nigerian pidgin English, see Anna Barbag-Stoll, *Social and Linguistic History of Nigerian Pidgin English* (Tübingen, Germany: Stauffenberg, 1983), p. 70. Norma A. Niles's remarks about joint African and English influences on Barbadian are in "Provincial English Dialects and Barbadian English" (Ph.D. dissertation, University of Michigan, Ann Arbor, 1980), p. 147. On Jamaican data, see Frederic G. Cassidy, "Multiple Etymologies in Jamaican Creole," *American Speech*, 41 (1966), pp. 211–215.

Ernie Smith's remarks are in *Ebonics: The Historical Development of African-American Language*, cited above, pp. 29–30. William E. Welmers is quoted from *African Language Structures* (Berkeley: University of California Press, 1973), pp. 53 and 71–72. Don Winford's discussion of *r* deletion and other pronunciation features is in "On the Origins of African American Vernacular English—A Creolist Perspective, Part II: Linguistic Features," *Diachronica*, 15 (1998), pp. 102–103. McWhorter's remarks about the deletion of *r* and *l* are in *The Word on the Street*, cited above, p. 173. For more on deleting *b, d,* and *g,* see John R. Rickford, "The Insights of the Mesolect," in David DeCamp and Ian F. Hancock, eds., *Pidgins and Creoles: Current Trends and Prospects* (Washington, D.C.: Georgetown University Press, 1974). The comments about monophthongal [e] and [o] are from Erik R. Thomas and Guy Bailey, "Parallels between Vowel Subsystems of African American Vernacular English and Caribbean Anglophone Creoles," *Journal of Pidgin and Creole Languages*, 13 (1998), pp. 267 and 287.

With respect to British dialect sources, see Gilbert Schneider, *American Earlier Black English: Morphological and Syntactic Variables* (Tuscaloosa: University of Alabama Press, 1989), especially chap. 3, and references. Don Winford synthesizes and extends the work of Schneider and other researchers (including Crawford Feagin and Ralph Fasold) in a judicious manner in "On the Origins of African American Vernacular English—A Creolist Perspective, Part II: Linguistic Features," cited above; the example quoted from William Dunbar is in Winford, p. 131. A newer source, not yet in print as we're writing, is Shana Poplack, ed., *The English History of African American English* (Oxford: Blackwell, 1999), which we were not able to see before going to press. The Philadelphia man's *say* sentence was recorded by John Rickford in September 1972; the Gullah woman's *say* sentence was recorded by John Rickford on Daufuskie Island, South Carolina, in 1970; the Jamaican Creole *say* sentence is from Beryl Bailey, *Jamaican Creole Syntax* (New York: Cambridge University Press, 1966), p. 46. Turner's discussion of *say* is from *Africanisms in the Gullah Dialect*, cited above, p. 211. Asante's discussion of serial verbs and tense-aspect is in "African Elements in African-American English," cited above, pp. 26–31. For habituals, completives, and remote time constructions in African languages, see William Welmers, *African Language Structures,* cited above, pp. 345–352.

The discussion of copula absence here is based on John Rickford, "The Creole Origins of African American Vernacular English: Evidence from Copula Absence," in Salikoko S. Mufwene, John R. Rickford, Guy Bailey, and John Baugh, eds., *African American English* (London: Routledge, 1998), pp. 154–200, which should be consulted for the sources of the data cited and for other details. As we were correcting page proofs, a new study by Danielle Martin and Sali Tagliamante ("Oh, It Beautiful: Copula Variability in Britain"), presented at "New Ways of Analyzing Variation," an October 1999 conference in Toronto, *does* show historical and contemporary evidence of copula absence in Britain, although at lower levels in the one dialect for which frequency data are available (zero *is* = 2 percent, zero *are* = 25 percent) than attested in Spoken Soul or in the Caribbean creoles. For discussion of black-white differences with respect to copula absence and other grammatical features in coastal North Carolina, see Walt Wolfram, Erik R. Thomas, and Elaine W. Green, "The Regional Context of Earlier African-American Speech: Evidence for Reconstructing the Development of AAVE," to appear in *Language in Society,* 29 (2000). The discussion of grammatical differences between an old white man and an old black woman on a South Carolina Sea Island is in John R. Rickford, "Ethnicity as a Sociolinguistic Boundary," *American Speech,* 60 (1985), pp. 90–125. For discussion of black-white working-class similarities in copula absence in a community where class trumps race, see Renee A. Blake, "All o' We Is One? Race, Class, and Language in a Barbados Community" (Ph.D. dissertation, Department of Linguistics, Stanford University, May 1997).

The Ewe sentence without a copula ("Tree the tall") is from Lorenzo Dow Turner, *Africanisms in the Gullah Dialect,* cited above, p. 216. Ewe (or Gbe) is a tone language spoken in parts of Togo, Benin, and Ghana; subscript $_1$ = low tone; subscript $_3$ = high tone. In the table showing frequency of copula absence in creole and African American diaspora languages, the decimal figures represent probability weights calculated from percentages by a variable-rule computer program that takes multiple factors into consideration simultaneously. The ex-slave narrative recordings mentioned are sixteen interviews with former slaves born around the middle of the nineteenth century, recorded mainly between 1935 and 1942 (two in 1971). They are preserved in the Archive of Folk Song at the Library of Congress. Eleven of the recordings are transcribed and discussed by various scholars in Guy Bailey, Natalie Maynor, and Patricia Cukor-Avila, eds., *The Emergence of Black English,* cited above. One new source that uses the ex-slave narrative recordings to argue for creole origins for Black English is David Sutcliffe, "Gone with the Wind? Evidence for Nineteenth-Century African American Speech," *Links and Letters* 5 (1998), pp. 127–145. Darrin Howe's discussion of negation in early Black English is in "Negation and the History of African American English," *Language Variation and Change,* 9 (1997), pp. 267–294.

The divergence hypothesis was first presented in William Labov and Wendell A. Harris, "De Facto Segregation of Black and White Vernaculars," cited above, pp. 1–24. The Texas strand of this research is best summarized in Guy Bailey, "A Perspective on African-American English," in Dennis R. Preston, ed., *American Dialect Research* (Amsterdam and Philadelphia: John Benjamins, 1993), pp. 287– 318, and in Guy Bailey and Natalie Maynor, "The Divergence Controversy,"

American Speech, 64 (1989), pp. 12–39. Critiques of the hypothesis can be found in Ralph W. Fasold, William Labov, Fay Boyd Vaughn-Cooke, Guy Bailey, Walt Wolfram, Arthur K. Spears, and John R. Rickford, "Are Black and White Vernaculars Diverging?" *American Speech,* 62 (1987), pp. 3–80, and in Ron Butters, *The Death of Black English: Divergence and Convergence in Black and White Vernaculars* (Frankfurt: Peter Lang, 1989).

Evidence that Spoken Soul is converging with white vernaculars and Standard English in terms of increasing pronunciation of unstressed initial syllables comes from Fay Boyd Vaughn-Cooke's contribution to "Are Black and White Vernaculars Diverging?", *American Speech,* 62 (1987), pp. 12–32, and in earlier works of hers cited there. Evidence for convergence in terms of the pronunciation of the final vowel in words like *fifty* is presented in Keith Denning, "Convergence with Divergence: A Sound Change in Vernacular Black English," *Language Variation and Change,* 1 (1989), pp. 145–168. For evidence on convergence with respect to the nonmarking of past tense, see John R. Rickford, "Grammatical Variation and Divergence in Vernacular Black English," in Marinel Gerritsen and Dieter Stein, eds., *Internal and External Factors in Syntactic Change* (Berlin and New York: Mouton, 1991), pp. 175–200.

For the latest in the divergence controversy, see William Labov, "Coexistent Systems in African American Vernacular English," in Salikoko S. Mufwene, John R. Rickford, Guy Bailey, and John Baugh, eds., *African American English,* cited above, pp. 110–153. Labov elaborates on the claim that "many important features of the modern dialect [AAVE] are creations of the twentieth century and not an inheritance of the nineteenth." But see John Victor Singler, "What's Not New in AAVE," *American Speech,* 73 (1998), pp. 227–256, for the argument that the presence of supposedly twentieth-century features of Spoken Soul in Liberian Settler English—formed in the nineteenth century—suggests that they are relatively "old" features.

Part Four
The Ebonics Firestorm

9. *Education*

Jesse Jackson's comment in the epigraph was made at a December 30, 1996, meeting with Oakland School District personnel and others before he publicly modified his position on the Ebonics resolution. The Terry Meier epigraph is from "Teaching Teachers About Black Communications," in Theresa Perry and Lisa Delpit, eds., *The Real Ebonics Debate: Power, Language, and the Education of African American Children* (Boston: Beacon Press, 1998), p. 106.

Statistics on the performance of white and black students nationwide in 1992–1994 are from the testimony of Michael Casserly, executive director of the Council of Great City Schools, before Senator Arlen Specter's U.S. Senate panel on Ebonics in January 1997. Casserly's testimony, which included data on the performance of various ethnic groups, covered fifty large urban public school districts, and hundreds and hundreds of schools. Statistics on the performance of African American students in Oakland—released to the media when the Ebonics firestorm arose—are from the December 1996 report of the Task Force on the

Education of African American Students, Oakland Unified School District, p. 5; the recommendations cited here are from pp. 3 and 6. The December 1, 1996, *Sunday Times* (London) report about Oakland's pending resolution was in the article "Parents Force Schools to Halt 'Dumbing of America,' " by James Adams, a Washington correspondent. The account of the December 30, 1996, meetings at Oakland School District headquarters is based on the notes and recollections of John R. Rickford and Angela E. Rickford, who were there along with other linguists and educators. The original wording of the Oakland resolutions is from the minutes of the Oakland school board meeting held on December 18, 1996; the revised wording is from the minutes of the school board meeting held on January 15, 1997. Both versions are reprinted in full in J. David Ramirez, Terrence G. Wiley, Gerda de Klerk, and Enid Lee, eds., *Ebonics in the Urban Education Debate* (Long Beach: Center for Language Minority Education and Research, California State University Long Beach, 1999), pp. 103–106 and 117–118.

Robert D. Twiggs's ideas are detailed in *Pan-African Language in the Western Hemisphere: A Redefinition of Black Dialect as a Language and the Culture of Black Dialect* (North Quincy, Mass.: Christopher, 1973). Robert L. Williams's discussion of Ebonics and the proceedings of the 1973 conference at which the term was developed are in his edited *Ebonics: The True Language of Black Folks* (St. Louis: Robert L. Williams and Associates, 1975). Ernie Smith's 1995 article "Bilingualism and the African American Child" is in Marie A. Ice and Marilyn A. Saunders-Lucas, eds., *Reading: The Blending of Theory and Practice* (Bakersfield: California State University, 1995), vol. 3; quotations here are from pp. 90–91 and 93. Hubert Devonish's comment about the wording "West and Niger-Congo languages" is on page 68 of "Walking Around the Language Barrier: A Carribean View of the Ebonics Controversy," in *Small Axe: A Journal of Criticism* 2, (Sept. 1997): pp. 63–76.

For the full text of California Assembly Bill 1206, introduced by Martinez on February 28, 1997, to prohibit the use of bilingual education funds "for the purpose of recognition of, or instruction in, any dialect, idiom or language derived from English," see: http://www.sen.ca.goc/www/leginfo/SearchText.html. State Superintendent Eastin's remarks are reprinted from the *San Jose Mercury*, December 20, 1996, p. 1A, in an article by Frances Dinkelspiel, "Black Language Policy in Oakland: Talk of the Town."

Coverage of the Oakland Task Force's revised May 1997 recommendations was provided in many newspapers, including the *New York Times* ("'Ebonics' Omitted in Oakland School Report," by Peter Applebome, May 6, 1997, p. A12); the *Oakland Tribune* ("Positive Response to Proposal for Education without Ebonics," by Jonathan Schorr, May 6, 1997, pp. A1, A9); and the *San Francisco Chronicle* ("Renamed Ebonics Plan Introduced in Oakland Schools," by Lori Olszewski, May 6, 1997, p. A18). The quotations from Sylvester Hodges are from the *Oakland Tribune* report, p. A-9. Etta Hollins's books include *Culture in School Learning* (Mahwah, N.J.: Erlbaum, 1996), *Preparing Teachers for Cultural Diversity,* ed. with Joyce E. King and Warren C. Hayman (New York: Teachers College Press, 1997); and *Racial and Ethnic Identity in School Practices,* ed. with Rosa Hernandez (Mahwah, N.J.: Erlbaum, 1999). For preliminary results from the research on decoding errors, see W. Labov, B. Baker, S. Bullock, L. Ross, and M. Brown, "A Graphemic-Phonemic Analysis of the Reading Errors of Inner-City Children" (http://www.ling.upenn.edu/~labov/home.html); William Labov and Bettina Baker, "Raising Reading Levels of African American Students in Inner-City Schools:

A Progress Report" (manuscript, Linguistics Laboratory, University of Pennsylvania, 1999); and Andrea Kortenhoven, "An Analysis of Reading Errors by African American and Latino Third Graders in East Palo Alto, California" (manuscript, Department of Linguistics, Stanford University, 1999).

For the full text of the Linguistic Society of America's January 1997 resolution on the Ebonics issue, see: http://www.stanford.edu/~rickford/ or http://www.lsadc.org. For a more detailed discussion of the research evidence relating to Ebonics in education, see John R. Rickford, "Using the Vernacular to Teach the Standard," in J. David Ramirez, Terrence G. Wiley, Gerda de Klerk, and Enid Lee, eds., *Ebonics in the Urban Education Debate*, cited above, pp. 23–41. The article is reprinted in John R. Rickford, *African American Vernacular English* (Oxford: Blackwell, 1999), pp. 329–347. Other recent books that deal with African American English and education include John Baugh, *Out of the Mouths of Slaves: African American Language and Educational Malpractice* (Austin: University of Texas Press, 1999); Theresa Perry and Lisa Delpit, eds., *The Real Ebonics Debate: Power, Language, and the Education of African-American Children*, cited above, a revised version of the fall 1997 (vol. 12, no. 1) issue of the journal *Rethinking Schools;* J. David Ramirez, Terrence G. Wiley, Gerda de Klerk, and Enid Lee, eds., *Ebonics in the Urban Education Debate*, cited above; Carolyn Temple Adger, Donna Christian, and Orlando Taylor, eds., *Making the Connection: Language and Academic Achievement among African American Students* (Washington, D.C.: Center for Applied Linguistics, and McHenry, Ill: Delta Systems, 1999); Geneva Smitherman, *Talkin That Talk: Language, Culture and Education in African America* (London and New York: Routledge, 2000); and Walt Wolfram, Carolyn Temple Adger, and Donna Christian, eds., *Dialects in Schools and Communities* (Mahwah, N.J.: Erlbaum, 1999).

Ann McCormick Piestrup's study was published as "Black Dialect Interference and Accommodation of Reading Instruction in First Grade," *Monographs of the Language Behavior Research Laboratory*, no. 4 (University of California, Berkeley, 1973). For a review of the attitudes of teachers to the language of children, including black vernacular, see Frederick Williams, *Explorations of the Linguistic Attitudes of Teachers* (Rowley, Mass.: Newbury House, 1976). For the harmful effects of negative attitudes, see Jacqueline Jordan Irvine, *Black Students and School Failure: Policies, Practices, and Prescriptions* (New York: Greenwood Press, 1990), and Robert T. Tauber, *Self-fulfilling Prophecy: A Practical Guide to Its Use in Education* (Westport, Conn.: Praeger, Tauber, 1996). The contrastive analysis book by H. H. Parker and M. I. Crist is *Teaching Minorities to Play the Corporate Language Game* (Columbia: University of South Carolina, National Resource Center for the Freshman Year Experience and Students in Transition, 1995). For one of the earliest Caribbean proposals to use contrastive analysis with creole to teach Standard English, see Robert B. Le Page's article "Problems to Be Faced in the Use of English as a Medium of Education in Four West Indian Territories," in Joshua A. Fishman, Charles A. Ferguson, and Jyotirindra Das Gupta, eds., *Language Problems of Developing Countries* (New York: John Wiley, 1968), pp. 431–443.

For a good introduction to contrastive analysis with vernacular and Standard English, see Irwin Feigenbaum, "The Use of Nonstandard English in Teaching Standard: Contrast and Comparison," in Ralph W. Fasold and Roger W. Shuy, eds., *Teaching Standard English in the Inner City* (Washington, D.C.: Center for Applied Linguistics, 1970), pp. 87–104. The Los Angeles bidialectal program, directed by Noma LeMoine, and known for years as the "Language Development Program for African American Students," has, in the wake of state propositions

209 and 227, been renamed and reconceptualized as the "Academic English Mastery Program for Speakers of Non-Standard Language Forms." For further information, see Noma LeMoine and the Los Angeles Unified School District, *English for Your Success: A Handbook of Successful Strategies for Educators* (Maywood, N.J.: The People's Publishing, 1999), and the four Curriculum Activity Guides that accompany it. Kelli Harris-Wright discusses the DeKalb County experiment and provides data on its success in her paper "Enhancing Bidialectalism in Urban African American Students" in Carolyn T. Adger, Donna Christian, and Orlando Taylor, eds., *Making the Connection: Language and Academic Achievement among African American Students* (McHenry, Ill.: Delta Systems and Center for Applied Linguistics, 1999). Doug Cummings is quoted from the *Atlanta Constitution*, January 9, 1997, p. B1. For details of the Aurora University experiment with contrastive analysis, see Hanni U. Taylor, *Standard English, Black English, and Bidialectalism* (New York: Peter Lang, 1989).

For a recent overview of dialect-reader approaches, see John R. Rickford and Angela E. Rickford, "Dialect Readers Revisited," *Linguistics and Education*, 7 (1995), pp. 107–128. For the Swedish dialect-reader study, see Tore Österberg, *Bilingualism and the First School Language—An Educational Problem Illustrated by Results from a Swedish Language Area* (Umeå, Sweden: Våsterbottens Tryckeri, 1961). The Norwegian experiment is described in Tove Bull, "Teaching School Beginners to Read and Write in Their Vernacular," in *Tromsø Linguistics in the Eighties*, 11 (1990), pp. 69–84. For discussion of and data on the Bridge experiment, see Gary A. Simpkins and Charlesetta Simpkins, "Cross-Cultural Approach to Curriculum Development," in Geneva Smitherman, ed., *Black English and the Education of Black Children and Youth* (Detroit: Wayne State University Center for Black Studies, 1981), pp. 221–240. Gary Simpkins is working with others on an updated version of the Bridge readers. For a discussion that includes positive remarks about the Bridge readers, but suggests other ways of taking knowledge of black vernacular into account in teaching reading, see William Labov, "Can Reading Failure Be Reversed? A Linguistic Approach to the Question," in *Literacy among African-American Youth: Issues in Learning, Teaching, and Schooling* (Creskill, N.J.: Hampton Press, 1995).

On the rationale for teaching African American children initially in their vernacular, see William Stewart, "On the Use of Negro Dialect in the Teaching of Reading," in Joan C. Baratz and Roger W. Shuy, eds., *Teaching Black Children to Read* (Washington D.C.: Center for Applied Linguistics, 1969), pp. 156–219. Many other articles in this book, and in its companion piece, *Teaching Standard English in the Inner City*, cited above, should be of interest to the inner-city teacher, even today. John McWhorter's critique of dialect-reader and other approaches that make special provisions for dialect speakers is in *Word on the Street: Fact and Fable about American English* (New York: Plenum, 1998), pp. 201–261.

10. *The Media*

The epigraph about language prejudice is from Wayne O'Neil's 1997 article "If Ebonics Isn't a Language, Then Tell Me, What Is?" reprinted in Theresa Perry and Lisa Delpit, eds., *The Real Ebonics Debate: Power, Language, and the Education of African American Children* (Boston: Beacon Press, 1998), p. 42. The epigraph from Theresa Perry is from the same source, p. 13.

The *San Francisco Chronicle* article announcing the landmark policy, "Oakland Schools OK Black English," by L. Olszewski, appeared on December 19, 1996, p. A1. Oprah Winfrey discussed Standard and Black English on a November 19, 1987, broadcast (No. W309), of her television show. For a discussion of Winfrey's stance toward Spoken Soul in this broadcast, see Rosina Lippi-Green, *English with an Accent: Language, Ideology, and Discrimination in the United States* (London: Routledge, 1997), pp. 193–196. "Lingering Conflict in the Schools: Black Dialect vs. Standard Speech," by Felicia R. Lee, was published in the *New York Times,* January 5, 1994. The *60 Minutes* segment on Black English, entitled "The Language Factor," appeared in March 1995. Walter M. Brasch presented his "cyclical theory" in *Black English and the Mass Media* (Lanham, Md.: University Press of America, 1981).

Neil Peirce's piece on Labov's divergence theory, "Bilingual Black English Isn't the Problem," was published in the *Inquirer Magazine* (of the *Philadelphia Inquirer*), May 5, 1985, p. 12. The *Philadelphia Daily News* article "Order to OK 'Black English' in Schools Comes under Fire" was published on August 11, 1969. The quotation outlining the nature of the original lawsuit in the Ann Arbor "King" case is from Geneva Smitherman, "What Go Round Come Round: King in Perspective," in *Harvard Educational Review* (Feb. 1981), pp. 40–56. Reprinted in G. Smitherman, *Talkin That Talk: Language, Culture and Education in African America,* cited above, pp. 132–149. Judge Joiner's quotation is taken from Reginald Stuart, "Help Ordered for Pupils Talking 'Black English,'" *New York Times,* July 13, 1979, p. A8.

Carl Rowan's comments are from "'Black English' Isn't 'Foreign,'" *Philadelphia Bulletin,* July 11, 1979. Vernon E. Jordan Jr.'s comments on the Ann Arbor decision are from "Teacher Preconceptions at Crux of Black English Problem," in *Detroit Free Press* (Dec. 7, 1979), p. 11A. For a full listing of the media's coverage of the King case, see Richard W. Bailey, "Press Coverage of the King Case," in Geneva Smitherman, ed., *Black English and the Education of Black Children and Youth* (Detroit: Center for Black Studies, Wayne State University, 1981), pp. 359–389. Labov's comments on Ebonics as an emotional subject are in "The Ebonics Uproar," *Kansas City Star,* January 9, 1997. Dillard refers to the same pervasive suggestion that Black English has been "made up" in his book *Black English* (New York: Random House, 1972), pp. 11ff. Jesse Jackson's comments on NBC's *Meet the Press* were quoted in *USA Today,* December 23, 1996. The *Rolanda* show featuring Ebonics was recorded on January 17, 1997, and broadcast later in amended form.

For a discussion of the deleterious contributions of headline writers to press coverage of the Ebonics controversy, see Geoffrey Nunberg, "Double Standards," *Natural Language and Linguistic Theory,* 15, 3 (1997). The *Times-Picayune* headline was published December 20, 1996, in the state edition, p. A1. The *Sacramento Bee* headline was published December 20, 1996, p. A24. The *Toronto Star* article "Ebonics' Garbled Message," by K. Kenna, was published on March 3, 1997, p. B5. "Voice of Inner City Streets Is Defended and Criticized," by S. A. Holmes, was published in the *New York Times* on December 30, 1996, p. A7.

The town hall meeting was covered by S. Kleffman in "Ebonics' Town Hall Support," *San Jose Mercury News,* January 9, 1997, p. 1B. The comments of the white accountant and the black welder are from A. Rojas, "Strong Opinions on Ebonics Policy," *San Francisco Chronicle,* December 23, 1996, p. A13.

The Education Trust report that African American and Latino students were losing ground was reported in the *New York Times* article "Report: Minorities Slipping Behind" written by Peter Applebome and published on December 29, 1996, p. A6. The notion of Ebonics as a universal classroom hurdle was explored by R. Sanchez in "Ebonics: A Way to Close the Learning Gap?" *Washington Post,* January 6, 1997, p. A1. The U.S. Department of Education report was cited in S. Kleffman, "Ebonics Furor Draws National Attention to Black Students' Needs," *San Jose Mercury News,* January 5, 1997, p. 1B.

The *Oakland Tribune* reprinted the Oakland School Board's Ebonics resolution on December 29, 1996, p. A9. K. De Witt wrote about Ebonics' pervasiveness in "Not So Separate: Ebonics, Language of Richard Nixon," *New York Times,* December 29, 1996. The insightful *Washington Post* article by R. Weiss was "Among Linguists, Black English Gets Respect," and was published on January 6, 1997, p. A10.

The instructional strategies of the Standard English Proficiency Program were examined by S. Kleffman in "Ebonics Debate Rages," *San Jose Mercury News,* February 14, 1997, p. B1. Peter Applebome's article "Dispute over Ebonics Reflects a Volatile Mix" appeared in *New York Times,* March 1, 1997.

The *International Workers Bulletin* article was "Who Is Promoting Ebonics and Why?" by J. Mackler, published January 13, 1997. *Socialist Action,* 15, 2 (February 1997) published "The Debate on Ebonics: What's Behind the Fury Generated by 'Black English,'" p. 4. Thomas Sowell's column "Black English (Ebonics) Is an Obsolete White Dialect" appeared in the *Detroit News,* January 19, 1997, p. 7B.

Walter Williams's column "'I Be' Talk Has No Ties to Any African Language" appeared in the *Detroit Free Press* on December 26, 1996. Bayard Rustin's "Won't They Ever Learn?" appeared in the *New York Times* on August 1, 1971. George Will's comments on the ABC program *This Week with David Brinkley* were aired on December 29, 1996. Rachel L. Jones's "Not White, Just Right" appeared in *Newsweek,* February 10, 1997, pp. 12–13. Bill Johnson called Ebonics a "linguistic nightmare" in "It's Time to Let Black English Rest in Peace," *Detroit News,* January 3, 1997.

The *New York Times* op-ed column that condemned the "Ebonic plague" was written by Frank Rich and published on January 8, 1997, p. A15. (Others made this invidious implicit comparison with the bubonic plague.) Derrick Z. Jackson suggested that Ebonics was just good business in "Black Slang, White Jive," which the *Boston Globe* published on January 3, 1997, p. A27. Ishmael Reed's *Newsday* piece "The Art of Black English" was in the *San Jose Mercury News,* January 10, 1997. Chauncey Bailey ripped into the Oakland school board on the January 16, 1997, edition of the KQED radio program *Forum.* Nicholas Stix's "Ebonics: Bridge to Illiteracy" appeared in *Liberty* 10, 6 (July 1997), pp. 45–49. To view some of the research on Black English as a bridge to Standard English that Stix distorted in his article, see John Rickford's web page, or www.stanford.edu/~rickford/. See also John Rickford, "Using the Vernacular to Teach the Standard," in his *African American Vernacular English* (Oxford: Blackwell, 1999), pp. 329–347.

Jack E. White's "Ebonics According to Buckwheat" appeared in *Time* on January 13, 1997. *Vanity Fair* contributor Christopher Hitchens wrote "Hooked on Ebonics," which was published in March 1997. Louis Menand wrote "Johnny Be Good: Ebonics and the Language of Cultural Separatism," for the *New Yorker,* January 13, 1997. The *San Diego Union-Tribune* published Rosemary Harris's "The Backlash against Black English Ignores the Beauty of the Words" on January 12, 1997, p. D6.

Leonard Pitts took a more moderate position in "Ebonics Can Be a Bridge to Success," *San Jose Mercury News*, January 9, 1997. *Essence* contributor Khephra Burns wrote "Yakkity Yak, Don't Talk Black!" published in March 1997, p. 150. The *Oakland Tribune* editorial "The First Lessons of a Controversial Idea" appeared on December 29, 1996, p. C8. The *New York Times* op-ed column that maintained everyone was looking down on Ebonics was "The Ebonic Plague," cited above.

The expressed policy against giving away advertising space is from a letter to "Concerned Linguists and Educators" c/o Dr. Geneva Smitherman, written December 18, 1998, by Daniel H. Cohen, senior vice-president of advertising for the *New York Times*. Data on the use of *has* and *have* among black teenagers in New York City is from William Labov, Paul Cohen, Clarence Robins, and John Lewis, *A Study of the Non-Standard English of Negro and Puerto Rican Speakers in New York City* (New York: Columbia University Press, 1968), vol. 1, p. 247. In Labov et al's data, *have* was used for *has* in thirty-five of fifty-two possible cases; *has* was used for *have* in not one of 114 possible cases. For coverage of the flap created by its publication of the "I has a dream" ad, see Lynn Schnaiberg, "Anti-Ebonics Ad Was Mistake, Head Start Group Says," *Education Week*, October 28, 1998.

11. *Ebonics "Humor"*

The epigraph quoting Jerrie C. Scott is from "The Serious Side of Ebonics Humor," *Journal of English Linguistics*, 26, 2 (June 1998), pp. 137–155. The second is from Maggie Ronkin and Helen Karn, "Mock Ebonics: Linguistic Racism in Parodies of Ebonics on the Internet," *Journal of Sociolinguistics*, 3, 3 (1999), pp. 360–380. It should be noted that these two papers and this chapter were written independently of one another, although a few of our examples and sources overlap.

John Leo's column appeared on January 20, 1997. For information on variation between *be* and *be's* or *bees*, see Cynthia Bernstein, "A Variant of 'Invariant' Be," *American Speech* 63, 2 (1988), pp. 119–124. She notes, among other things, that in the *Linguistic Atlas of the Gulf States* samples, speakers under forty-nine years old never used *bees*, while more than half (56 percent) of those forty-nine and over did. Bill Cosby's "We Be Toys" joke was recounted in the *Wall Street Journal*, January 10, 1997.

The data on Thunderbirds' use of *be* came from William Labov, Paul Cohen, Clarence Robins, and John Lewis, *A Study of the Non-Standard English of Negro and Puerto Rican Speakers in New York City* (New York: Columbia University Press, 1968), p. 236. The Detroit data are reported in Walt Wolfram, *A Linguistic Description of Detroit Negro Speech* (Washington, D.C.: Center for Applied Linguistics, 1969), p. 198. Foxy Boston's speech is discussed in John Rickford and Faye McNair-Knox, "Addressee and Topic-Influenced Style Shift," in Douglas Biber and Edward Finegan, eds., *Perspectives on Register* (Oxford: Oxford University Press, 1994), pp. 235–276, and reprinted in Rickford's *African American Vernacular English* (Malden, Mass.: Blackwell, 1999), pp. 112–153. The Texas data on *be* is in Guy Bailey and Natalie Maynor, "Decreolization?", *Language in Society*, 16 (1987), pp. 449–474.

For more information on the discourse marker "Know what I'm saying," see Dawn Hannah, "(Do) (y)(ou) (kn)ow (wha)(t) (I) ('m) sa(y)(i)(n)(g)?: A Case of Phonological Reduction and Pragmatic Expansion" (Stanford University, Department of Linguistics, 1996). Despite the emphasis in this chapter on the habitual meaning of invariant *be,* note that the form is sometimes used for extended duratives, nonhabitual actions drawn out in time. See Guy Bailey and Natalie Maynor, "Decreolization?", cited above. Patricia Smith's *Oakland Tribune* column appeared on December 29, 1996, and Bill Cosby's comment in the *Wall Street Journal* is from January 10, 1997. The William Raspberry excerpt is from the *Knoxville News-Sentinel,* December 26, 1996. *Hollywood Shuffle,* starring and directed by Robert Townsend, was produced in 1987 and distributed by MCEG/Sterling. *Airplane!,* directed by David Zucker, Jim Abrahams, and Jerry Zucker, was produced in 1980.

William Stewart's version of "The Night Before Christmas" is presented and discussed in "On the Use of Negro Dialect in the Teaching of Reading," in Joan C. Baratz and Roger W. Shuy, eds., *Teaching Black Children to Read* (Washington, D.C.: Center for Applied Linguistics, 1969), pp. 156–219. Moore's poem is a perennial favorite of translators. For a translation into Gullah, see Virginia Geraty, *Gullah Night Before Christmas* (Gretna, La.: Pelican, 1998). The first stanza: " 'E bin de night befo' Chris'mus en' eenside we house, / Eb'ryt'ing settle down, eb'n de mouse. / De cump'ny done lef' f'um de bighouse at las', / En' de fambly all gone tuh Middlenight Mass."

The translation filters used on the www.novusordo.com/indexn.htm and www.AtlantaGA.com/ebonics.htm websites appear to be similar or identical to Jive, from mod.sources.games (Tektronix, Inc., games-request@tekred.TEK.COM). According to Bill Randle, the moderator of mod.sources.games: "Jive and valspeak [a filter for converting English texts to Valley talk] are filters that take an ordinary text file and change selected words into jive (or valspeak). The original author of these programs is not listed in the source code; they were submitted to mod.sources.games by Adams Douglas (adamsd@crash.UUCP)."

Maggie Ronkin and Helen E. Karn are quoted from their paper on "Mock Ebonics," cited above.

I. B. White's *The Old, Fat, White Guy's Guide to Ebonics* (Chatsworth, Calif.: CCC Publications, 1997) was perhaps the first book on Ebonics to be produced in the wake of the controversy. Significantly, it was a comedy piece. For Sterling Brown's discussion of the "brute" and other literary stereotypes, see "Negro Characters As Seen by White Authors," originally published in *Journal of Negro Education,* 2 (January 1933), pp. 180–201, then reprinted in James A. Emanuel and Theodore L. Gross, eds., *Dark Symphony* (New York: The Free Press, 1968).

The statistics about the percentages of African Americans executed for rape between 1930 and 1967 are from the *Statistical Abstract of the United States* (1115th ed., Washington D.C., Bureau of the Census, 1995), p. 220. The criminal justice statistics on African American males between ages twenty and twenty-nine were compiled by the Sentencing Project, and reported by Charisse Jones, "Crime and Punishment: Is Race the Issue?" *New York Times,* October 28, 1995, pp. 1, 9.

The "Ebonics Loan Application" is from Jerrie Scott, "The Serious Side of Ebonics Humor," cited above, p. 142. Keith Lovett's Ebonics joke book *Hooked on Ebonics* was published by St. Simons Press, Atlanta.

Paradoxically, the same website with the cruel caricature of the "Ebonics Olympic Games" (novusordo.com/elympic.html; no longer active) included a link to a website with a linguistically informed and educationally reasoned discussion of "Black English: Its History and Its Role in the Education of Our Children" (www.princeton.edu/~bclewis/blacktalk.html).

Part Five
The Double Self

12. *The Crucible of Identity*

The W. E. B. Du Bois epigraph is from *The Souls of Black Folk* (Chicago: A. C. Mc-Clurg, 1903). The Derek Walcott epigraph is excerpted from "A Far Cry from Africa," in the collection *In a Green Night: Poems 1948–1960* (London, Cape, 1969). For the California elementary school conversation, we are grateful to Angela E. Rickford.

The quotation from Ellen Bouchard Ryan is from "Why Do Low-Prestige Language Varieties Persist?" in Howard Giles and Robert N. St. Clair, eds., *Language and Social Psychology* (Oxford: Blackwell, 1979), pp. 145–158. For conflicting attitudes to pidgins and creoles, see John R. Rickford and Elizabeth Closs Traugott, "Symbol of Powerlessness and Degeneracy, or Symbol of Solidarity and Truth? Paradoxical Attitudes toward Pidgins and Creoles," in Sidney Greenbaum, ed., *The English Language Today* (Oxford: Pergamon, 1985), pp. 252–261.

The quotations from Signithia Fordham and John Ogbu are from pp. 181–182 and 186 of their article "Black Students' School Success: Coping with the Burden of 'Acting White,'" *Urban Review,* 18, 3 (1986). Ogbu's notion of opposition identity is also explained in this work. The quotations from black teenagers in East Palo Alto and Redwood City, California, are from John R. Rickford, "Grammatical Variation and Divergence in Vernacular Black English," in Marinel Gerritsen and Dieter Stein, eds., *Internal and External Factors in Syntactic Change* (Berlin: Mouton, 1992), pp. 175–200, reprinted in Rickford's *African American Vernacular English,* cited above, pp. 261–280.

A Ph.D. dissertation that deals with the diffusion of African American language to white American youth is Mary Bucholtz, *Borrowed Blackness: Language, Racialization, and White Identity in an Urban High School* (Department of Linguistics, University of California, Berkeley, 1997). Another, covering the diffusion of hip-hop culture to the world beyond America, is Halifu Osumare, *African Aesthetics, American Culture: Dancing towards a Global Culture* (Department of American Studies, University of Hawaii, Manoa, 1999).

Mary Hoover's article is "Community Attitudes toward Black English," *Language in Society,* 7 (1978), pp. 65–87. The Eliot quotation is from *Notes towards the Definition of Culture* (London: Faber & Faber, 1948), p. 57. The Cleanth Brooks quotation is from *The Language of the American South* (Athens: University of Georgia Press, 1985), p. 2. The black professor at a midwestern university is quoted in Barbara L. Speicher and Seane M. McMahon, "Some African American Perspectives on Black English Vernacular," *Language in Society,* 21 (1992), pp. 383–407. Toni Morrison is quoted from p. 27 of Thomas LeClair, "A Conversation with Toni Morrison: 'The Language Must Not Sweat,'" *The New Republic,* March 21, 1981. The study by Jacquelyn Rahman is entitled "Black Attitudes to Black English, Standard and Vernacular" (manuscript, Department of Linguistics, Stanford University, 1999).

The quotations from Malcolm X, which appear in Mary Hoover's "Community Attitudes," cited above, are from *The Autobiography of Malcolm X* by Alex Haley (New York: Grove Press, 1965). The excerpt from Frederick Douglass's address is reprinted from Henry Louis Gates Jr. and Nellie Y. McKay, eds., *The Norton Anthology of African American Literature* (New York: W.W. Norton, 1997), p. 386.

Index

This index does not include material from the Notes section (pages 231–258).

Permissions